DALITS–ECONOMY AND SOCIETY
A Study of Tamil Nadu

DALITS–ECONOMY AND SOCIETY
A Study of Tamil Nadu

M. Thangaraj

KALPAZ

ISBN: 978-93-8639=736-2
Price: ₹

First Published 2018

Published by

Kalpaz Publications
C-30, Satyawati Nagar,
Delhi - 110052
E-mail: kalpaz@hotmail.com Ph.: 9212142040

Printed at : G. Print Process, Delhi

Cataloging in Publication Data--DK

Courtesy: D.K. Agencies (P) Ltd. <docinfo@dkagencies.com>

Thangaraj, M., author.
Dalits : economy and society : a study of Tamil Nadu / M. Thangaraj.
pages cm
Includes bibliographical references.
ISBN 9789386397362 (HB)

1. Dalits--India--Tamil Nadu--Social conditions. 2. Dalits--India--Tamil Nadu--Economic conditions. 3. Dalits--Government policy--India--Tamil Nadu. I. Title.

LCC HT720.T43 2017 | DDC 305.5688095482 23

Contents

Foreword

This book by Professor Thangraj is another academic contribution by him on the issue of Dalits in Tamil Nadu, on which he has been researching for quite long time in his academic engagement. The book discusses the economic and social status of Dalits in Tamil Nadu. Beside Scheduled Castes, it also examines the status of Scheduled Tribes and Women. In economic status, it examines the occupational diversification of SCs, STs and women. In that it deals with ownership of agricultural land and enterprises. In social sector it examines the situation with respect to education and health including the working of government programmes. The book thus brings an insight on these aspects with a recent data and indicates the policy implications.

In the economic status, it looks at the changes in land ownership in Tamil Nadu. It came with the results that although the land reform legislations were enacted mainly to redistribute land to the landless and other poor, but failed to change the agrarian structure. The Hindu Succession Act also could not deliver justice to women in getting their ancestral land, as the land owned by women continued to be abysmally low even after several years of the enactment of Hindu Succession Act in Tamil Nadu. The percentage of land owned by women is disproportionately low considering their crucial contribution to agriculture. These legislations could not improve the land owned by the SCs as they continued to be low even after fifty-five years of implementation of land reform legislations in the State. Of those SCs who owned some land, most of them are small holdings. The wells and tube wells owned by the ST/SC farmers is disproportionately low in Tamil Nadu. The proportion of well and tube wells fitted with electric pump sets was also low among the SCs compared with Others in 2005-06 and 2010-11. Distribution of area irrigated by diverse sources of irrigation viz. wells and tube wells was very low among SCs and STs as compared to Others in Tamil Nadu.

The occupational diversification among social groups has been limited. About 71 per cent and 79 per cent of the SC and ST rural workforce respectively continue to be employed in agricultural sector. In 2001, only 15 per cent of the SCs rural workers were engaged in cultivation as against the corresponding figures of 47 per cent of STs and 35 per cent non-SC/ST rural workers. By 2011, this proportion declined to 10 per cent of the SC rural workers, 34 per cent of STs and 27 per cent of non-SCs/STs among rural workers. The NSS household data also substantiates the limited diversification of occupation of SCs and STs compared with others group in rural area. The proportion of workforce engaged in household industry has declined.

The SCs in urban areas in Tamil Nadu also occupy relatively disadvantageous position as compared to OBCs, as the percentage of self-employed SC workers was lower by about 10 percentage point in 2009-2010. As regards the casual labourers, the percentage share was higher by about 20 percentage point than the corresponding figures for OBCs. The inter group variation in the percentage of regular wage earners/salaried was much lower among SCs, STs and OBCs which indicate the positive role of the reservation policy for the SCs, STs and OBCs in Tamil Nadu. However, the proportion of workforce engaged in regular wage/salaried has declined among SCs, STs and OBCs. But the decline in regular wage/salaried was higher among SCs. This indicates that the brunt of slackening public sector employment during the economic reform period has fallen more heavily on SCs.

The author also examines the educational status of the Scheduled Castes in Tamil Nadu in reasonable detail. Analysis of the literacy rates by social groups reveals that the rate of literacy has gone up substantially for all social groups in 2011 as compared to 1991. The rate of literacy was high among the non-SCs/STs as compared to SCs and STs. The enrolment has gone up in the recent past, but the proportion of enrolment is still low among the Scheduled Castes and Scheduled Tribes in Tamil Nadu. The rate of drop-outs has come down for all population, including the Scheduled Castes and Scheduled Tribes in 2005 as compared to 2001. The schools run by the government have enrolled more students as compared to the schools under private management. The attendance rate, completion rate and transition rate are low among the SCs as compared to non-SCs/STs. The data relating to repetition rate was high among the SCs as compared to non-SCs/STs at the school levels. Analysis of data by gender shows that repetition rate was high among the boys, completion rate was high among the girls and the transition rate remains more or less the same for both the boys and girls.

The discussion on health status brings out the situation of SC and ST persons. Mortality rates among children belonging to all social groups have declined in Tamil Nadu. The children who received Vitamin 'A' supplementation among SCs was however low. The percentage of women who have received antenatal care was low among SC women. The delivery assisted by doctors is also low among the SC women compared with OBC women. The food consumption by women viz. milk/curd, green leafy vegetables and fruits was low among SCs as compared to OBCs and Others.

Prevalence of anemia was much higher among women and children belonging to SCs. The prevalence of acute respiratory infection (ARI) was slightly high among the children belonging to SCs as compared to OBCs. The lower percentage of SC children received vaccination both in 1998-99 and 2005-06.

The books also discusses the implementation of the SC-Sub Plan (SC-SP) in Tamil Nadu and points out the limitation in its implementations. The funds allotted under the scheme have been inadequate and less than the proportion of the Scheduled Caste population in the State. The hope of the deprived section of the people with regard to the effective implementation of the SC-SP still remains a distant dream, due to lack of political will on the part of administrative machinery.

In the social aspects, the book examines the situation with respect to atrocity. It indicates that the rate of pendency in disposal of cases for crimes has gone up. The conviction rate has also come down. It is to be noted that the highest percentage of atrocities cases were reported in Thirunelveli and Madurai districts. The Scheduled Castes and Scheduled Tribes (Prevention of Atrocity) Act, 1989 is an important milestone for the SCs as it aims to prevent atrocities on the SCs and STs and to eradicate the untouchability, but this law has not been effectively implemented in Tamil Nadu.

Thus, the book is wide in its coverage in so far as it deals with the multiple aspect of the economic and social status of Scheduled Castes and scheduled Tribes and women. It has brought out insight on the current status. It is therefore useful for researchers, student and policy-making organisation in Tamil Nadu.

Sukhadeo Thorat
Professor Emeritus,
Jawaharlal Nehru University, Delhi

Acknowledgements

I wish to express my sincere gratitude to Indian Council for Social Science Research (ICSSR), Ministry of Human Resource Development, Government of India, New Delhi, for financial support for two years (from 1st July 2014 to 30th June 2016) under ICSSR - Mahatma Gandhi National Fellowship. I would like to express my heartfelt thanks to Professor Sukhadeo Thorat, former Chairman, ICSSR and Dr. Ramesh Dadhich, former Member Secretary for their financial, academic and moral support.

I thank Mr. D. Babu, my former student, Department of Economics, for his help and support in data processing and typographical work. I extend my gratitude to Mr. Noordhin, Research Scholar, New College, Chennai for his help in data analysis. I also wish to extend my thanks to Dr. Abdul Raheem, Associate Professor, New College, Chennai for his help and encouragement and my former Doctoral Scholar Dr. S. Vijayalakshmi, Justice Basheer Ahamed College, Chennai for her comments on the earlier version of the report.

I am grateful to Professor R. Thandavan, former Vice-Chancellor, Dr Jawahar, former Registrar, Dr. Ravindran, Director, Chepauk Campus Office and Staff Members of

Chepauk Campus Director's Office, University of Madras for providing logistical support and facilities for conducting the project work. I wish to express my gratitude to all those who co-operated in the completion of this study. I am grateful to Professor Sukhadeo Thorat for his foreword for this book. I would like to extend my sincere thanks to Mr. Amit Garg, Director, Kalpaz Publications for taking interest in bringing out this volume at a short notice.

M. Thangaraj
Former Professor and Head
Department of Economics,
Former ICSSR-Mahatma Gandhi National Fellow
University of Madras

1

Introduction

The people belonging to the Scheduled Caste (Dalit) have been prohibited from the mainstream socio-economic activities. They have been put into a lot of discrimination and oppression from time immemorial. They were treated as slaves. They are not treated equally on par with Others by the caste Hindus even to-day. The Colonial Government in India, Christian Missionaries and the post-independence government in India have extended several ameliorative programmes for their upliftment. Even after seven decades of independence in India, there is no marked change in their sources of livelihood and occupational status. They continue to work in the agriculture as wage labour and other occupations, such as, casual work, scavenging and menial occupations.

Eleventh five year plan has emphasised the inclusive growth. The concept of inclusive growth is broader than welfare programmes implemented by the government. Inclusive growth demands that all social groups in India have equal access to the services provided by the state and equal opportunity for the upward economic and social mobility. It is also necessary to ensure that there is no discrimination against any section of the society. Twelfth five year plan also adopted the policy of the inclusive growth.

Majority of the population in India is living in the rural area and agriculture is the mainstay for most of the people in rural India. Land is the basic source of livelihood for most of the rural people in India. The people who depend on land may be classified as land owners, tenants and agricultural workers. The observed pattern of land distribution exhibits an unequal distribution of landholdings. Information relating to landholdings by social groups indicates that the people belonging to Scheduled Castes (SCs) have been, by and large, excluded from getting access to land ownership.

Available studies on the issues relating to the SCs show that there are some fragmentary evidences that the status of the SCs have improved on the economic front due to welfare measures implemented by the government. But these studies have not come out clearly, even cursorily, as how far the people belonging to the SCs have been able to get benefit from the government programmes. Recent caste clashes that occurred in Tamil Nadu abundantly make it clear that caste-Hindus unable to tolerate even there is small change in the economic development of the SCs. Hence, there is a need for an in-depth study covering all issues of the socio-economic factors.

Objectives of the Study

The proposed study on "Dalits-Economy and Society: A Study of Tamil Nadu" would examine the current socio-economic status of the SCs (Dalits) in Tamil Nadu. The specific objectives of the study are given below.

1. To study the access to land by the SCs in Tamil Nadu,
2. To analyse the occupational characteristics of the SCs in Tamil Nadu,

3. To investigate the schemes available with reference to entrepreneurship development in Tamil Nadu,
4. To examine the educational status of the SCs in Tamil Nadu,
5. To analyse the status of health and consumption expenditure of the SCs in Tamil Nadu,
6. To evaluate the nature and functioning of the SC-Sub Plan in Tamil Nadu, and
7. To study the nature, causes and types of atrocities on SCs in Tamil Nadu.

Methodology

Data on landholdings by social groups were collected from Agricultural Census for two points of time viz. 2006-06 and 2010-11. Data on educational level of the SCs were collected from Census of India and Selected Educational Statistics for two points of time viz. 2001 and 2011. Data on occupational characteristics were obtained from Census of India 2001 and 2011 and also from NSS reports. Data on Entrepreneurship were collected from the Reports of the Government of India and Tamil Nadu like MSME, TAHDCO, etc. Data on health status and consumer expenditure were collected from the NSS Reports and National Family Health Survey (NFHS). Information relating to the implantation of SC-Sub Plan were collected from the reports of the Budget Documents, Government of Tamil Nadu and Audit Report (General and Social Sector) for the year ended in 31 March 2012. Data on nature and causes of atrocities on Scheduled Castes were collected from the annual reports of the National Crime Record Bureau (NCRB) and Crime Review, 2014.

Tools of Analysis

The study has used the following statistical tools for analysis of data for obtaining meaningful disparity measurements.

1. Access Index, 2. Simple disparity index and 3. Simple gap, i.e., a gap between a social group and the reference group.

Scope of the Study

The purpose of the study is to evaluate the socio-economic status of the Scheduled Castes in Tamil Nadu. The outcome of the proposed study would throw light on the effectiveness of the existing welfare programmes in the changed economic scenario and to suggest suitable policy measures for the upliftment of the Scheduled Castes.

Chapterisation

The first and introductory chapter describes briefly about the theme of the study with focus on socio-economic conditions of the Scheduled Caste, objectives of the study, methodology adopted and tools of analysis. Chapter two examines the issues pertaining to land, caste and gender in Tamil Nadu. Occupational diversification among social groups has been examined in chapter three. Issues pertaining to entrepreneurship development programme have been elaborately discussed in chapter four. Chapter five evaluates the educational status of the Scheduled Castes in Tamil Nadu. Health status and monthly per capita consumption (MPCE) expenditure have been analysed in chapter six. The chapter seven examines the nature and functioning of SC-Sub Plan in Tamil Nadu. The nature and types of atrocities committed on Scheduled Castes have been examined in chapter eight. Chapter nine presents the broad summary, conclusions and policy implications.

References

1. Thangaraj M. "Land and caste in Tamil Nadu", in *Land reforms in India-Tamil Nadu: An Unfinished task,* (Ed.), M. Thangaraj, Sage publications,, New Delhi, 2003.

2. Thangaraj, M. "Access to land by Scheduled Castes and Scheduled Tribes in India", in *Dalits and the State*, (Ed.) Ghanshyam Shah, Concept Publishing Company, New Delhi, 2002.

3. Thangaraj, M. "State and NGO Interventions in the distribution of land to the poor: A study of Tamil Nadu" in *Agrarian reforms, land markets and rural poor*, (Ed.) Narasimha Reddy, Concept Publishing Company, New Delhi, 2009.

4. Thangaraj, M. "Economic development of the Scheduled Castes and Scheduled Tribes: A study of Tamil Nadu" in *Perspectives on economic development and social change* (Ed.) Yagati China Roa, Rawat Publications, New Delhi, 2009.

5. Thangaraj, M. "Special component plan for the Scheduled Castes in Tamil Nadu", Social Action, Vol. 57, No. 1, January-March 2007.

6. Thangaraj, M. "Analysis of Literacy by Social Groups in India", Indian Journal of Adult Education, Vol. 56, No. 4, October-December, 1995.

7. Thangaraj, M. "Demographic and Occupational Characteristics of the Scheduled Castes and the Scheduled Tribes in India", *MIDS Working Paper*, No. 134, September 1995.

2

Land, Caste and Gender in Tamil Nadu

Land is an important productive asset in rural India. Land is the backbone of agriculture. It serves as the base for all living beings. Nearly two-thirds of work-force is directly or indirectly depends on agriculture for their livelihood. About one-fifth of National Income is derived from agricultural sector. Agriculture is a risky and most uncertain economic activity, as it heavily depends upon the vagarious of monsoon. Land market is a significant economic activity and may be classified into land sales market and land lease market both in rural and urban areas. Land reform is one of the regulating mechanisms of the agrarian activity which may be classified into: 1. Reforms aimed at changing ownership pattern (redistributive reform), 2. Reforms dealing with leasing of land (tenancy/tenure reform) in Tamil Nadu.

Objectives of the Study

Major objective of the study is to provide a comprehensive and systematic analysis relating to land, caste and gender. The specific objectives of the study are as follows:

1. To examine access to land by social groups.
2. To analyse the access to land by women.
3. To study the access to irrigation by social groups.
4. To investigate the land use pattern by social groups.

Data

Data relating to access to land operated by social groups for Tamil Nadu were collected from All India Report on Agricultural Census for two points of time viz. 2005-06 and 2010-11 and the information on population were collected from the Census of India, 2011.

Tools of Analysis

A simple access index has been used for the data analysis for this study.

Characteristics of Land

- Land is power i.e., it provides social and economic power to the land owners.
- There is a nexus between landlords and politics.
- Land is considered as status symbol in India.
- Right to landed property from predecessor and right to inherit the property by the successor.
- Access to land is limited. Women and SCs do not have adequate access to land.
- Caste and class coincides in India.
- Skewed distribution of land among the cultivators.
- The word land is associated with exploitation. Landlords often exploit agricultural workers.
- Landlords do not have the will to implement the minimum wage for agricultural workers. For instance,

a violent clash that took place in 1968 in Kilvenmani village, erstwhile Thanjavur District, where 42 agricultural workers from SCs were burnt alive by landlords belonging to upper castes for the simple reason that agricultural workers demanded an addition of half a measure of paddy during the paddy harvest.

- Debate on inverse relationship between land size and productivity is still going on and it remains inconclusive.
- Institutional (Mutt, Temples and Public Trusts) control over land still continues.

Institutional Holdings

The government of Tamil Nadu permits the Institutions to own/control of the land. Institutions are permitted to hold land in excess of ceiling limit. The data presented in Table 2.1 clearly indicate that nearly two per cent of the land is operated (owned) by Institutions viz. Temples, Mutts and Public Trusts. Kings and individuals gifted land to these institutions for the upkeep of the temples and charitable institutions.

Table 2.1:Distribution of Landholdings: All Social Groups in Tamil Nadu – 2010-11 and 2005-06

Category	*2010-11*		*2005-06*	
	Number	*Area (Ha)*	*Number*	*Area (Ha)*
Individual and Joint	8098747 (99.76)	6355623 (97.95)	8173904 (99.77)	6687815 (98.01)
Institutional	19477 (0.24)	132747 (2.05)	19069 (0.23)	136132 (1.99)
Total	**8118224 (100.00)**	**6488370 (100.00)**	**8192973 (100.00)**	**6823948 (100.00)**

Note: Figures in brackets indicate the percentages.

Source: www.agricensus

1. Land and Caste

The SCs are socially and economically exploited by upper castes. They are excluded from the mainstream socio-economic activities, such as, access to safe drinking water, food, shelter and clothing. They are also denied access to ownership of land and education. The laws of Manu states that 'the dwelling of Untouchables should be outside the village; dogs and donkeys should be their wealth. Their clothing should be clothes of the dead and they should wander constantly' (The Laws of Manu, 1991, p. 242). Thus, right to own property is systematically denied to SCs. Landlessness is a pervasive feature of SCs households in rural India.

Table 2.2: Distribution of Landholdings and Land Operated by Social Groups in Tamil Nadu – 2010-11 and 2005-06

Category	*Population 2011*	*2010-11*		*2005-06*	
		Number	*Area (ha)*	*Number*	*Area (ha)*
Scheduled Castes	20.01 %	873499 (10.76)	492306 (7.59)	884241 (10.79)	503341 (7.38)
Scheduled Tribes	1.10 %	74414 (0.92)	74684 (1.12)	68632 (0.84)	75210 (1.10)
Others	78.89 %	7150834 (88.08)	5788634 (89.22)	7221031 (88.14)	6109265 (89.53)
Institutional	-	19477 (0.24)	132747 (2.05)	19069 (0.23)	136132 (1.99)
Total	**100 %**	**8118224 (100.00)**	**6488370 (100.00)**	**8192973 (100.00)**	**6823948 (100.00)**

Sources: 1. www.agricensus; 2. Census of India, 2011.

A brief note on access index

One of the top priorities of post-independence India after 1947 has ben to break up large feudal landholdings and distribute the ceiling surplus land among the poor. Many state governments have enacted ceiling on Land Holding Act during the early 1960s in India. Yet the successive governments have lacked the political will to do so. As a result, a major part of the work-force among the SCs is still depending on agriculture as landless wage labourers in India.

The data presented in Table 2.2 show the land operated by social groups. The data clearly indicate that there was unequal distribution of land by social groups. The land is mostly held by the upper caste landlords in Tamil Nadu. The land operated by the SCs was only 7.6 per cent, while the percentage of SCs population was 20.01 per cent. It is significant to note that the lands operated by the SCs were in the nature of small holdings.

A brief note on access index

The magnitude of access to land by social groups has been examined in terms of simple index of access which is defined as follows:

1. $a_i = \frac{l_i}{p_i}$ Where a_i = access index

   l_i = percentage of land operated by community i to total land

   p_i = percentage of community i to total population

2. $l_i = \frac{L_i}{L}$ Where L_i = Amount of land operated community i

   L = Σ Li total land operated by all communities

3. $p_i = \frac{P_i}{P}$ Where P_i = Population of the community i

   P = Σ Pi = Total population

4. $a_i = \frac{L_i/L}{P_i/P}$

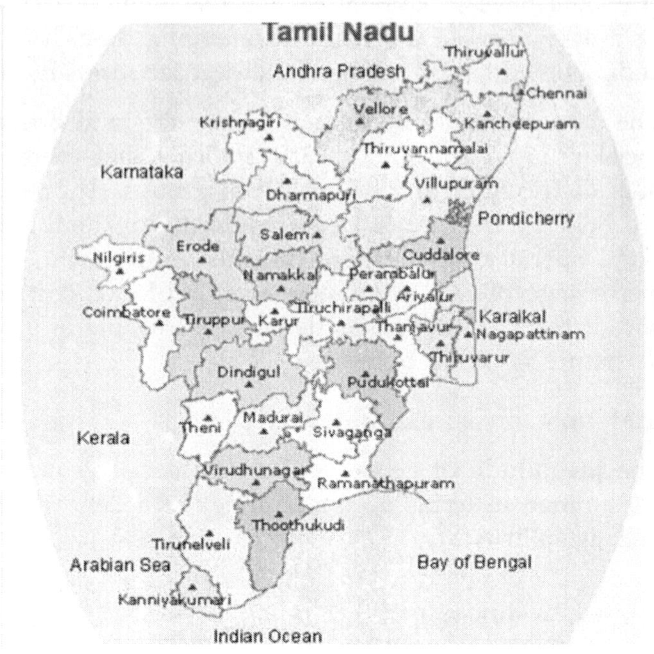

Figure 2.1: Map of Tamil Nadu

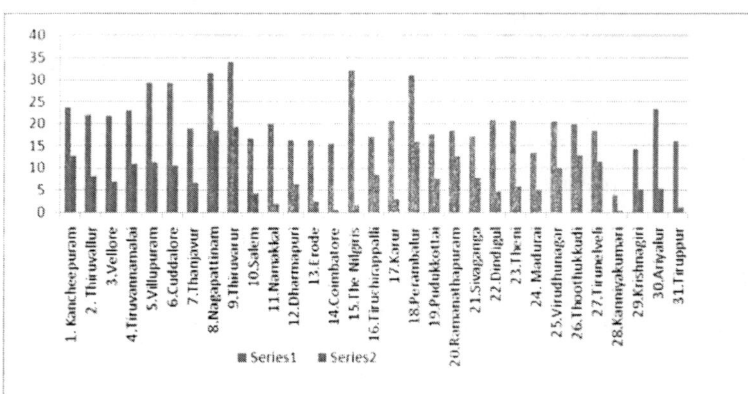

Figure 2.2: Percentage of population and the percentage of land operated by the SCs

Source: Appendix: 2.5.

Note: Series 1 represents the percentage of population

Series 2 represents the percentage of land operated

The access index is equal to one then it indicates that there is perfect equality between the proportion of the community i to the total population and proportion of land operated by the community i to the total land operated. If the access is less than 1, then it shows that the proportion of the land operated by the community i was less than the proportion of the community i to the total population. If the index is more than 1, then it indicates the high access to land i.e. the proportion of land operated by the community i to the total land operated was more than the proportion of population of the community i to the total population. The data presented in Table 2.3 show that the access to land by Scheduled Castes was low as compared to other social groups.

Table 2.3: Access to Land by Social groups

Socual Groups	*2010-11*	*2005-05*
Scheduled Castes	0.38	0.37
Scheduled Tribes	1.02	1.00
Others	1.13	1.13

Source: computed from Table 1.2.

The percentage distribution of land operated by social groups and population by social groups is given in Tables 2.4 and 2.5 at the district level. A close look at the data show that there was a variation in both the population and the area of land operated at the district level. It is significant to note that there was uneven distribution of land operated by the SCs in Tamil Nadu. The percentage of land operated by the SCs was less than their population percentage in all districts in Tamil Nadu. It is disheartening to note that the land operated by the SCs was too low in western part of Tamil Nadu, viz. Namakkal (1.9 per cent), Erode (2.5 per cent), Coimbatore (0.6 per cent), The Nilgiris (1.7 per cent, Karur (3.1 per cent) and Thiruppur with 1.1 per cent. It is striking to note that in the Nilgiris district where the population of of the SCs was the highest with 32.08 per cent of the land operated by the SCs was only 1.7 per cent of the land.

2. Land and Women

Number of days at work in agriculture is high among female workers than that of male workers. Women are, by and large, denied equal rights to access, inherit, or own property/land. Indian tradition dictates that sons inherit family property. Many women fear to ask for her to have a share in the ancestral property, as would cause conflict within the family.

Property Rights Acts

Colonial government and post-independence governments in India have enacted laws to inherit property by women. They are:

1. Hindu Law of Inheritance Act, 1929.
2. Hindu Women's Right to Property Act (XVIII of), 1937.
3. The Hindu Succession Act 1956, (Enacted by the Government of India).
4. The Hindu Succession (Tamil Nadu Amendment) Act, 1989.

Hindu Law of Inheritance Act, 1929: This Act brings woman into the scheme of inheritance. This Act conferred inheritance rights on three female heirs i.e. son's daughter, daughter's daughter and sister.

Hindu Women's Right to Property Act (XVIII of), 1937: The Act of 1937 enables the widow to succeed along with the son and to take a share equal to that of the son.

The Hindu Succession Act 1956, (Enacted by the Government of India): Daughters were given equal rights as sons in their father's self-earned property, if the father

Table 2.4: Percentage distribution of landholdings by Social Groups and by districts in Tamil Nadu – 2010-11

2010-11		*SC*		*ST*		*Others*		*Institutional*		*All*	
		Number	*Area*	*Number*	*Area*	*Number*	*Area*	*Number*	*Area*	*Number*	*Area*
1	Kancheepuram	18.5	12.6	0.1	0.1	80.4	83.3	0.9	4.0	100.0	100.0
2	Tiruvallur	12.1	8.2	0.1	0.2	86.9	89.1	0.8	2.5	100.0	100.0
3	Vellore	8.7	6.9	1.8	3.5	89.5	89.3	0.1	0.3	100.0	100.0
4	Tiruvannamalai	13.2	10.9	2.6	3.3	84.0	85.2	0.2	0.5	100.0	100.0
5	Villupuram	15.3	11.3	1.6	2.5	83.0	85.6	0.1	0.5	100.0	100.0
6	Cuddalore	16.1	10.6	0.1	0.1	83.8	88.9	0.0	0.4	100.0	100.0
7	Thanjavur	9.5	6.7	0.0	0.0	90.4	92.3	0.1	0.9	100.0	100.0
8	Nagapatinam	24.9	18.5	0.0	0.0	75.0	81.0	0.0	0.5	100.0	100.0
9	Thiruvarur	27.0	19.3	0.0	0.0	73.0	79.8	0.1	0.9	100.0	100.0
10	Salem	5.6	4.2	6.0	7.3	88.4	88.1	0.0	0.4	100.0	100.0
11	Namakkal	3.1	1.9	4.6	5.4	92.2	92.4	0.1	0.3	100.0	100.0
12	Dharmapuri	8.0	6.4	3.0	2.7	89.0	90.7	0.1	0.2	100.0	100.0
13	Erode	3.4	2.5	0.6	0.5	95.9	96.2	0.1	0.8	100.0	100.0
14	Coimbatore	1.5	0.6	0.4	0.2	97.1	90.2	0.9	9.0	100.0	100.0
15	The Nilgris	5.4	1.7	4.6	2.9	89.4	53.9	0.5	41.6	100.0	100.0
16	Tiruchirapalli	10.6	8.4	0.8	1.3	88.4	89.1	0.2	1.1	100.0	100.0

contd...

	2010-11	SC		ST		Others		Institutional		All	
		Number	*Area*	*Number*	*Area*	*Number*	*Area*	*Number*	*Area*	*Number*	*Area*
16	Tiruchirapalli	10.6	8.4	0.8	1.3	88.4	89.1	0.2	1.1	100.0	100.0
17	Karur	7.2	3.1	0.0	0.0	92.5	96.2	0.3	0.7	100.0	100.0
18	Perambalur	21.0	15.9	0.2	0.4	78.8	83.5	0.0	0.2	100.0	100.0
19	Pudukkottai	10.5	7.6	0.0	0.0	89.4	91.7	0.1	0.7	100.0	100.0
20	Ramanathapuram	15.1	12.7	0.0	0.0	84.8	86.4	0.1	0.9	100.0	100.0
21	Sivagangai	10.4	7.8	0.0	0.0	89.5	91.2	0.1	1.0	100.0	100.0
22	Dindigul	7.6	4.8	0.0	0.0	92.0	93.6	0.3	1.7	100.0	100.0
23	Theni	8.7	5.9	0.0	0.0	91.2	90.1	0.1	4.0	100.0	100.0
24	Madurai	5.7	4.9	0.0	0.0	93.8	93.4	0.5	1.7	100.0	100.0
25	Virudhunagar	13.9	9.9	0.0	0.0	85.8	86.8	0.3	3.3	100.0	100.0
26	Thoothukudi	16.1	12.8	0.0	0.0	83.2	84.5	0.6	2.7	100.0	100.0
27	Tirunelveli	15.3	11.4	0.0	0.0	84.4	84.1	0.3	4.5	100.0	100.0
28	Kannyakumari	0.4	0.4	0.0	0.0	98.9	95.1	0.7	4.5	100.0	100.0
29	Krishnagiri	6.8	5.2	0.1	0.1	92.9	94.1	0.1	0.6	100.0	100.0
30	Ariyalur	8.6	5.3	0.1	0.1	91.2	94.3	0.1	0.3	100.0	100.0
31	Tiruppur	2.9	1.1	0.0	0.0	96.8	97.7	0.3	1.2	100.0	100.0
	State	10.8	7.6	0.9	1.2	88.1	89.2	0.2	2.0	100.0	100.0

Source: www.agricensus

Table 2.5: Distribution of Population by social groups in Tamil Nadu: 2011

	Population (in numbers)				*Percentage of population*			
	SC	*ST*	*Others*	*All*	*SC*	*ST*	*Others*	*All*
Tamil Nadu	14438445	794697	56913888	72147030	20.01	1.10	78.89	100
Chennai	779667	10061	3857004	4646732	16.78	0.22	83.00	100
1. Kancheepuram	948081	41210	3008961	3998252	23.71	1.03	75.26	100
2. Thiruvallur	821646	47243	2859215	3728104	22.04	1.27	76.69	100
3. Cuddalore	763944	15702	1826268	2605914	29.32	0.60	70.08	100
4. Villupuram	1015716	74859	2368298	3458873	29.37	2.16	68.47	100
5. Vellore	860212	72955	3003164	3936331	21.85	1.85	76.29	100
6. Tiruvannamalai	565329	90954	1808592	2464875	22.94	3.69	73.37	100
7. Salem	580512	119369	2782175	3482056	16.67	3.43	79.90	100
8 Namakkal	345392	57059	1324150	1726601	20.00	3.30	76.69	100
9. Dharmapuri	245392	63044	1198407	1506843	16.29	4.18	79.53	100
10. Krishnagiri	267386	22388	1590035	1879809	14.22	1.19	84.58	100
11. Erode	369483	21880	1860381	2251744	16.41	0.97	82.62	100
12. Coimbatore	535911	28342	2893792	3458045	15.50	0.82	83.68	100
13. Tiruppur	395876	5458	2077718	2479052	15.97	0.22	83.81	100
14. The Nilgiris	235878	32813	466703	735394	32.08	4.46	63.46	100
15. Tiruchirappalli	466561	18198	2237531	2722290	17.14	0.67	82.19	100

contd...

	Population (in numbers)				*Percentage of population*			
	SC	*ST*	*Others*	*All*	*SC*	*ST*	*Others*	*All*
16. Karur	221385	575	842533	1064493	20.80	0.05	79.15	100
17. Perambalur	175289	2584	387350	565223	31.01	0.46	68.53	100
18. Ariyalur	176230	10722	567942	754894	23.34	1.42	75.23	100
19. Thanjavur	455062	3561	1947267	2405890	18.91	0.15	80.94	100
20. Nagapattinam	509767	3756	1102927	1616450	31.54	0.23	68.23	100
21. Thiruvarur	430927	3034	830316	1264277	34.08	0.24	65.68	100
22. Pudukkottai	284804	1283	1332258	1618345	17.60	0.08	82.32	100
23. Madurai	408976	11096	2618180	3038252	13.46	0.37	86.17	100
24. Theni	258200	1835	985864	1245899	20.72	0.15	79.13	100
25. Dindigul	452376	8064	1699335	2159775	20.95	0.37	78.68	100
26. Ramanathapuram	249008	1105	1103332	1353445	18.40	0.08	81.52	100
27. Virudhunagar	399831	2294	1540163	1942288	20.59	0.12	79.30	100
28. Sivaganga	227746	790	1110565	1339101	17.01	0.06	82.93	100
29. Tirunelveli	569714	10270	2497249	3077233	18.51	0.33	81.15	100
30. Thoothukkudi	347895	4911	1397370	1750176	19.88	0.28	79.84	100
31.Kanniyakumari	74249	7282	1788843	1870374	3.97	0.39	95.64	100

Source: Census of India – 2011

died intestate. They, however, had no rights to ancestral property.

The Hindu Succession (Tamil Nadu Amendment) Act, 1989 gives equal rights to women as men in ancestral property. Daughters can also force a partition of ancestral property, if the share is denied or delayed.

In 2005 the Government of India amended its inheritance laws (Hindu Succession Amendment) to ensure daughters (married/unmarried women have equal share in their parental/ancestral property as that of male heirs. This Act applied all over India and also in the State of Tamil Nadu.

Women Empowerment through Property Rights

Studies have shown that when women secure rights to land:

1. Their family nutrition and health status improves;
2. Their children are more likely to receive an education and stay in school longer;
3. They are less likely to be victims of domestic violence;
4. Women may have better access to micro-credit;
5. Women's participation in household decision-making increases.

Case Study (Times of India Report)

Only 13 per cent of women whose parents own land have inherited or expect to inherit land and the biggest opposition to women inheriting land comes from brothers followed by parents. Over 60 per cent of the women renounced their rights to inherit any land by signing no-objection certificates. These facts were revealed in a three state survey conducted in Bihar, Madhya Pradesh and Andhra Pradesh to ascertain how successful the legislation granting Indian women equal rights to inherit land from their parents and what the formal and informal barriers were to the implementation of the Hindu Succession (Amendment) Act 2005 (Times of India, March 4, 2014).

The Hindu Succession Act 1956 that covers inheritance and succession of property of Hindus, Sikhs, Buddhists and Jains comprising 83.6 per cent of the Indian population was amended in 2005 to grant rights to women to inherit agricultural land of the parents and husband. This amendment happened almost a decade after five southern states namely, Maharashtra, Kerala, Andhra Pradesh, Karnataka and Tamil Nadu had amended their succession laws to allow women to inherit agricultural land subject to various conditionalities.

Hostile attitudes towards women inheriting the land

Parents would not like to bequeath land to daughters.

Brothers do not wish sisters to inherit land.

Community does not recognise women's right to inherit land.

The Government of India amended its inheritance laws to ensure daughters to have equal rights to inherit their parent's land and property. But these laws seem to be having little impact even today.

Stridhana Land

Tamil Nadu Ceiling on land holdings Act, 1961 states that "stridhana land means any land held on the date of the commencement of this Act by any female member of a family in her own name". This Act came into force from 6th April 1960. Stridhana land up to 10 standard acre was allowed to be retained outside the family pool (Table 2.6).

Table 2.6: Current status of ceiling on landholdings

Person or Family	Family consisting of not more than 5 members	15 standard acres
	For each additional member	5 standard acres
	Overall ceiling area	30 standard acres
	Additionally Stridhana Land	
	Female members holding land on the date of commencement of the Act	10 Standard Acres

Source: http://www.landreforms.tn.gov.in/LandReforms.html

Land Purchase Scheme

Recognising the importance of land, Government of Tamil Nadu have announced a scheme on "Land purchase scheme" in 2003 (2003-04 Budget) to benefit exclusively for women in Tamil Nadu. Under this scheme, financial assistance is being given to 6000 SC women and 1000 ST women in a year. The aim of the schemes is to improve the land holdings of Schedule Castes and Scheduled Tribes and to enhance their socio-economic status in the state. The government have also issued orders for the exemption of 100 per cent stamp duty for the registration of the land purchased under the scheme.

Subsidy

A maximum 30 per cent of the project cost or Rs 2.25 lakhs whichever is less may be released as subsidy to each beneficiary. The cost of land should be fixed as per the government guidelines. The subsidy released as back end subsidy.

Table 2.7: Land Purchase Scheme: Achievement

Year	*Achievement*	*Fin (In Lakhs)*			*Acres of Land Purchased*		
	Number	*Subsidy*	*Loan*	*Total*	*Dry*	*Wet*	*Total*
2004-05	488	434.15	445.06	879.21	930.37	742.00	1672.37
2005-06	622	555.70	574.88	1130.58	1060.06	1141.74	2201.80
2006-07	2259	562.51	617.92	1180.43	834.64	1890.57	2725.21
2007-08	742	343.71	351.09	694.80	556.36	601.27	1157.63
2008-09	973	345.63	443.89	789.52	522.79	670.23	1193.02
2009-10	1298	392.16	445.45	837.61	191.88	767.51	959.39
2010-11	658	244.18	259.66	503.84	132.83	400.50	533.33
2011-12	133	69.31	160.48	229.795	50.27	83.95 1	34.22
Total	**7173**	**2947.35**	**3298.43**	**6245.785**	**4279.20**	**6297.77**	**10576.97**

Source: S. Jayapal, "Social Welfare Programmes of Scheduled Castes in Tamil Nadu", M.Phil. Dissertation, Department of Economics, University of Madras, 2012

Eligibility

- The applicant shall be a member of the Scheduled Caste Women.
- The applicant should be in the age group of 18 -55.
- The annual family income of the applicant should not exceed Rs 1.00 lakh.
- The applicant should not own any agricultural land.
- The occupation of the applicant should be agriculture.
- Applicants and their family members should not have availed any subsidy so far.

Conditions

- Applicants themselves should select the land to be purchased.
- The lands have to be purchased from the land owners who do not belong to Scheduled Caste.
- The land purchased shall be registered only in the name of applicant.
- The land purchased shall not be sold out within twenty years.
- The applicant who has the land registered in his name can alone take up land development activities.
- The land development activities of digging of open well, bore well and electrification of pump sets shall be taken up as per the NABARD guidelines.
- The feasibility certificate shall be obtained from geologist in respect of digging of open well / bore well.
- The applicant and her family members should not have sold / transferred their lands to others during the last five years.

As per the notification of the government, 6000 SCs women would financed for purchase of land in 2003-04. Till 2011-12 i.e. eight years of the implementation of the scheme, only 7,173 beneficiaries purchased 10576.97 acres of land under this scheme. If this scheme is genuinely implemented by the government, 72,000 women would have benefited and more than 1,00,000 acres of land would have been bought under this scheme by the SCs women alone. Thus, the data presented in Table 2.7 clearly point out that the land purchase scheme in not implemented properly.

Land Operated by Women

The workforce engaged in agriculture is more among the female workers as compared to their male counterparts. "Women constitute nearly 40 per cent of the agricultural workforce in the country. More importantly, 75 per cent of all female workforce and 85 per cent of all rural female workforce in the country today is involved in agriculture and this percentage is rising. Further, rural households are increasingly becoming de-facto female headed households, due to widowhood, desertion, or male out-migration". Draft National Land Reforms Policy (24th July, 2013), Department of Land Resources, Ministry of Rural Development, Government of India.

Women form nearly half (49.91 per cent in 2011) of the total population in Tamil Nadu. The data as given in Tables 2.8, 2.9, 2.10 and 2.11 provide information relating to landholdings by gender and by social groups viz. SCs, STs, Others and all social groups. The data explicate that the land operated by women was very low as compared to their male counterparts in all social groups. There was a marginal increase in the land operated by females in 2010-11 as compared to 2005-06. It is significant to note that the SCs women are slightly better off, as percentage of land operated by SCs females was slightly more.

Table 2.8: Distribution of Landholdings by gender: Scheduled Castes – 2010-11 and 2005-06

	2010-11		*2005-06*	
Category	*Number*	*Area (Ha)*	*Number*	*Area (Ha)*
Males	704764 (80.68)	402228 (81.70)	722543 (81.72)	417185 (82.88)
Females	168735 (19.32)	90077 (18.30)	161698 (18.28)	86156 (17.12)
Total	**873499 (100.00)**	**492306 (100.00)**	**884241 (100.00)**	**503341 (100.00)**

Source: www.agricensus

Table 2.9: Distribution of Landholdings by gender: Scheduled Tribes – 2010-11 and 2005-06

	2010-11		*2005-06*	
Category	*Number*	*Area (Ha)*	*Number*	*Area (Ha)*
Males	61276 (82.35)	63305 (84.76)	57834 (84.27)	64769 (86.12)
Females	13138 (17.65)	11379 (15.24)	10798 (15.73)	10440 (13.88)
Total	**74414 (100.00)**	**74684 (100.00)**	**68632 (100.00)**	**75210 (100.00)**

Source: www.agricensus

Table 2.10: Distribution of Landholdings by gender: Others – 2010-11 and 2005-06

	2010-11		*2005-06*	
Category	*Number*	*Area (Ha)*	*Number*	*Area (Ha)*
Males	5781730 (80.85)	4834472 (83.52)	5866728 (81.25)	5139005 (84.12)
Females	1369104 (19.15)	954161 (16.48)	1354303 (18.75)	970260 (15.88)
Total	**7150834 (100.00)**	**5788634 (100.00)**	**7221031 (100)**	**6109265 (100)**

Source: www.agricensus

Table 2.11: Distribution of landholdings by gender: All Social groups

	2010-11		*2005-06*	
Category	*Number*	*Area (Ha)*	*Number*	*Area (Ha)*
Males	6547770 (80.8)	5300004 (83.4)	6647105 (81.3)	5620959 (84.0)
Females	1550977 (19.2)	1055617 (16.6)	1526799 (18.7)	1066856 (16.0)
Total	**8098747 (100.0)**	**6355621 (100.0)**	**8173904 (100.0)**	**6687816 (100.0)**

Source: www.agricensus

Data on distribution of land operated among social groups by women and by districts are given in Appendices 2.1, 2.2, 2.3 and 2.4. The data clearly demonstrate that land operated by SCs women among SCs was the highest in the Nilgiris district with 32 per cent and the lowest in Namakkal district with 14 per cent of the land. While in the case of land operated by 'Others' women among 'Others' was the highest in Kanyakumari district with 27.3 per cent and the lowest in Erode district with 10.1 per cent if the land in 2010-11. Thus, the data clearly indicate that there is a variation among women by social groups in Tamil Nadu.

Landholdings by size classes

Indian agriculture is characterised by a large number of small holdings and a small number of large holdings. Distribution of land operated by males and females by the size classes of operational holdings as given in Tables 2.12, 2.13, 2.14 and 2.15 illustrate the difference between the males and females by social groups. The land operated by females was high in the marginal holdings. The analysis of data by social groups shows that the land operated by the SC females was high in the marginal holdings and very low in the large holdings as compared to STs and Others. This indicates that the inequality in the distribution of land holdings was low among the Scheduled Castes in Tamil Nadu.

Table 2.12: Distribution of Landholdings by size class of holdings: All Social Groups – 2010-11

Category	*Males*		*Female*		*Total*	
	Number	*Area (Ha)*	*Number*	*Area (Ha)*	*Number*	*Area (Ha)*
Marginal	4996103 (70.30)	1837625 (31.67)	1259486 (81.21)	450290 (42.66)	6255589 (77.24)	2287915 (36.00)
Small	981687 (14.99)	1367714 (25.80)	196962 (12.30)	272122 (25.78)	1178649 (14.55)	1639836 (25.80)
Semi-medium	426503 (6.51)	1152113 (21.74)	73463 (4.74)	196752 (18.64)	499966 (6.17)	1348865 (21.22)
Medium	129714 (1.98)	729711 (13.77)	19179 (1.24)	107165 (10.15)	148893 (1.84)	836876 (13.17)
Large	13763 (0.21)	212844 (4.02)	1887 (0.12)	29288 (2.77)	15650 (0.19)	242132 (3.81)
All classes	**6547770 (100.00)**	**5300004 (100.00)**	**1550977 (100.00)**	**1055617 (100.00)**	**8098747 (100.00)**	**6355621 (100.00)**

Source: www.agricensus

Table 2.13: Distribution of Landholdings by size class of holdings: Scheduled Castes – 2010-11

Category	*Males*		*Female*	
	Number	*Area (Ha)*	*Number*	*Area (Ha)*
Marginal	599165 (85.02)	211785 (52.65)	147088 (87.17)	52682 (58.49)
Small	79371 (11.26)	108352 (26.94)	16818 (9.97)	22953 (25.48)
Semi-medium	22260 (3.10)	58377 (14.51)	4230 (2,50)	10968 (12.18)
Medium	3740 (0.53)	20350 (5.06)	569 (0.34)	3125 (3.47)
Large	228 (0.00)	3364 (0.84)	230 (0.00)	354 (0.39)
All classes	**704764 (100.00)**	**402228 (100.00)**	**168735 (100.00)**	**90077 (100.00)**

Source: www.agricensus

Table 2.14: Distribution of Landholdings by size class of holdings: Scheduled Tribes – 2010-11

Category	*Males*		*Female*	
	Number	*Area (Ha)*	*Number*	*Area (Ha)*
Marginal	39026 (63.69)	17699 (27.94)	9275 (70.60)	4195 (36.87)
Small	14767 (24.10)	20651 (32.62)	2802 (21.33)	3841 (33.77)
Semi-medium	5949 (9.71)	15835 (25.01)	893 (6.80)	2316 (20.36)
Medium	1444 (2.35)	7855 (12.41)	155 (1.18)	827 (7.27)
Large	90 (0.15)	1263 (1.10)	13 (0.10)	199 (1.75)
All classes	**61276 (100.00)**	**63304 (100.00)**	**13138 (100.00)**	**11377 (100.00)**

Source: www.agricensus

Table 2.15: Distribution of Landholdings by size class of holdings: Others – 2010-11

Category	*Males*		*Female*	
	Number	*Area (Ha)*	*Number*	*Area (Ha)*
Marginal	4357912 (75.37)	1608137 (33.26)	1103123 (80.51)	393412 (41.23)
Small	887549 (15.35)	1238716 (25.62)	177342 (12.95)	245326 (25.71)
Semi-medium	398294 (2.69)	1077897 (22.30)	68340 (4.99)	183471 (19.22)
Medium	124530 (2.15)	701504 (14.51)	18455 (1.35)	103215 (10.82)
Large	13445 (2.33)	208218 (4.31)	1844 (0.13)	28735 (3.01)
All classes	**5781730 (100.00)**	**4834472 (100.00)**	**1369104 (100.00)**	**954164 (100.00)**

Source: www.agricensus

3. Access to Irrigation

Water is one of the social goods. Social goods are goods, the consumption of which is non-rival and non-excludability. Same benefits are available to all from the social goods without mutual interference. There is no regulatory mechanism in India as how much water can be used for agricultural and non-agricultural purposes. Water is being robbed by the water sellers who have pump-sets. Excessive extraction of water results in depletion of ground water.

India has a tropical climate and it receives rainfall less than four months in a year. It does not have potentiality to go for multiple cropping. Provision of irrigation facilities helps to cultivate superior crops. Provision of irrigation will considerably enhance agriculture production and productivity. With the introduction of irrigation, cultivable waste lands can be brought under cultivation and multiple cropping can be practiced.

A well is a hole dug in the ground to get the water. Well can be dug for drinking, bathing and cultivation. The depth of the well depends upon the soil quality and availability of water. A major part of the Peninsular India is not suitable for well irrigation due to hilly terrain, uneven surface and lack of underground water. Tube well is a deeper well from which water can be lifted with the help of pump sets operated by an electric motor or a diesel engine. Surface water (tanks and rivers) and Sub-surface water (ground water) are the major sources of water for agricultural purposes. Information relating to well and tube wells fitted with pump sets are being discussed in this section.

Installation of ground water structure requires heavy investment by farmers in the water scarce areas. Access to finance/credit is one of the ways to install ground water structure. Competitive deepening of bore wells leads rapid depletion of ground water. It may be hypothesised that access to bore well fitted with electric pump sets is low among the SC farmers as against Others in Tamil Nadu. The data presented in Tables 2.16 and 2.17 demonstrate the estimated number of wells and tube wells and the wells and tube wells fitted with pump-sets and without pump-sets in Tamil Nadu by social groups. It could be seen from the data that wells without pump sets is proportionately low among the SCs as compared to Others. It is evident from the data that about 90 per cent of the wells in use was under the control of Others with pump sets fitted with electric and diesel. Almost a similar picture is emerging from the data with regard to tube wells. The wells and tube wells controlled by the STs and SCs forms less that 10 per cent which is disproportionately low in Tamil Nadu. The proportion of well and tube wells fitted with electric pump sets was high among the Others and low among the SCs and STs in Tamil Nadu both in 2005-06 and 2010-11. It is significant to note that the Government of Tamil Nadu is supplying electricity at free of cost to the farmers and the SCs and STs are not having adequate access to the bore well fitted with the electricity.

Area of land irrigated by sources: Agriculture generally depends very much on monsoon and in India it is unpredictable. In water starved area, farmers have to supplement the ground water with the help of wells and bore wells. Access to water from wells and bore wells is not easy in India and farmers have to invest heavily to irrigate their land with wells and bore-wells. Distribution of area irrigated by diverse sources as given in Tables 2.18 and 2.19 clearly indicate that the sub-surface water viz. wells and tube wells was very low among the SCs and STs as compared to Others in Tamil Nadu. It is significant to note that the net area irrigated by different sources of irrigation has increased in 2010-11 as compared to 2005-06.

4. Land Use Pattern

Land is an important productive asset and also a major source of livelihood for most of the rural people in India.

Table 2.16 : Estimated number of wells and tube-wells in Tamil Nadu by social groups - 2005 – 06 (area in absolute hectares)

SOCIAL GROUPS	*Total Holdings*		*Number of Wells*					*Number of Tube wells*		
			in Use				*Not in Use*			
			With Pump sets			*Without Pump sets*				
	Number	*Area*	*Electric*	*Diesel*	*Total*			*Electric*	*Diesel*	*Total*
Others	7221031	6109265	1548522	268223	1816745	25186	18266	319496	153303	472799
STs	68632	75210	11975	3303	15278	415	39	650	149	799
SCs	884241	503341	139604	24896	164500	2808	1766	32572	20331	52903
Institutional	19069	136132	3025	449	3474	14	36	867	253	1120
All	**8192973**	**6823948**	**1703126**	**296871**	**1999997**	**28423**	**20107**	**353585**	**174036**	**527621**
Percentages										
Others	88.14	89.53	90.92	90.35	90.84	88.61	90.84	90.36	88.09	89.61
STs	0.84	1.10	0.70	1.11	0.76	1.46	0.19	0.18	0.09	0.15
SCs	10.79	7.38	8.20	8.39	8.23	9.88	8.78	9.21	11.68	10.03
Institutional	0.23	1.99	0.18	0.15	0.17	0.05	0.18	0.25	0.15	0.21
All	**100.00**	**100.00**	**100.00**	**100.00**	**100.00**	**100.00**	**100.00**	**100.00**	**100.00**	**100.00**

Source: www.agricensus

Table 2.17 : Estimated number of wells and tube-wells in Tamil Nadu by social groups - 2010 – 11 (area in absolute hectares)

SOCIAL GROUPS	*Total Holdings*		*Number of Wells*					*Number of Tube wells*		
			in Use				*Not in Use*			
			With Pump sets			*Without Pump sets*				
	Number	*Area*	*Electric*	*Diesel*	*Total*			*Electric*	*Diesel*	*Total*
Others	7150834	5788634	1476958	210140	1687098	13481	9009	587346	92558	679904
STs	74414	74684	8951	823	9774	8	21	757	0	757
SCs	873499	492306	82048	10756	92804	2860	1593	29125	2190	31315
Institutional	19477	132747	3308	260	3568	79	33	1678	15	1693
All	**8118224**	**6488370**	**1571265**	**221979**	**1793244**	**16428**	**10656**	**618906**	**94763**	**713669**
Percentages										
Others	88.08	89.22	94.00	94.67	94.08	82.06	84.54	94.90	97.67	95.27
STs	0.92	1.15	0.57	0.37	0.55	0.05	0.20	0.12	0.00	0.11
SCs	10.76	7.59	5.22	4.85	5.18	17.41	14.95	4.71	2.31	4.39
Institutional	0.24	2.05	0.21	0.12	0.20	0.48	0.31	0.27	0.02	0.24
All	**100.00**	**100.00**	**100.00**	**100.00**	**100.00**	**100.00**	**100.00**	**100.00**	**100.00**	**100.00**

Source: www.agricensus

Table 2.18: Estimated number of operational holdings by irrigation and area Irrigated by different sources in Tamil Nadu by social groups - 2005 – 06 (area in absolute hectares)

SOCIAL GROUPS	Total Holdings		Canals		Tanks		Wells		Tube wells		Other Sources		Exclusive Number of Holdings Receiving Irrigation	Total Net Irrigated Area
	Number	Area	No. of Holdings	Area Irrigated	No. of Holdings	Area Irrigated	No. of Holdings	Area Irrigated	No. of Holdings	Area Irrigated	No. of Holdings	Area Irrigated		
Others	7221031	6109265	896552	641674	963210	459497	1472478	1031852	361901	264570	56825	36546	3670864	2434139
STs	68632	75210	537	520	1933	1238	14682	12864	1442	1869	1428	804	19768	17294
SCs	884241	503341	128966	73375	150572	59240	149259	74809	41757	19085	5555	2265	469640	228775
Institutional	19069	136132	2607	12265	2742	4872	3119	10123	978	2694	397	3757	9629	33710
All	**8192973**	**6823948**	**1028662**	**727834**	**1118457**	**524848**	**1639538**	**1129648**	**406078**	**288216**	**64205**	**43372**	**4169901**	**2713918**
Percentages														
Others	88.14	89.53	87.16	88.16	86.12	87.55	89.81	91.34	89.12	91.80	88.51	84.26	88.03	89.69
STs	0.84	1.10	0.05	0.07	0.17	0.24	0.90	1.14	0.36	0.65	2.22	1.85	0.47	0.64
SCs	10.79	7.38	12.54	10.08	13.46	11.29	9.10	6.62	10.28	6.62	8.65	5.22	11.26	8.43
Institutional	0.23	1.99	0.25	1.69	0.25	0.93	0.19	0.90	0.24	0.93	0.62	8.66	0.23	1.24
All	**100.00**	**100.00**	**100.00**	**100.00**	**100.00**	**100.00**	**100.00**	**100.00**	**100.00**	**100.00**	**100.00**	**100.00**	**100.00**	**100.00**

Source: www.agricensus

Table 2.19: Estimated number of operational holdings by area irrigated by different sources in Tamil Nadu by social groups - 2010 –11 (area in absolute hectares)

SOCIAL GROUPS	*Total Holdings*		*Canals*		*Tanks*		*Wells*		*Tube wells*		*Other Sources*		*Exclusive Number of Holdings Receiving Irrigation*	Total Net Irrigated Area
	Number	*Area*	*No. of Holdings*	*Area Irrigated*	*No. of Holdings*	*Area Irrigated*	*No. of Holdings*	*Area Irrigated*	*No. of Holdings*	*Area Irrigated*	*No. of Holdings*	*Area Irrigated*		
Others	7150834	5788634	857457	618395	943181	431389	2157925	1413434	859436	488705	21659	10501	4770695	2962424
STs	74414	74684	957	279	337	162	15787	13253	782	494	6240	4321	23706	17609
SCs	873499	492306	148768	85159	147376	59459	143302	75786	54756	25280	3443	1126	492294	246809
Institutional	19477	132747	3347	7911	4490	8894	3265	6939	1507	3278	12	443	11993	27466
All	**8118224**	**6488370**	**1010169**	**711744**	**1095384**	**499905**	**2320279**	**1509412**	**916481**	**517758**	**31354**	**15490**	**5298688**	**3254308**
Percentages														
Others	88.08	89.22	84.88	86.88	86.11	86.29	93.00	93.64	93.78	94.39	69.08	67.79	90.04	91.03
STs	0.92	1.15	0.09	0.04	0.03	0.03	0.68	0.88	0.09	0.10	19.90	27.90	0.45	0.54
SCs	10.76	7.59	14.73	11.96	13.45	11.89	6.18	5.02	5.97	4.88	10.98	7.27	9.29	7.58
Institutional	0.24	2.05	0.33	1.11	0.41	1.78	0.14	0.46	0.16	0.63	0.04	2.86	0.23	0.84
All	**100.00**	**100.00**	**100.04**	**100.00**	**100.00**	**100.00**	**100.00**	**100.00**	**100.00**	**100.00**	**100.00**	**105.82**	**100.00**	**100.00**

Source: www.agricensus

The basic needs, such as, food, shelter, fuel, and clothing are directly obtained from land. It also provides multiple utilities to the owner or the user. The existing land use pattern is uneven, as the share of forest land to the total geographical area is lower than that of the minimum required for the protection of the environment from ecological degradation. The increasing needs consequent to growth of population require a revision or rectification of existing land use pattern. The data presented in Tables 2.20 and 2.21 exhibit the land use pattern by social groups. It is evident from the data that other uncultivated land excluding fallow land, fallow land other than current fallows, cultivable waste land, total uncultivated and land not available for cultivation was low among the SCs as compared to Others in Tamil Nadu. Hence, it may be concluded that the SCs were efficient in utilising land.

Land Reforms and the New Economic Policies

Section 37-A of the Ceiling on land holdings Act, Tamil Nadu, 1961 provides permission for industrial and commercial undertakings/corporate companies for contract and corporate farming to acquire or hold land in excess of ceiling limit. Section 37-B provides permission for the Public Trust for establishment of educational institutions and hospitals to acquire land excess over the ceiling limit. Many corporate companies private educational institutions have managed to acquire a huge quantity of land, as a result of this provision. Although these two provisions were in the Act since its inception i.e. from 1961, there was not many Institutions (private and corporate companies) to use these provisions due strict conditions laid down by the Government of Tamil Nadu. But it is only after the introduction of the New Economic Policies, the Government of Tamil Nadu granted permission to the Institutions to acquire land in excess of ceiling limit to many private and corporate companies.

Table 2.20: Estimated area of land use in Tamil Nadu by social groups - 2005 – 06 (area in absolute hectares)

SOCIAL GROUPS	*Total Holdings*		*Net Area Sown*	*Area Under Current Fallows*	*Net Cultivated Area*	*Other Uncultivated Land Excluding Fallow Land*	*Fallow Land Other than Current Fallows*	*Cultivable Waste Land*	*Total Uncultivated Land*	*Land Not Available for Cultivation*
Others	7221031	6109265	4345615	1587639	5933254	26106	51386	18191	95683	80328
STs	68632	75210	59475	14281	73756	339	729	52	1120	334
SCs	884241	503341	371291	124314	495606	1473	2661	1005	5139	2596
Institutional	19069	136132	104305	27344	131648	520	1869	287	2676	1808
All	**8192973**	**6823948**	**4880687**	**1753578**	**6634264**	**28438**	**56644**	**19536**	**104618**	**85066**
Percentages										
Others	88.14	89.53	89.04	90.54	89.43	91.80	90.72	93.12	91.46	94.43
STs	0.84	1.10	1.22	0.81	1.11	1.19	1.29	0.27	1.07	0.39
SCs	10.79	7.38	7.61	7.09	7.47	5.18	4.70	5.14	4.91	3.05
Institutional	0.23	1.99	2.14	1.56	1.98	1.83	3.30	1.47	2.56	2.13
All	**100.00**	**100.00**	**100.00**	**100.00**	**100.00**	**100.00**	**100.00**	**99.99**	**100.00**	**100.00**

Source: www.agricensus

Table 2.21: Estimated area of land use in Tamil Nadu by social groups - 2010 – 11 (area in absolute hectares)

Social Group	*Total Holdings*		*Net Area Sown*	*Area Under Current Fallows*	*Net Cultivated Area*	*Other Uncultivated Land Excluding Fallow Land*	*Fallow Land Other than Current Fallows*	*Cultivable Waste Land*	*Total Uncultivated Land*	*Land Not Available for Cultivation*
	Number	*Area*								
Others	7150834	5788634	4577833	913739	5491572	30944	84739	67731	183414	113647
STs	74414	74684	59519	14840	74359	43	12	6	61	264
SCs	873499	492306	374318	106009	480327	1507	4399	1296	7201	4778
Institutional	19477	132747	87949	23712	111662	5232	3872	2141	11245	9841
All	8118224	6488370	5099619	1058301	6157920	37726	93022	71173	201921	128529
Percentages										
Others	88.08	89.22	89.77	86.34	89.18	82.02	91.1	95.16	90.83	88.42
STs	0.92	1.15	1.17	1.4	1.21	0.11	0.01	0.01	0.03	0.21
SCs	10.76	7.59	7.34	10.02	7.8	3.99	4.73	1.82	3.57	3.72
Institutional	0.24	2.05	1.72	2.24	1.81	13.87	4.16	3.01	5.57	7.66
All	**100**	**100**	**100**	**100**	**100**	**100**	**100**	**100**	**100**	**100**

Source: www.agricensus

(i) Performance under Section 37-A (as on 31-03-2016)

Orders issued by the Government granting permission	172
Extent involved	47,099 acres
No. of applications received from Government after amendment 25.11.10	235
No. of proposals pending in Government for orders	23

Source: http://www.landreforms.tn.gov.in/LandReforms.html

(ii) Performance under Section 37-B (as on 31-03-2016)

Orders issued by the Government granting permission	
Prior to amendment	112
After amendment	23
No. of applications pending after amendment	642
No. of proposals pending in Government for orders	82

Source: http://www.landreforms.tn.gov.in/LandReforms.html

Conclusion

Land reform legislations were enacted mainly to redistribute land to the landless and other poor, but these legislations could not alter the agrarian structure as land operated by the SCs continued to be low even after fifty-five years of implementation of land reform legislations. The land operated by the SCs is in the nature of small holdings. The Hindu Succession Act could deliver justice to women in getting their ancestral land, as the land controlled by women continued to be abysmally low even after several years of the enactment of Hindu Succession Act in Tamil Nadu. The percentage of land owned by women is disproportionately small considering their crucial contribution to agriculture. There is a need for reframing land reform policies so that widows and deserted women would be given preference from government while distributing land to the beneficiaries.

The wells and tube wells controlled by the STs and SCs forms less than 10 per cent which is disproportionately low in Tamil Nadu. The proportion of well and tube wells fitted with electric pump sets was high among Others and low among SCs and STs in Tamil Nadu both in 2005-06 and 2010-11. Distribution of area irrigated by diverse sources of irrigation as given in Tables 1.18 and 1.19 clearly indicate that sub-surface water viz. wells and tube wells was very low among the SCs and STs as compared to Others in Tamil Nadu.

It is evident from the data that, other uncultivated land excluding fallow land, fallow land other than current fallows, cultivable waste land, total uncultivated and land not available for cultivation was low among SCs as compared to Others in Tamil Nadu which indicate that the SCs were efficient in utilising land.

References

1. Centre for Women Studies, *Property rights of women in Tamil Nadu,* Justice Basheer Ahmed Sayeed College for women, Chennai.
2. Dalit women right to land: A Fight for Survival, Dignity and Equality, Action Aid, Bangalore, India, April 2013.
3. Draft National Land Reforms Policy (24th July, 2013), Department of Land Resources, Ministry of Rural Development Government of India.
4. Krishnakumar, K., Tamil Selvan, P., "Role of Commercial Banks in Socio-Economic Development of SCs and STs (A Study with Special Reference to Tahdco Schemes in Tamil Nadu)" *Indian Journal of Applied Research,* Volume 4, No. 3, March, 2014.
5. Thangaraj, M, "Access to Land for the Scheduled Castes and Scheduled Tribes in India", *MIDS Working Paper,* No. 122, June 1994.

6. Thangaraj, M., "Land Use Pattern in Tamil Nadu", *MIDS Working Paper*, No. 107, June 1992.

7. The Tamil Nadu land reforms (Fixation of Ceiling on Land) Act, 1961, Government of Tamil Nadu, 1980.

8. Times of India, Barely one in ten women own land, brothers most anti sisters inheriting land: Survey, March 4, 2014.

Appendix 2.1: Distribution of landholdings by Scheduled Caste in Tamil Nadu – 2010-11

		Male		*Female*		*Total*		*Male*		*Female*	
		Number	*Area*	*Number*	*Area*	*Number*	*Area*	*Number %*	*Area %*	*Number %*	*Area %*
1	Kancheepuram	33346	15099	7438	3203	40784	18303	81.8	82.5	18.2	17.5
2	Tiruvallur	21793	8697	4735	1956	26528	10653	82.2	81.6	17.8	18.4
3	Vellore	26777	13879	6543	3322	33320	17202	80.4	80.7	19.6	19.3
4	Tiruvannamalai	48788	27481	10468	5856	59256	33338	82.3	82.4	17.7	17.6
5	Villupuram	79213	39816	15017	6900	94230	46716	84.1	85.2	15.9	14.8
6	Cuddalore	40781	19736	9286	4080	50067	23817	81.5	82.9	18.5	17.1
7	Thanjavur	21662	11200	6027	2905	27689	14105	78.2	79.4	21.8	20.6
8	Nagapatinam	33635	21626	9746	6031	43381	27657	77.5	78.2	22.5	21.8
9	Thiruvarur	32684	21949	8327	5209	41011	27159	79.7	80.8	20.3	19.2
10	Salem	14042	8736	3839	2358	17881	11095	78.5	78.7	21.5	21.3
11	Namakkal	6171	3431	1071	557	7242	3988	85.2	86.0	14.8	14.0
12	Dharmapuri	16706	10506	4716	2870	21422	13376	78.0	78.5	22.0	21.5
13	Erode	5733	5576	1047	995	6780	6572	84.6	84.8	15.4	15.1
14	Coimbatore	1667	1097	332	210	1999	1307	83.4	83.9	16.6	16.1
15	The Nilgiris	2397	941	1063	442	3460	1383	69.3	68.0	30.7	32.0
16	Tiruchirapalli	25194	16010	6668	3810	31862	19820	79.1	80.8	20.9	19.2
17	Karur	8432	5251	2138	1142	10570	6393	79.8	82.1	20.2	17.9
18	Perambalur	22983	13412	6721	3560	29704	16973	77.4	79.0	22.6	21.0
19	Pudukkottai	32798	14003	7132	2930	39930	16933	82.1	82.7	17.9	17.3
20	Ramanathapuram	46571	28911	12942	7206	59513	36118	78.3	80.0	21.7	20.0

contd...

		Male		*Female*		*Total*		*Male*		*Female*	
		Number	*Area*	*Number*	*Area*	*Number*	*Area*	*Number %*	*Area %*	*Number %*	*Area %*
21	Sivagangai	22348	10650	5462	2334	27810	12985	80.4	82.0	19.6	18.0
22	Dindigul	17796	11844	4765	3070	22561	14914	78.9	79.4	21.1	20.6
23	Theni	9004	6076	2142	1484	11146	7561	80.8	80.4	19.2	19.6
24	Madurai	13360	6677	3460	1565	16820	8242	79.4	81.0	20.6	19.0
25	Virudhunagar	22744	15399	4845	2786	27589	18186	82.4	84.7	17.6	15.3
26	Thoothukudi	25319	25079	6514	5732	31833	30812	79.5	81.4	20.5	18.6
27	Tirunelveli	37225	20616	7761	3434	44986	24051	82.7	85.7	17.3	14.3
28	Kannyakumari	1138	224	451	98	1589	322	71.6	69.6	28.4	30.4
29	Krishnagiri	15717	9667	3580	2129	19297	11796	81.4	82.0	18.6	18.0
30	Ariyalur	14804	5319	3375	1180	18179	6500	81.4	81.8	18.6	18.2
31	Tiruppur	3936	3307	1124	706	5060	4014	77.8	82.4	22.2	17.6
	State	**704764**	**402228**	**168735**	**90077**	**873499**	**492305**	**80.7**	**81.7**	**19.3**	**18.3**

Source: www.agricensus

Appendix 2.2: Distribution of landholdings by Scheduled Tribe in Tamil Nadu – 2010-11

		Male		*Female*		*Total*		*Male*		*Female*	
		Number	*Area*	*Number*	*Area*	*Number*	*Area*	*Number %*	*Area %*	*Number %*	*Area %*
1	Kancheepuram	138	110	47	17	185	127	74.6	86.6	25.4	13.4
2	Tiruvallur	204	152	96	51	300	204	68.0	74.5	32.0	25.0
3	Vellore	5920]	7757	897	926	6817	8684	-	89.3	13.2	10.7
4	Tiruvannamalai	9974	9005	1535	1192	11509	10197	86.7	88.3	13.3	11.7
5	Villupuram	7979	8907	1601	1617	9580	10524	83.3	84.6	16.7	15.4
6	Cuddalore	202	112	37	14	239	126	84.5	88.9	15.5	11.1
7	Thanjavur	19	20	10	10	29	30	65.5	66.7	34.5	33.3
8	Nagapatinam	0	0	0	0	0	0	0	0	0	0
9	Thiruvarur	1	1	4	4	5	5	20.0	20.0	80.0	80.0
10	Salem	15003	15778	3994	3731	18997	19510	79.0	80.9	21.0	19.1
11	Namakkal	8930	9792	1875	1812	10805	11604	82.6	84.4	17.4	15.6
12	Dharmapuri	6216	4503	1730	1050	7946	5553	78.2	81.1	21.8	18.9
13	Erode	967	1215	176	172	1143	1388	84.6	87.5	15.4	12.4
14	Coimbatore	397	464	114	97	511	561	77.7	82.7	22.3	17.3
15	The Nilgiris	2444	2014	546	290	2990	2304	81.7	87.4	18.3	12.6
16	Tiruchirapalli	2157	2831	267	238	2424	3069	89.0	92.2	11.0	7.8
17	Karur	0	0	0	0	0	0	0	0	0	0
18	Perambalur	195	324	34	50	229	374	85.2	86.6	14.8	13.4
19	Pudukkottai	33	11	2	0	35	11	94.3	100.0	5.7	0.0
20	Ramanathapuram	0	0	0	0	0	0	0	0	0	0
21	Sivagangai	0	0	0	0	0	0	0	0	0	0
22	Dindigul	18	11	8	4	26	16	69.2	68.8	30.8	25.0
23	Theni	22	19	9	7	31	26	71.0	73.1	29.0	26.9
24	Madurai	0	0	0	0	0	0	0	0	0	0

contd...

		Male		*Female*		*Total*		*Male*		*Female*	
		Number	*Area*	*Number*	*Area*	*Number*	*Area*	*Number %*	*Area%*	*Number %*	*Area %*
25	Virudhunagar	0	0	0	0	0	0	0	0	0	0
26	Thoothukudi	0	0	0	0	0	0	0	0	0	0
27	Tirunelveli	8	3	7	2	15	6	53.3	50.0	46.7	33.3
28	Kanniyakumari	25	2	12	1	37	3	67.6	66.7	32.4	33.3
29	Krishnagiri	215	168	55	35	270	204	79.6	82.4	20.4	17.2
30	Ariyalur	198	91	79	48	277	140	71.5	65.0	28.5	34.3
31	Tiruppur	11	5	3	2	14	7	78.6	71.4	21.4	28.6
	State	**61276**	**63305**	**13138**	**11378**	**74414**	**74683**	**82.3**	**84.8**	**17.7**	**15.2**

Source: www.agricensus

Appendix 2.3: Distribution of landholdings by Others in Tamil Nadu – 2010-11

		Male		*Female*		*Total*		*Male*		*Female*	
		Number	*Area*	*Number*	*Area*	*Number*	*Area*	*Number %*	*Area%*	*Number %*	*Area%*
1	Kancheepuram	139307	99190	37668	21639	176975	120830	78.7	82.1	21.3	17.9
2	Tiruvallur	154213	95852	36732	20319	190945	116171	80.8	82.5	19.2	17.5
3	Vellore	281008	184226	63678	38089	344686	222316	81.5	82.9	18.5	17.1
4	Tiruvannamalai	314942	222489	61660	37235	376602	259724	83.6	85.7	16.4	14.3
5	Villupuram	433134	308649	78017	44698	511151	353347	84.7	87.4	15.3	12.6
6	Cuddalore	214534	171048	45661	27708	260195	198757	82.5	86.1	17.5	13.9
7	Thanjavur	204156	157267	60443	36503	264599	193770	77.2	81.2	22.8	18.8
8	Nagapatinam	103600	98632	26809	22559	130409	121191	79.4	81.4	20.6	18.6
9	Thiruvarur	85873	89983	25150	22239	111023	112222	77.3	80.2	22.7	19.8
10	Salem	229928	196026	51317	38658	281245	234684	81.8	83.5	18.2	16.5
11	Namakkal	183127	169068	33368	27725	216495	196794	84.6	85.9	15.4	14.1
12	Dharmapuri	192326	155664	47384	32974	239710	188638	80.2	82.5	19.8	17.5
13	Erode	167484	229997	21897	25876	189381	255874	88.4	89.9	11.6	10.1
14	Coimbatore	100690	172989	26900	41146	127590	214136	78.9	80.8	21.1	19.2
15	The Nilgiris	47176	35650	10402	7634	57578	43284	81.9	82.4	18.1	17.6
16	Tiruchirapalli	222174	177611	44647	31723	266821	209335	83.3	84.8	16.7	15.2
17	Karur	112436	170955	22677	27942	135113	198898	83.2	86.0	16.8	14.0
18	Perambalur	86640	71798	24883	17129	111523	88928	77.7	80.7	22.3	19.3
19	Pudukkottai	275304	172511	63254	31774	338558	204286	81.3	84.4	18.7	15.6

contd...

		Male		Female		Total		Male		Female	
		Number	Area	Number	Area	Number	Area	Number %	Area%	Number %	Area%
20	Ramanathapuram	251471	193575	82410	52283	333881	245859	75.3	78.7	24.7	21.3
21	Sivagangai	194887	127318	45393	24087	240280	151406	81.1	84.1	18.9	15.9
22	Dindigul	215241	239298	56533	52604	271774	291902	79.2	82.0	20.8	18.0
23	Theni	94306	93629	23023	22227	117329	115857	80.4	80.8	19.6	19.2
24	Madurai	209702	122554	65661	35804	275363	158359	76.2	77.4	23.8	22.6
25	Virudhunagar	139245	133235	31059	26652	170304	159888	81.8	83.3	18.2	16.7
26	Thoothukudi	129877	163172	34166	39858	164043	203030	79.2	80.4	20.8	19.6
27	Tirunelveli	209553	154343	37798	23766	247351	178110	84.7	86.7	15.3	13.3
28	Kanniyakumari	276605	57762	99434	21662	376039	79424	73.6	72.7	26.4	27.3
29	Krishnagiri	214853	178659	46972	34749	261825	213409	82.1	83.7	17.9	16.3
30	Ariyalur	156797	97915	35644	18010	192441	115926	81.5	84.5	18.5	15.5
31	Tiruppur	141141	293391	28464	48875	169605	342266	83.2	85.7	16.8	14.3
	State	**5781730**	**4834472**	**1369104**	**954161**	**7150834**	**5788633**	**80.9**	**83.5**	**19.1**	**16.5**

Source: www.agricensus

Appendix 2.4: Distribution of landholdings by All Social Groups in Tamil Nadu – 2010-11

2010-11		All Male		All Female		All Total		All Male		All Female	
		Number	Area	Number	Area	Number	Area	Number %	Area %	Number %	Area %
1	Kancheepuram	172791	114400	45153	24860	220026	145068	78.5	78.9	20.5	17.1
2	Tiruvallur	176210	104702	41563	22327	219609	130341	80.2	80.3	18.9	17.1
3	Vellore	313705	205864	71118	42338	385085	248953	81.5	82.7	18.5	17.0
4	Tiruvannamalai	373704	258975	73663	44284	448365	304801	83.3	85.0	16.4	14.5
5	Villupuram	520326	357372	94635	53216	615543	412766	84.5	86.6	15.4	12.9
6	Cuddalore	255517	190897	54984	31803	310644	223642	82.3	85.4	17.7	14.2
7	Thanjavur	225837	168487	66480	39419	292656	209849	77.2	80.3	22.7	18.8
8	Nagapatinam	137235	120258	36555	28590	173876	149538	78.9	80.4	21.0	19.1
9	Thiruvarur	118558	111933	33481	27453	152127	140613	77.9	79.6	22.0	19.5
10	Salem	258973	220541	59150	44748	318159	266465	81.4	82.8	18.6	16.8
11	Namakkal	198228	182292	36314	30095	234802	213075	84.4	85.6	15.5	14.1
12	Dharmapuri	215248	170673	53830	36895	269288	207998	79.9	82.1	20.0	17.7
13	Erode	174184	236790	23120	27045	197532	266013	88.2	89.0	11.7	10.2
14	Coimbatore	102754	174552	27346	41453	131341	237305	78.2	73.6	20.8	17.5
15	The Nilgiris	52017	38606	12011	8366	64369	80376	80.8	48.0	18.7	10.4
16	Tiruchirapalli	249525	196452	51582	35772	301666	234844	82.7	83.7	17.1	15.2
17	Karur	120868	176206	24815	29085	146051	206824	82.8	85.2	17.0	14.1
18	Perambalur	109818	85535	31638	20740	141525	106471	77.6	80.3	22.4	19.5
19	Pudukkottai	308135	186526	70388	34705	378796	222712	81.3	83.8	18.6	15.6
20	Ramanathapuram	298042	222487	95352	59489	393888	284427	75.7	78.2	24.2	20.9
21	Sivagangai	217235	137969	50855	26422	268366	166050	80.9	83.1	18.9	15.9
22	Dindigul	233055	251155	61306	55679	295249	312026	78.9	80.5	20.8	17.8
23	Theni	103332	99726	25174	23719	128694	128652	80.3	77.5	19.6	18.4
24	Madurai	223062	129232	69121	37369	293578	169534	76.0	76.2	23.5	22.0

contd...

2010-11		All Male		All Female		All Total		All Male		All Female	
		Number	*Area*	*Number*	*Area*	*Number*	*Area*	*Number %*	*Area %*	*Number %*	*Area %*
25	Virudhunagar	161989	148635	35904	29439	198451	184215	81.6	80.7	18.1	16.0
26	Thoothukudi	155196	188251	40680	45591	197131	240403	78.7	78.3	20.6	19.0
27	Tirunelveli	246786	174963	45566	27204	293237	211761	84.2	82.6	15.5	12.8
28	Kanniyakumari	277768	57988	99897	21761	380248	83480	73.0	69.5	26.3	26.1
29	Krishnagiri	230785	188495	50607	36914	281733	226766	81.9	83.1	18.0	16.3
30	Ariyalur	171799	103326	39098	19239	211007	122974	81.4	84.0	18.5	15.6
31	Tiruppur	145088	296704	29591	49584	175182	350413	82.8	84.7	16.9	14.2
	State	**6547770**	**5300005**	**1550977**	**1055617**	**8118224**	**6488370**	**80.7**	**81.7**	**19.1**	**16.3**

Source: www.agricensus

Appendix 2.5: Percentage distribution of population and percentage of land operated by the Scheduled Caste in Tamil Nadu

Districts	*Percentage of Population*	*Percentage of land operated*
1. Kancheepuram	23.71	12.6
2. Thiruvallur	22.04	8.2
3. Vellore	21.85	6.9
4. Tiruvannamalai	22.94	10.9
5.Villupuram	29.37	11.3
6. Cuddalore	29.32	10.6
7. Thanjavur	18.91	6.7
8. Nagapattinam	31.54	18.5
9. Thiruvarur	34.08	19.3
10. Salem	16.67	4.2
11. Namakkal	20	1.9
12. Dharmapuri	16.29	6.4
13. Erode	16.41	2.5
14. Coimbatore	15.5	0.6
15. The Nilgiris	32.08	1.7
16. Tiruchirappalli	17.14	8.4
17. Karur	20.8	3.1
18. Perambalur	31.01	15.9
19. Pudukkottai	17.6	7.6
20. Ramanathapuram	18.4	12.7
21. Sivaganga	17.01	7.8
22. Dindigul	20.95	4.8
23. Theni	20.72	5.9
24. Madurai	13.46	4.9
25. Virudhunagar	20.59	9.9
26. Thoothukkudi	19.88	12.8
27. Tirunelveli	18.51	11.4
28. Kanniyakumari	3.97	0.1
29. Krishnagiri	14.22	5.2
30. Ariyalur	23.34	5.3
31. Tiruppur	15.97	1.1

Source: Computed.

3

Occupational Diversification in Tamil Nadu

Census of India and National Sample Survey Organisation (NSSO) classify the Indian population into economically active population and economically non-active population. Economically active population is also known as workforce or labour force. Economically inactivate population constitutes, children, students, household workers, old aged people, etc. Economic development of any country depends upon the size and the quality of the labour force. In the less developed countries like India, a majority of the workers are engaged in the primary sector. On the country, a majority of workers in the developed country are employed in non-agricultural sectors viz. industrial and tertiary sectors.

Agriculture continues to be the mainstay of the Indian population, although some trends towards occupational diversification of rural workers from agricultural to non-agricultural sector. The Scheduled Castes (SCs) have been denied property rights. Caste system as a system of occupational assignment has been relegated them to the peripheral occupations and hence, economic immobility. Several welfare programmes have been conceived and implemented by the government to promote the emancipation and economic mobility among the SCs. It is worthwhile to evaluate the impact of such policy interventions on the occupational status of the SCs in Tamil Nadu.

Objectives of the Study

The aim of the chapter is to investigate the changes in the livelihood pattern among social groups in Tamil Nadu. Specifically, this chapter examines three major aspects of occupational diversification, viz. (1) shift from agricultural to non-agricultural occupations in rural areas, (2) pattern of diversification within agricultural sector and (3) changes in occupation pattern in urban areas.

Data Base

The study uses two sets of data sources for delineating the occupational pattern among social groups viz. Population Census and National Sample Survey (NSS). The population Census provides information on labour force participation. Workers are classified into main workers and marginal workers. It further categorised work-force on the basis of nine-fold industrial classification. Only main work-force is considered for this study for the periods 2001 and 2011. The typology NSS data is different. Workers are categorised as self-employed in agriculture (SEA), agricultural workers. Self-employed in non-agriculture (SENA), other labourers and other workers. Workers in urban areas are classified into four segments viz. self-employed, wage and salaried workers, casual labourers and other households. NSS data for periods 2004-05 and 2009-10 were used to conduct an analysis for this study.

Concepts

1. NSS

Self-Employed: Persons who operated their own farm or non-farm enterprises or were engaged independently in a profession or trade on own-account or with one or few partners were deemed to be self-employed in household enterprises. The essential feature of the self-employed is that they have autonomy (i.e., how, where and when to produce) and economic independence (i.e., market, scale of operation and money) for carrying out their operation. The remuneration received by them comprised two part-share of their labour and profit of the enterprises. In other words, their remuneration was determined wholly or mainly by sales or profit of the goods or services which were produced.

Regular salaried/wage employee: These were persons who worked in other farm or non-farm enterprise (both household and non-household) and, in return, received salary or wages on a regular basis (i.e. not on the basis of daily or periodic renewal of work contract). This category included not only person getting time wage but also persons receiving piece wage or salary and paid apprentices, both full time and part-time.

Casual Wage Labour: A person who was casually engaged in other's farm or non-farm enterprises (both household and non-household) and, in return, received wage according to the terms of the daily or periodic work contract, was a casual wage labour.

Rural Labour: Manual labour working in agricultural and non-agricultural occupations in return for wages paid either in cash or in kind (excluding exchange labour) either of casual or regular basis and living in rural areas, was taken as rural labour.

Agricultural Labour: A person was considered as agricultural labour, if he/she followed one or more of agricultural occupations in the capacity of a wage paid manual labour, whether paid in cash or kind or both:

1. Farming,
2. Dairy farming,
3. Production of any horticultural commodity,
4. Raising of any livestock, bees or poultry,
5. Any practice performed on a farm as incidental to or in conjunction with farm operations (including forestry and timbering) and the preparation for market and delivery to storage or to market or to carriage for transportation to market of farm produce.

2. Census

Cultivators: Census of India, 1991 defines cultivator as person "if he or she engaged either as employer, single worker or family in cultivation of land owned or held from government or held from private person or institution for payment in money, kind or share. Cultivation includes supervision or direction of cultivation".

Agricultural Labour: Census of India 1991 defines agricultural labour as "a person who works on another person's land for wage in money, or share is regarded as an agricultural labour. He or she has no risk in cultivation, but he or she merely works on another person's land for wage. An agricultural labour has no right of lease or contract on land on which he or she works".

Household Industry: Household industry defined as "an industry conducted by the head of the household himself and/or by the member of the household at home or within the village in rural areas and only within the precincts of the house where the household lives in urban areas". Household industry relates to Production, Processing, Servicing, repairing or making and selling (but not merely selling) of goods.

Other Workers: All workers, i.e., Those who have been engaged in some economic activity during the year preceding enumerations who are not cultivators or agricultural labourers or household industry workers are 'Other Workers'. The type of workers that come under this category includes factory workers, plantation workers, those in trade, commerce, business, transport, mining, construction, political or social work, all government servants, municipal employees, teacher, priests, entertainment artists, etc.

Main Worker: Census of India 1991 define the main worker as 'person who had worked for the major part of the year' and 'major part of the year is defined as six months (183 days) or more.

Marginal Workers: Marginal workers are those who worked any time at all the year preceding the enumeration but did not work for a major part of the year i,e,. those who worked for less than 183 days or six months.

Coverage

Data on labour force or occupational analysis was made both at the rural and urban areas in Tamil Nadu.

Tools of Analysis

Change in the occupational diversification was studied with the help of Simple Disparity Index.

Difference in the selected variable between SCs and others, STs and others are apparent. In a bid to measure these disparities, the following measure is used.

$$\text{Simple Disparity (A, B)} = \frac{\text{Variable of group A}}{\text{Variable of group B}}$$

This index measures the performance of groups A relative to group B. Here group A refers to the group for which the diversification is estimated. If the value in group A is high relative to that in group B, then the index will have a high value, more than 1. As the value in group A decreases relative to that in group B, the value of the index decrees, reaching the value 1, when the access to occupation among the two groups is equal. Any deviation from 1 is thus a measure of disparity between the groups. The deprived groups viz. SCs/STs have been labeled as separate groups. Consequently, the value of the index will normally be higher than 1 and higher the value represents higher the disparity against the SC/ST groups.

Distribution of Rural Workforce

This section examines the pattern and trends in the distribution of rural workforce in agriculture and non-agriculture sectors. The state level analysis is presented on the basis of NSS and Census data.

Census Data

The workforce is predominantly employed in agriculture in Tamil Nadu. In the case of SCs and STs, the dependence on this traditional sector is more predominant than non-SCs-STs (Table 3.1). Over the year, the proportion has declined to 70.64 per cent in 2011 from 78.19 per cent in 2001 for SCs. The percentage of STs workers has also marginally declined. Nearly four-fifths (79.28 per cent) of the total work force depends upon agricultural sector among STs.

Table 3.1: Percentage of rural main workers in agricultural sector in Tamil Nadu

Social groups	*Percentage of rural main workers in agricultural sector*	
	2001	*2011*
SCs	2578880 (78.19)	2693383 (70.64)
STs	204112 (79.88)	242241 (79.28)
Non-SCs/STs	6833309 (63.64)	6843693 (60.98)
Total	**9616301** **(67.29)**	**9779316** **(73.75)**

Source: Primary Census Abstract of Tamil Nadu, 2001 and 2011.

NSS Report on Employment and Unemployment Survey

The NSS data substantiates the pattern of occupational shift from agricultural to non-agricultural sector among the SCs, STs and OBCs during the period 2004-05 to 2009-10 (Table 3.2). The magnitude of the shift was reported to be more prominent among the SCs and STs households, and hence the inter-sectoral group disparity among them was accentuated marginally during 2004-05 to 2009-10 (Table 3.3). The data distinctly indicate the heavy dependence of SCs and STs work force on agricultural sector and persistence of disparities among SCs and OBC/Others, as a large proportion of SCs and STs workers are engaged in the traditional sector in comparison to the proportion of OBC/Others workforce.

Table 3.2: Distribution of rural household workers engaged in agricultural and non-agricultural sector by social groups in Tamil Nadu: Per 1000 workers

Social groups	*Agricultural Sector*			*Non-agricultural Sectors*		
	Percentage share		*Net Change*	*Percentage share*		*Net Change*
	2004-05	*2009-10*	*2004-05 to 2009-10*	*2004-05*	*2009-10*	*2004-05 to 2009-10*
ST	76.0	68.4	-7.6	24.0	31.7	+7.7
SC	66.0	60.4	-5.6	33.9	39.6	+5.7
OBC	52.8	51.4	-1.4	47.2	48.6	+1.4
Others	27.9	31.5	+3.6	72.2	68.4	-3.8
All	**56.0**	**53.5**	**-2.5**	**43.9**	**46.5**	**+2.6**

Source: Employment and unemployment situation among social groups in India-2004-05, NSS 61st Report, July 2004-June 2005, Ministry of Statistics and Programme Implementation, Government of India, October 2006.

Table 3.3: Disparity ratio of workers engaged in agriculture and non-agriculture

Social groups	*Agricultural Sector*		*Non-agricultural Sectors*	
	2004-05	*2009-10*	*2004-05*	*2009-10*
SC/ST	0.87	0.88	1.41	1.25
SC/OBC	1.27	1.18	0.72	0.81
SC/Others	2.37	1.92	0.47	0.58

Source: Computed from Table 3.2.

Rural Occupational Pattern: Agricultural Sector

The Census of India classifies the rural workers engaged in agricultural sector as cultivators and agricultural labourers. NSS categorises rural agricultural households as self-employed in agriculture (SEA) and agricultural labourers. The former category in either classification denotes access to rural households to their own asset, such as land, while the latter category shows the dependence on wage labour. The distribution of rural workforce employed as cultivator to the total workforce by social groups (Table 3.4) highlights the fact that cultivation is the major economic activity for STs and non-SCs/STs, while rural SCs workers in agricultural sector predominantly work as wage labourers. In 2011, only 10.49 per cent SCs workers were cultivators as against 34.33 per cent STs rural workers and 26.92 non-SCs/STs rural workers. A majority of the SCs workers in rural areas have traditionally served as agricultural labourers, as their engagement in this occupation has been rather favoured by upper castes. Moreover, due to their lack of education and technical skill, their absorption in other jobs has been difficult. As agricultural labourers, they are unorganised and have neither social nor economic security. During the decade 2001-2011, there has been decline in the proportion of cultivators among all social groups and increase in the proportion agricultural workers among all social groups, except the SCs.

The inter-social group disparities in the nature of agricultural occupation were also evident from the NSS household data (Table 3.5). The proportion of rural household engaged in self-employed in agriculture was low and the proportion of rural households engaged as agricultural labourer was high among the SCs in 2009-10. Between 2004-05 and 2009-10, the outreach of rural households to land resources worsened, as indicated by the declining proportion of SEA and marginal rise in the percentage of agricultural labour households in Tamil Nadu. The data as given in Table 3.5A clearly indicate there is a disparity among the workers engaged in self-employed in agriculture and agricultural labours.

Table 3.4: Percentage of rural cultivators and agricultural labourers in Tamil Nadu

	Cultivator		*Agricultural workers*	
Social groups	*2001*	*2011*	*2001*	*2011*
SCs	503026 (15.25)	399881 (10.49)	2075854 (62.94)	2293502 (60.15)
STs	121151 (47.41)	104889 (34.33)	82961 (32.47)	137352 (44.95)
Non-SCs/STs	3792022 (35.32)	3021604 (26.92)	3041287 (28.33)	3822089 (34.06
Total	**4416199 (30.90)**	**3526374 (22.99)**	**5200102 (36.39)**	**6252943 (40.76)**

Source: Primary Census Abstract of Tamil Nadu, 2001 and 2011.

Table 3.5: Distribution of rural household workers engaged in Self-employed in Agriculture and Agricultural Labourers by social groups in Tamil Nadu: per 100

Social groups	*Self employed in Agriculture*			*Agricultural Labourers*		
	Percentage share		*Net Change*	*Percentage share*		*Net Change*
	2004-05	*2009-10*	*2004-05 to 2009-10*	*2004-05*	*2009-10*	*2004-05 to 2009-10*
ST	10.0	21.1	+11.1	66.0	47.3	-18.7
SC	10.1	7.8	-2.3	55.9	52.6	-3.3
OBC	24.4	21.0	-3.4	28.4	30.4	+2.0
Others	19.8	17.5	-2.3	8.1	14.0	+5.9
All	**20.5**	**17.8**	**-2.7**	**35.5**	**35.7**	**+0.2**

Source: Employment and unemployment situation among social groups in India-2004-05, NSS 61st Report, July 2004-June 2005, Ministry of Statistics and Programme Implementation, Government of India, October 2006.

Table 3.5A: Disparity Ratio of rural household workers engaged in Self-employed in Agriculture and Agricultural Labourers by social groups in Tamil Nadu: per 100

Social groups	*Self employed in Agriculture*		*Agricultural Labourers*	
	Percentage share		*Percentage share*	
	2004-05	*2009-10*	*2004-05*	*2009-10*
SC/ST	1.01	0.37	0.85	1.11
SC/OBC	0.41	0.37	0.51	0.58
SC/Others	0.51	0.45	0.29	0.46
SC/All	**0.49**	**0.44**	**4.38**	**2.55**

Source: Computed from Table 3.5.

Rural Occupational Pattern: Non-agricultural Sector

The sectoral occupational diversification trends brought out earlier indicated the same shift in rural workforce from agricultural to non-agricultural sector. The Census of India classifies non-agricultural workforce into two groups viz. (1) those who engaged in household industry and (2) Other workers. Household industry relates to the production, processing, servicing, repairing or making and selling of goods. The concept of household industry signifies that workers engaged in the household industry have some access to capital. In contrast, non-agricultural workers classified as 'Other workers' are those who are engaged in factory, plantation, trade, commerce, transport, mining, construction, etc., have negligible access to capital.

The Census data indicate that household industry accounts for a very small proportion of rural non-agricultural workers, engaging less than four per cent of the total rural main workers. The rural labour force shifting out of agricultural occupation has been absorbed in non-agricultural sector as 'Other workers' rather than household industry, as is evident from the rising proportion of 'other workers' during the past one decade and near stagnation in the share of household industry during the same period.

Table 3.6: Distribution of workers engaged in non-agricultural sector to total rural main workers by social groups in Tamil Nadu

	Household Industry		*Other workers*	
Social groups	*2001*	*2011*	*2001*	*2011*
SCs	68377 (2.07)	57013 (1.50)	651087 (19.74)	1062345 (27.86)
STs	5059 (1.98)	3631 (1.19)	46370 (18.15)	59680 (19.53)
Non-SCs/STs	614727 (5.73)	494975 (4.41)	3288631 (30.63)	3882155 (34.60)
Total	**688154 (4.82)**	**555619 (3.68)**	**3986088 (27.89)**	**5004180 (32.62)**

Source: Primary Census Abstract of Tamil Nadu, 2001 and 2011.

The sectoral occupational diversification brought out earlier indicated the shift in rural workforce from agricultural to non-agricultural sector. The NSS classification of non-agricultural workers SENA, other labourers (Manual workers) and others provides additional insight into the limited access to SC households to capital resources (Table 3.7). It is evident from the data that the proportion of households engaged in self-employed in non-agriculture was low among the SCs as compared to other social groups. The data further show that the proportion of households engaged in manual work was the highest among the SCs in Tamil Nadu. Thus, the data clearly indicate the relatively disadvantageous position of SCs with regard to non-agricultural sector. The data presented in Table 3.7A clearly indicate there is a disparity among the workers engaged in self-employed in non-agriculture, other labourers (Manual workers) and Others.

Table 3.7: Distribution of rural household workers engaged in Self-employed in Non-Agriculture and Other Labourers and others by social groups in Tamil Nadu: per 1000

Social groups	*Self- employed in Non-Agriculture (SENA)*			*Other Labourers (Manual workers)*			*Others*		
	Percentage share		*Net Change*	*Percentage share*		*Net Change*	*Percentage share*		*Net Change*
	2004-05	*2009-10*	*2004-05 to 2009-10*	*2004-05*	*2009-10*	*2004-05 to 2009-10*	*2004-05*	*2009-10*	*2004-05 to 2009-10*
ST	8.7	19.8	+11.1	15.3	9.0	-6.3	0	2.9	+2.9
SC	7.6	4.2	-3.4	15.5	24.2	+8.7	10.8	11.2	+0.4
OBC	15.6	14.0	-1.6	17.1	22.0	+4.9	14.5	12.6	-1.9
Others	22.3	18.9	-3.4	10.9	24.0	+13.1	39.0	25.5	-3.5
All	**13.5**	**11.8**	**-1.7**	**16.6**	**22.4**	**+5.8**	**13.8**	**12.3**	**-1.5**

Source: Employment and unemployment situation among social groups in India -2004-05, NSS 61st Report, July 2004-June 2005, Ministry of Statistics and Programme Implementation, Government of India, October 2006.

Table 3.7A: Disparity Ratio of rural household workers engaged in Self-employed in Non-Agriculture and Other Labourers and others by social groups in Tamil Nadu: per 1000

Social groups	*Self-employed in Non-agriculture (SENA)*		*Other Labourers (Manual workers)*		*Others*	
	Percentage share		*Percentage share*		*Percentage share*	
	2004-05	*2009-10*	*2004-05*	*2009-10*	*2004-05*	*2009-10*
SC/ST	0.87	0.21	1.01	2.69	0	3.86
SC/OBC	0.49	0.30	0.91	1.10	0.74	0.89
SC/Others	0.34	0.22	1.42	1.01	0.28	0.44
SC/All	**0.56**	**0.36**	**0.93**	**1.08**	**0.78**	**0.91**

Source: Computed from Table 3.7.

Urban Occupational Pattern

Given the limited availability of agricultural land in urban areas, the workforce in urban areas is predominantly engaged

Table 3.8: Distribution of urban household workers engaged in Self-employed, wages/salaried, casual labour and others by social groups in Tamil Nadu: per 1000

Social groups	*Self-employed*			*Wage/salaried*			*Casual labour*			*Others*		
	Percentage share		*Net Change*	*Percentage share*		*Net Change*	*Percentage share*		*Net Change*	*Percentage share*		*Net Change*
	2004-05	2009-10	2004-05 to 2009-10	2004-05	2009-10	2004-05 to 2009-10	2004-05	2009-10	2004-05 to 2009-10	2004-05	2009-10	2004-05 to 2009-10
ST	31.7	49.9	+18.2	29.2	33.0	+3.8	3.5	14.3	+10.8	35.6	2.8	-32.8
SC	18.8	18.3	-0.5	44.4	31.8	-12.6	25.5	41.0	+15.5	11.3	8.8	-2.5
OBC	35.5	28.6	-6.9	43.2	37.7	-5.5	12.7	21.7	+9.0	8.6	12.0	+3.4
Others	31.8	18.6	-13.2	45.2	56.9	+11.7	1.4	3.5	+2.4	21.6	21.1	-0.5
All	**32.8**	**26.8**	**-6.0**	**43.4**	**38.3**	**-5.1**	**13.3**	**22.8**	**+9.5**	**10.5**	**12.2**	**+1.7**

Source: Employment and unemployment situation among social groups in India -2004-05, NSS 61st Report, July 2004-June 2005, Ministry of Statistics and Programme Implementation, Government of India, October 2006.

Table 3.8A: Disparity Ratio of urban household workers engaged in Self-employed, wages/salaried, casual labour and others by social groups in Tamil Nadu: per 1000

Social groups	*Self-employed*		*Wage/salaried*		*Casual labour*		*Others*	
	Percentage share		*Percentage share*		*Percentage share*		*Percentage share*	
	2004-05	*2009-10*	*2004-05*	*2009-10*	*2004-05*	*2009-10*	*2004-05*	*2009-10*
SC/ST	0.59	0.37	1.52	0.96	7.29	2.87	0.32	3.14
SC/OBC	0.53	0.64	1.03	0.84	2.01	1.89	1.31	0.73
SC/Others	0.59	0.98	0.98	0.56	18.21	11.71	0.52	0.42
SC/All	**0.57**	**0.68**	**1.02**	**0.83**	**1.92**	**1.80**	**1.08**	**0.72**

Source: Computed from Table 3.8

in non-agricultural activities. The NSS categorisation of urban workforce into self-employed, regular wages/salaried, casual labourers and others brings out very interesting features of the urban occupational pattern across social groups (Table 3.8). As expected, the percentage of self-employed among SCs and STs was much lower, while that of casual workers was much higher than non-SCs/STs. The inter-sectoral group variations in the percentage of regular wage earners/salaried indicates the positive role of reservation policy for the SCs/STs. The data presented in Table 3.8A clearly shows that there is a disparity among the workers engaged self-employed in agriculture and agricultural labours.

Summary

Although the trend towards occupational diversification of rural workforce across all social groups observed during the study period, 71 per cent and 79 per cent of the SCs and STs rural workforce respectively continue to be employed in agricultural sector and their dependence on this traditional sector is more prominent as compared to the non-SCs/STs with 61 per cent of the work-force in 2011. The disparity index of SCs as compared to non-SCs/STs workers remained above 1 which indicates a higher percentage of SCs workforce as against non-SCs/STs workforce.

A majority of the SC workers (60 per cent in 2009-10) in rural areas work as agricultural workers. Traditionally, SCs have been discriminated against possession of land and cultivation is the major economic activity for both STs and non-SCs/STs. In 2001, only 15 per cent of the SCs rural workers engaged in cultivation as against the corresponding figures of 47 per cent of STs and 35 per cent non-SCs/STs rural workers. By 2011, this proportion declined to 10 per cent of the SCs rural workers 34 per cent of STs and 27 per cent and non-SCs/STs among rural workers. NSS household data also substantiates the inter-social group disparities in rural occupation pattern that is SCs workforce constitutes 52.6 per cent, OBCs workforce with 30.4 per cent as against 35.7 per cent among all agricultural worker households.

The non-agricultural rural workforce has limited access to capital, as only 1.50 per cent is employed in household industry and 27.86 per cent engaged in 'other workers' among SCs. The proportion of workforce engaged in household industry has declined, while the proportion of 'other workers' has increased for all social groups in 2011. However during the study period, the proportion 'other workers' has increased sharply among SCs and STs. Further, the labour force displaced from agricultural sector is not absorbed in rural household industry but are engaged in 'other workers' with limited access to capital.

The SCs in urban areas in Tamil Nadu also occupy relatively disadvantageous position as compared to OBCs, as the percentage of self-employed SCs workers is lower about 10 percentage point in 2009-2010. As regards the casual labourers is higher about 20 percentage point than the corresponding figures for OBCs. The inter-group variation in the percentage of regular wage earners/salaried is much lower among SCs, STs and OBCs which indicate the positive role of the reservation policy for the SCs, STs and OBCs in Tamil Nadu. However, the proportion of workforce engaged in regular wage/salaried has declined among SCs, STs and OBCs, but the decline in regular wage/salaried is higher among SCs. This indicates that the brunt of slackening public employment during the economic reform period has fallen more heavily on SCs.

References

1. Kamble, N.D., *The Scheduled Castes,* Ashish Publishing House, New Delhi,1982.

2. Parvathamma, C. *Scheduled castes and Tribes: A Socio-economic Survey,* Ashish Publishing House, New Delhi, 1984.

3. Thangaraj, M., Demographic and occupational characteristics of the Scheduled Castes and Scheduled Tribes in India", *Madras Institute of Development Studies,* Working paper No.134, 1995.

4. Thangaraj, M., "Occupational Pattern", in Thorat Sukhadeo and Nidhi Sadana Sabharwal (Ed*), Bridging the Social Gap: Perspectives on Dalit Empowerment,* Sage Publications, New Delhi, 2014.

5. Thorat Sukhadeo, "Oppression and Dalit: Dalit Discrimination in the 1990s", *Economic and Political Weekly,* February 2002.

4

Entrepreneurship Development Programmes in Tamil Nadu

The work-force in India is largely depending on agriculture for survival as land owners, cultivators, tenants and agricultural workers. Over 60 per cent of the workforce is engaged in agriculture, but the share of agriculture to the GDP is only 14 per cent. There is a disguised unemployment in agriculture, and there is a need to shift the surplus work-force from agriculture to the non-agricultural activities. Most of the surplus labourers are unskilled/semi-skilled. They have to be trained and make them employable. Government and non-governmental organisations are providing skills/training and also offer financial assistance for taking up self-employment to the unskilled/semi-skilled workers in India. Educational institutions like IIT, NIT and colleges have also started offering the skill and training to the students and educated youths.

The sectoral share in GDP clearly shows that the share of agriculture has come down drastically to about

14 per cent, while the share of non-agricultural sector viz. industry has not witnessed any major change and has contributed significantly. While the share of service sector has increased (Table 4.1).

Table 4.1: Sectoral share in GDP

	Sector	*1999-2000*	*2007-08*	*2012-13*	*2013-14 (p)*
1	Agriculture and allied	23.2	16.8	13.9	13.9
2	Industry	26.8	28.7	27.3	26.1
3	Services	50.0	54.4	58.8	59.9

Source: Economic Survey, Government of India – 2013-14.

The issues addressed to in this paper are: 1. Entrepreneur Development Institutes in India and Tamil Nadu, 2. Entrepreneur development programmes and economic development programmes implemented by National Scheduled Castes Financial Development Corporation (NSFDC), New Delhi and the Tamil Nadu Adi-Dravidar Housing and Development Corporation (TAHDCO), and Dalit Indian Chamber of Commerce and Industry (DICCI), and 3. Entrepreneurship and Development programmes implemented by other state controlled agencies in Tamil Nadu.

Objective of the Study

The broad objective of the study is to examine the entrepreneurship development programmes for non-agricultural employment in Tamil Nadu. This paper specifically addresses the steps taken up by both the Government of India and the Government of Tamil Nadu to promote non-agricultural employment opportunities of the work-force.

Data Base

Data were collected on 1. Entrepreneur Development Institutes in India and Tamil Nadu, 2. Entrepreneur development programmes and economic development programmes implemented by National Scheduled Castes Financial Development Corporation (NSFDC), New Delhi and the Tamil Nadu Adi-Dravidar Housing and Development Corporation (TAHDCO), and Dalit Indian Chamber of Commerce and Industry (DICCI), and 3. Entrepreneurship and Development programmes implemented by other state controlled agencies in Tamil Nadu were collected from the respective websites.

Definition of Entrepreneur

The word entrepreneur originates from the French word, entreprendre, which means "to undertake." In a business context, it means to start a business. The Merriam-Webster Dictionary presents the definition of an entrepreneur as 'one who organises, manages, and assumes the risks of a business or enterprise'. Entrepreneur is someone who exercises initiative by organising a venture to take benefit of an opportunity and, as the decision maker, decides what, how, and how much of a good or services will be produced.

According to Economist Joseph Alois Schumpeter (1883-1950), "Entrepreneurs are not necessarily motivated by profit but regard it as a standard for measuring achievement or success". Schumpeter discovered that they (1) greatly value self-reliance, (2) strive for distinction through excellence, (3) are highly optimistic (otherwise nothing would be undertaken), and (4) always favour challenges of medium risk (neither too easy, nor ruinous) (http://www.business-dictionary.com/definition/entrepreneur.html).

Financial Institutions

The following financial institutions were in the forefront in the initial years after independence in providing financial assistance to the entrepreneurial development programmes in India. They are:

- Industrial Development Bank of India (IDBI),
- Industrial Credit and Investment Corporation of India (ICICI),
- Industrial Finance Corporation of India (IFCI), and
- State Bank of India (SBI).

Entrepreneur Development/Training Institutes

One of the significant developments of the post-independent India is to provide entrepreneur development/training to the citizens for taking up self-employment. The Ministry of Industries, Government of India, has initiated several steps in this direction. State Government also entered in this venture on the advice of the Government of India.

National Institutes

The Ministry of Micro, Small and Medium Enterprises (MSMEs) has set up three national-level apex Entrepreneurship Development Institutes (EDIs). They are: 1. National Institute for Micro, Small and Medium Enterprises (NI-MSME), Hyderabad; 2. Indian Institute of Entrepreneurship (IIE), Guwahati and 3. National Institute for Entrepreneurship and Small Business Development (NIESBUD), Noida.

National Institute for Entrepreneurship and Small Business Development (NIESBUD), Noida

NIESBUD is an apex body under the Government of India for coordinating and overseeing the activities of various institutions/agencies engaged in entrepreneurship development particularly in the area of small industry and small business. The Institute started functioning from 6th July, 1983.

The policy, direction and guidance to the Institute is provided by its Governing Council whose Chairman is the

Minister of MSME. The Executive Committee consisting of Secretary (Micro, Small and Medium Enterprises) as its Chairman and Director General of the Institute as its Member-Secretary, executes the policies and decisions of the Governing Council through its whole-time Director General.

The NIESBUD is a premier organisation of Ministry of MSME engaged in training, consultancy, research, etc. in order to promote entrepreneurship. The major activities of the Institute are Training of Trainers, Management Development Programme, Entrepreneurship-cum-Skill Development Programme, Entrepreneurship Development Programme and Cluster Intervention. The Institute has conducted a total 14,793 different training programmes covering 3,80,655 participants which includes 171 International programmes with 2,790 participants from more than 125 countries till December 2014.

The objectives of the NIESBUD are as follows:

- To evolve standardised materials and processes for selection, training, support and sustenance of entrepreneurs, potential and existing.
- To help/support and affiliate institutions/organisations in carrying out training and other entrepreneurship development related activities.
- To serve as an apex national level resource institute for accelerating the process of entrepreneurship development ensuring its impact across the country and among all strata of the society.
- To provide vital information and support to trainers, promoters and entrepreneurs by organising research and documentation activities relevant to entrepreneurship development.
- To train the trainers, promoters and consultants in various areas of entrepreneurship development.

- To offer consultancy nationally/internationally for promotion of entrepreneurship and small business development.
- To provide national/international forums for interaction and exchange of experiences helpful for policy formulation and modification at various levels.
- To share international experience and expertise in entrepreneurship development.
- To share experience and expertise in entrepreneurship development across national frontiers.

Training Programmes of NIESBUD

I. Trainers' Training Programmes

1. Enterprise Launching and Management
2. EMT Accreditation Programmes
3. Barefoot Managers
4. Self-Employment / PMRY
5. Project Formulation and Appraisal
6. Planning and Organising EDPs.

II. Small Business Promoters' Programmes

1. Entrepreneurship Orientation for Weaker Sections/ DWACRA Functionaries
2. Grassroot Management Training
3. Women Empowerment through Enterprise Development
4. Orientation Programmes for Voluntary Organisations
5. Small Business Development
6. Micro-Enterprise for Women/SC/ST/Weaker Section
7. TRYSEM/ISB Beneficiaries.

III. Development Officers' Orientation Programmes

1. DICs-Managers and General Managers
2. SIDO (Small Industries Development Officers)
3. Voluntary Organisations
4. Income-Generating Activities
5. ITI/Vocational Institute Instructors and Principals
6. KVIC (Khadi and Village Industries Commission)
7. Performance Improvement and Personal Effectiveness
8. Techniques for Identification and Selection of Entrepreneurs.

IV. Continuing Education Programmes for SSI Entrepreneurs

1. Working Capital Assessment and Management
2. Opportunity Identification and Guidance
3. Managing and Controlling Small Business Accounts
4. Marketing Strategies for small Entrepreneurs
5. Managing Finance
6. Creative Selling and Promotion for Small Enterprise
7. Marketing Survey Methods
8. TQM for Small Business
9. Business Forecasting Techniques
10. Export Marketing for SSI Entrepreneurs
11. Accounting Business and Industry
12. Strategic Management for Small Entrepreneurs
13. Managing Finance SSI

14. Effective Business Communication for Small Business Owners
15. Leadership and Team Building Skills for Small Business Owners
16. Computers for Small Entrepreneurs
17. Opportunity and Support for Expansion, Diversification and Modernisation of Small Enterprises
18. Small Enterprise Management Assistants Programme (Barefoot Managers)
19. Enhancing Productivity and Improving Quality.

V. International Training Programmes

1. Small Business Creation and Development for Women Entrepreneurs
2. Development of Entrepreneurship and Entrepreneurial Skills
3. Entrepreneurship for Small, Business Trainers/ Promoters
4. Entrepreneurship Development for Business Entrants
5. Micro-Enterprise Development
6. Case Development
7. Curriculum Development
8. Entrepreneurship Development and Promotion of Income-Generating Activities
9. Business Advisors' Training Programmes
10. Small Business Planning and Promotion.

VI. Entrepreneurship Development Programmes

These are done on-campus in Delhi or off campus in different locations. These are of two types :

(a) Target specific such as

- General
- Women
- Science and Technology Graduates
- School Leavers
- SC/OBC
- Ex-Servicemen (Veterans)
- Self-Employment SEEUY (Scheme for Educated Unemployed Youth), TRYSEM, PMRY etc.

(b) Product/Process Oriented

- Leather
- Builders Hardware
- Food
- Plastics
- Chemicals
- Sports Goods
- Readymade Garments
- Electronics
- Information Technology etc.

Indian Institute of Entrepreneurship, Guwahati

With an aim to undertake training, research and consultancy activities in small and micro enterprises focusing on entrepreneurship development, the Indian Institute of Entrepreneurship (IIE) was established in the year 1993 in Guwahati by the Ministry of MSME, Government of India as an autonomous National Institute. The institute began its operation from April 1994 with the North East Council (NEC),

Governments of Assam, Arunachal Pradesh and Nagaland and SIDBI as its other stakeholders.

The policy direction and guidance to the institute is provided by its Board of Management whose Chairman is the Secretary to Government of India, Ministry of MSME. The Governing Council of the Institute is headed by Chairman, NEC and the Executive Committee is headed by the Secretary, Ministry of MSME, Government of India.

Objectives

1. To promote and develop entrepreneurship.
2. To conduct research and provide consultancy for entrepreneurship development.
3. To coordinate and collaborate with other organisations in undertaking training, research and other activities to increase outreach of the institute.
4. To provide consultancy and monitoring service to MSMEs/ potential entrepreneurs and enhancing employability of participants.
5. To promote greater use of information technology in the activities/ functions of the IIE.
6. To comply with statutory responsibility.

Functions

1. Designing and organising training activities for different target group and undertaking research in the relevant to entrepreneurship.
2. Improving the efficiency, effectiveness and delivery of the change agents and development practitioners i.e. trainers, support organisations engaged in enterprise building. etc.
3. Provide consultancy service to the prospective and existing entrepreneurs.

4. Increasing the outreach of activities of the institute through collaborative activities and increasing their effectiveness through use of different tools of information technology.

Programme

1. Training
2. Research
3. Consultancy
4. Seminar and Workshop
5. Projects

Training Programme

1. Entrepreneurship Awareness Programme
2. Workshop on Job and Placement
3. Workshop on Entrepreneurship Awareness Programme
4. Entrepreneurship Orientation Programme (EOP)
5. EDP under PMEGP scheme
6. EDP under PMEGP scheme of KVIC
7. Informative Session on German Senior Expert Service (SES)
8. SDP on CATIA
9. Certificate in Computer Application
10. Mobile phone repairing and Maintenance
11. Senior Experten Service- By IIE Indo German Chambers of Commerce.

National Institute for Micro, Small and Medium Enterprises (NI-MSME), Hyderabad

NI-MSME was originally set up as Central Industrial Extension Training Institute (CIETI) in New Delhi in 1960 as a Department under the Ministry of Industry and Commerce, Government of India. It was decided to keep it free from the tardy and impeding administrative controls and procedures, so that the Institute can play a pivotal role in the promotion of small enterprise. Therefore, the Institute was shifted to Hyderabad in 1962, and was renamed as Small Industry Extension Training Institute (SIETI). SIETI is managed by Governing Council, appointed by the Government of India.

Centre of Excellence

SIETI was conferred the status of national institute by the Government of India with the charter of assisting in the promotion of Small Enterprises mainly by creating a pro-business environment. In 1984, the UNIDO had recognised SIETI as an institute of meritorious performance under its Centres of Excellence Scheme subsequently; it was also accorded the national status in the same year. To cope with the pressure of globalisation, the Government of India has enacted the MSMED Bill in the Parliament, which became effective from 2nd October 2006. Accordingly, the Institute, in order to reflect the expanded focus of its objectives with name was rechristened as NI-MSME from 11th April 2007 and re-designed its structure and organisation.

MINISTRY OF MSME, GOVERNMENT OF INDIA

There are 30 MSME-DIs and 28 Branch MSME-DIs set up in state capitals and other industrial cities all over the country. The main activities of these institutions are as follows:

1. Assistance/Consultancy to Prospective Entrepreneurs
2. Assistance/Consultancy rendered to existing units
3. Preparation of State Industrial Profiles
4. Preparation/Updation of District Industrial Potential Surveys

5. Project Profiles
6. Entrepreneurship Development Programmes
7. Motivational Campaigns
8. Production Index
9. Management Development Programmes
10. Skill Development Programmes
11. Energy Conservation
12. Pollution Control
13. Quality Control and Upgradation
14. Export Promotion
15. Ancillary Development
16. Common Facility Workshop/Lab
17. Preparation of Directory of Specific Industry
18. Intensive Technical Assistance
19. Coordination with DICs
20. Linkage with State Government Functionaries
21. Market Surveys
22. Other Action Plan Activities assigned by Headquarters.

National Small Industries Corporation Ltd (NSIC)

NSIC is an ISO 9001-2008 certified Government of India Enterprise under Ministry of Micro, Small and Medium Enterprises (MSME). NSIC has been working to fulfil its mission of promoting, aiding and fostering the growth of small industries and industry related micro, small and medium enterprises in the country. Over a period of five decades of transition, growth and development, NSIC has proved its strength within the country and abroad by promoting modernisation, upgradation of technology, quality consciousness, strengthening linkages with large medium enterprises and enhancing exports - projects and products from small enterprises.

NSIC operates through countrywide network of offices and Technical Centres in the country. To manage operations in African countries, NSIC operates from its office in Johannesburg, South Africa. In addition, NSIC has set up Training cum Incubation Centre and with a large professional manpower, NSIC provides a package of services as per the needs of MSME sector.

NSIC carries forward its mission to assist small enterprises with a set of specially tailored schemes designed to put them in a competitive and advantageous position. The schemes comprise of facilitating marketing support, credit support, technology support and other support services.

NSIC Technical Services Centres are located at the following places

Name of the Centre	*Focus area*
Chennai	Leather and Footware
Howrah	General Engineering
Hyderabad	Electronics and Computer Application
New Delhi	Machine Tools and related activities
Rajkot	Energy Audit and Energy Conservation activities
Rajpura (Pb)	Domestic Electrical Appliances
Aligarh (UP)	Lock Cluster and Die and Tool making

DEVELOPMENT INSTITUTES IN TAMIL NADU

MSME Development Institute (MSME-DI), Chennai

The Micro Small and Medium Enterprises Development Institute (MSME-DI), Chennai, was established in the year 1954. Office of DC (MSME) is the apex body for formulating SSI policies in the country and it implements promotional activities through its country wide network of MSME DIs, Br. MSME DIs, Field Testing Stations, Prototype Development Centres and Tool Rooms etc.

MSME-DI, Chennai assists existing and prospective entrepreneurs by providing techno-managerial consultancy services and training in various areas. Br. MSME DI, Coimbatore and Tuticorin with an attached Workshop at Tirunelveli were established in the years 1984.

Training Programme

- Entrepreneur Programme
- Skill development Programme
- Seminar/Workshop
- Trade Fair/Exhibition/B2B Meet

Online Information

- EM Filing (SSI Registration)
- Export/Import Guidance
- Reimbursement Status

Branches

- Chennai
- Coimbatore
- Tirunelveli, and
- Tuticorin

STEPS TO START AN ENTERPRISE

Step-1: Decision to be Self-employed

- Economic gains
- From job seeker to job-creator

- Sovereign status than a subservient role
- Image of prestige and status
- Inner satisfaction.

Step-2: Product Selection

- Look up for all possible trade publications and secondary data.
- Consult with specialists/ resource persons from MSME-DIs, SSIDC, CSIR, NRDC, DoIs, APCTT etc. Extensive use of Internet is also suggested.
- Undertake a market survey for the proposed product/ services proposed to be manufactured/ service rendered.
- Assess technology sources, raw materials availability, suppliers of required machinery and equipments. Total investment required for the project, promoter's contribution need to be estimated. Analyse your personal strengths and weaknesses are other considerations. Assess your capacity to invest from own sources and resourcefulness to offer collateral security.

Step-3: Preparation of Preliminary Project Report (PPR)

- Prepare a PPR to get an overall idea regarding the financial requirements namely, working capital and fixed capital and total investment. PPR will serve as a basic document to assess the technical feasibility and financial viability of the project. PPR will contain all elements of the project such as requirement of machinery, power, labour and raw materials and profitability estimates.

Step-4: Decide On the form of Ownership

- Sole proprietary

- Partnership
- Co-operative society
- Private limited company
- Public limited company understand the merits and de-merits of each form of ownership and their legal requirements and procedures of registrations.

Step-5: Locationional Considerations

- Nearness to the market
- Easy access to sources of raw materials
- Availability of power
- Availability of skilled labours locally
- Incentives and facilities offered by Government
- Transportation

Step-6: Procurement of Land and Buildings

- Decide on whether to construct buildings/work sheds or to hire them on monthly rent or by long-term leasing
- Check with State industries promotion agencies/ corporations, if they could provide land/ ready- built work sheds in the developed industrial estates.

Step-7: Procurement of Machinery/Equipments

- Identify suppliers of machinery/equipment.
- Invite quotations clearly specifying type, size, capacity of each machines. Terms of sale, warranty and guarantee terms and conditions of payment together with technical catalogues and compare them.
- Explore possibilities for obtaining machinery on hire purchase basis under the Schemes of National Small Industries Corporation (NSIC).

Step-8: Preparation of Detailed Project Report

Detailed project report or bankable project report or business plan is an important document. This should include every minor detail about the project with profitability estimates and projected balance sheet and repayment (of loan) schedules. Cash flow statement, estimate of working capital will also be included. The other general chapters would contain

- Introduction
- Demand and market analysis
- Requirement of land, raw materials, machinery, labour, power, finances.
- Be realistic and honest. Let the report not be rosy.

Step-9: Filing of Entrepreneur Memorandum (EM)

- Part one of EM is synonymous with erstwhile Provisional registration Permanent registration or EM Part -II will be done later after the commencement of commercial production.The District Industries Centre/ Jt. Director of Industries or MSME-DI can be contacted for the purpose. Online EM filing can also be done by the entrepreneur himself/herself.

Step-10: Processing for Financial Assistance

- Identify credit requirements. Study the schemes operated by various agencies and commercial banks / TIIC. Government funded schemes like PMEGP and conditions of assistance must be clearly understood. Approach the appropriate agency with detailed project report. Call on the financier and appraise him about the viability of the project. Submit all relevant documents, as demanded. Arrange for promoters contribution. As loan will be disbursed in installments, ensure cash flow.

Step-11: Obtaining Statutory Licenses and Clearances

- Obtain all necessary clearances/ permits/ registrations and licenses, where required from local bodies and statutory organisations.

Step-12: Procurement of Basic Infrastructure Requirements

- Procure machinery, install them on the site
- Arrange for power, water and fuel connection
- Recruit personnel, train them
- Procure raw materials.

Step-13: Trail Production

- Conduct trail runs. Review the processing methods and techniques, improve upon them, if scope exists. Perfect and standardise the process.

Step-14: Commercial Production

- Commercial production commences. File Entrepreneurs Memorandum Part II. Process your application for Government Subsidies and incentives. Establish Total Quality Management System. Obtain ISI [BIS] marking, if applicable. Try to be an ISO 9000 certified company.

Step-15: Establish Your Market Network

- Workout a marketing plan, establish distribution network, if needed
- Workout a pricing strategy compatible to the existing market trend
- Workout schemes for sales promotion.

Step-16: Performance Review

- Review your operations. Review cash flow. Review production performances. Identify problem areas, if any. Correct them instantly. Adhere to the repayment plans, as envisaged in the project report. In case of defaults/ deviations consult your financier. Do not flinch in the face of difficulties.

Step-17: Modernisation And Technology Upgradation

- Explore possibilities modernisation and technology upgradation. Remember, improvement and developments are continuous processes.

Step-18: Avoiding Sickness

- Beware of pit-falls. Business crises are not unusual. Tackle them with patience and perseverance. Seek expert advice. Take financiers, suppliers and distributors into confidence. Do not hide facts.

For more clear understanding on the procedures involved in starting an enterprise, Entrepreneurs are advised to refer the guide book titled "A Handbook for New Entrepreneurs" published by MSME-DI.

GUIDANCE TO THE ENTERPRISE

Here entrepreneurs can get information about

- How to improve your Business
- Vendor Registration with Buyer
- How to save
- How to do Export
- What are latest Events / Seminars / Exhibitions

- What are the schemes available for Existing Entrepreneur.
- Quality
- Common facility service

Marketing Information

- Vendor Registration - B2B Meet / Vendor Development Programmeee
- Latest Events / Seminars / Exhibitions
- Cluster Development Programme
- International Trade Fair
- Training Programme.

Export

- What is the procedure to Import and Export
- Online Export Guidance

Schemes

- What are the Schemes available for Existing Industry
- Quality
- Online ISO Application status for Reimbursement
- ISO Consultancy
- ISO Reimbursement
- Training Programmes.

Entrepreneurship Development Institutes in Tamil Nadu

1. Entrepreneurship Development Institute (EDI)

Entrepreneurship Development Institute (EDI) was established in 2001 in Chennai. It is an apex organisation in the field of entrepreneurship education and self-employment promotion in Tamil Nadu. EDI was constituted by Government of Tamil Nadu and is administered by Department of Micro, Small and Medium Enterprises (MSME). EDI has embarked on a multipronged strategy to be executed in the next few years which involves a series of programmes to be introduced with the objective of promoting Entrepreneurship in small scale industrial sector in Tamil Nadu. The different training programmes which are provided by the department will certainly help the individuals who have an ambition to start their own enterprise. EDI is partnering with the best HR and training companies in the country to deliver these programmes. These companies have experienced trainers in specific domains who will be able to deliver the programmes in an effective manner.

Sponsoring Agencies

- Development Commissioner (SSI), New Delhi
- Department of Science and Technology - GOI
- Department of Industries and Commerce (DI and C)
- Tamil Nadu Industrial Investment Corporation (TIIC)
- Small Industries Development Corporation (SIDCO)
- National Bank for Agriculture and Rural Development (NABARD)
- Small Industries Development Bank of India (SIDBI)
- Tamil Nadu Adi Dravidar Housing Development Corporation (TAHDCO)

2. Centre for Entrepreneurship Development (CED), Tamil Nadu

Centre for Entrepreneurship Development (Tamil Nadu) is a Public Charitable Trust and functioning as an independent state level entrepreneurship development institution recognised by the Ministry of Small Scale Industry, Government of India, New Delhi and Industries Department, Government of Tamil Nadu, Chennai. CED was established in 2009 and is located in Madurai (Head Office).

Objectives of the CED

1. To promote self-employment and entrepreneurship culture in Tamil Nadu.
2. To enhance employability of educated youth through industry specific skill training.
3. Women empowerment.
4. NGO capacity building for mass employment generation in the rural areas.

   CED has implemented Entrepreneurship Development Training Scheme for different target groups like Science and Technology Graduates, SC/ST candidates, Women, Rural Youth and Sector Specific Programmes like Coir, Food Processing, Medicinal and Aromatic Plants, Information Technology, Non-Conventional Energy etc. sponsored by the different agencies of Government of India and Government of Tamil Nadu. CED has entered into strategic tie-up with Industry Associations, Chambers of Commerce, Testing Laboratories for advanced training and placement. It is also working with various Government Agencies such as TAHDCO, BC/MBC Corporation, etc. to avail funding assistance and to provide free training to the poor students and candidates of marginalised communities.

ENTREPRENEURSHIP DEVELOPMENT PROGRAMME FOR SCHEDULED CASTES AND SCHEDULED TRIBES

1. National Scheduled Castes Finance and Development Corporation (Ministry of Social Justice and Empowerment, Government of India)

NSFDC was setup by the Government of India on February 08, 1989 with the name National Scheduled Castes and Scheduled Tribes Finance and Development Corporation (NSFDC). It was incorporated as a fully owned Government Company under Section 8 of the Companies Act, 2013. It has been assigned the task for financing, facilitating and mobilising funds for the economic empowerment of persons living below Double of the Poverty Line (DPL). It provides financial assistance for income generating schemes for the target group through State Channelising Agencies (SCAs) which are nominated by respective State/UT Government. This is managed by a Board of Directors with representation from Central Government, State Scheduled Castes Development Corporations, Financial Institutions and non-official members representing Scheduled Castes.

Financing Programmes

1. **Credit based schemes.**
2. **Non-credit based schemes**

- Allocation of NSFDC Funds
- Allocation of Funds and Security.

Notional Allocation of NSFDC Funds to be Disbursed

1. At the beginning of the each financial year, NSFDC shall notionally allocate funds to the SCAs, in proportion to the Scheduled Caste population of the

country represented by the respective State/UT Administration. The SCAs are, in turn, required to further make district-wise allocation in accordance with the same principle.

2. The status of notional allocation vis-à-vis actual for each financial year, as on 31st August, shall be reviewed by NSFDC before 15th of September of that year, and in case allocated funds have not been availed by any SCA, the funds earmarked for the SCA may be re-allocated to other States(s)/UT(s).

3. Unit Cost for Term Loan

Sr. No.	*Unit Cost*	*Percentage of Notional Allocation*
a.	Projects costing up to Rs 0.50 lakh	30
b.	Projects costing above Rs 0.50 lakh and up to Rs 1.00 lakh	30
c.	Projects costing above Rs 1.00 lakh and up to Rs 5.00 lakh	30
d.	Projects costing above Rs 5.00 lakh and up to Rs 10.00 lakh	5
e.	Projects costing above Rs 10.00 lakh and up to Rs 30.00 lakh	5

Note:

(i) At the time of notional allocation of funds to SCAs at the beginning of financial year, funds equivalent to 50 per cent of notional allocation for projects costing up to Rs 1.00 lakh of each SCA, shall be released to the SCAs in advance, after receipt of Action Plan, to implement projects costing up to Rs 1.00 lakh in the prescribed ratio. The SCAs shall furnish utilisation of these funds within 90 days of its release by NSFDC.

(ii) In addition, 50 per cent of the notional allocation separately made for Micro Credit Finance (MCF) and

Mahila Samriddhi Yojana (MSY) schemes for each SCA shall also be released in advance on receipt of Action Plan for implementation of these schemes which are to be utilized within 90 days from date of disbursement.

(iii) The release of these funds to SCAs shall however be subject to fulfillment of Clause 12.1(iii) regarding availability of adequate Government Guarantee cover and Clause 12.2 (i) and (ii) regarding 80 per cent satisfactory level of fund utilisation and repayment of overdues not more than one year as at end of preceding financial year

4. Social Priorities

Further, the SCAs are required to endeavour to cover target groups in accordance with the priorities laid down as under:

i. Educated unemployed/underemployed 50 per cent

ii. Women 40 per cent

iii. Others 20 per cent

5. Sectoral Priorities

The SCAs are required to endeavour to achieve sectoral priorities in accordance with the percentages listed below:

Sectors Allocation

(i) Agriculture and Allied 50 per cent

(ii) Service 40 per cent

(iii) Industry 10 per cent

6. Security

(i) SCAs shall provide Government Guarantee/Bank Guarantee to the NSFDC for the funds sanctioned to them, preferably as block guarantee.

ii. Security for the Seed Capital Assistance shall be the same as determined by the Term Lending Institutions.

AVAILING ASSISTANCE

Procedure for availing assistance

1. For term loan schemes costing up to Rs 2.00 lakh and Micro-Credit Schemes costing upto Rs 0.50 lakh per unit, no separate application is required. Sanction and Disbursement would be done for these schemes on receipt of Action Plan from SCAs having details such as name of schemes, number of units and beneficiaries, total cost, subsidy, SCA's share per unit, NSFDC share per unit and total NSFDC's share.
2. Applications for availing term loan from NSFDC under schemes costing above Rs 2.00 lakh through its SCAs should be submitted in the formats prescribed hereunder:
   - (i) Format of application for financial assistance for Non-farming and other activities (Form 1: Annexure -II).
   - (ii) Format of application for financial assistance for Farming activities (Form 2: Annexure-III).
   - (iii) Format of application for financial assistance for Transport Sector (Form 3: Annexure-IV).
   - (iv) http://www.nsfdc.nic.in/writereaddata/annexure4.docThese formats have detailed checklist of points to be covered while submitting the proposals to NSFDC.
3. Eligible applicants shall submit their project proposals to the SCAs as per the formats applicable to them and SCA shall forwarded this to NSFDC.
4. The SCAs, while recommending proposals to the NSFDC within the eligibility criteria, shall undertake their willingness to:

(i) Implement the schemes as sanctioned by NSFDC.

(ii) Provide their share of financial assistance and subsidy as applicable.

(iii) Monitor the project implementation and repay the loan.

(iv) Provide Government Guarantee/Bank Guarantee towards the assistance sought from NSFDC

5. The SCAs would, thereafter, take the following steps:

(i) Compulsory registration of applications.

(ii) All applications, thus registered, to be examined in a time-bound manner by a duly constituted Selection Committee. The suitability of candidates should be judged on the basis of their experience in the line/ educational qualifications.

(iii) The reasons for selection/rejection to be necessarily maintained in all such cases.

(iv) Selections/rejections to be necessarily communicated to the applicants as soon as possible.

(v) Arrange for a field verification for any High Cost Scheme (with NSFDC's share exceeding Rs 5.00 lakhs), and forwarded such Project proposals along with Field Verification Report, giving the findings on and recommendation of the Field Officer.

(vi) Applications having project-cost exceeding Rs 5.00 lakhs should necessarily accompany Affidavits prescribed at Annexure - V. Such affidavits are also to be obtained under group proposals having NSFDC's Share of Rs 5.00 lakhs or more. This requirement is in addition to the submission of caste and income certificates by the Applicants in all cases.

(vii) Selections to be made in proportion to the sanctioned units with wait listing on first come first served basis.

(viii) Sanctions to be communicated to the beneficiaries as soon as the 'Letter of Intent' of a scheme is received from the NSFDC.

(ix) Sanction Letter to the beneficiary to include all the terms and conditions contained in the Letter of Intent as well as the documents required from him/her.

(x) In selection of assets (within the sanctioned parameters), choice of beneficiaries to be a prime consideration.

Disbursement of Funds

NSFDC funds for sanctioned schemes are disbursed only on specific request from the SCAs. The disbursements are subject to the fulfilment of conditions, some of which are given below:

1. Execution of General Loan Agreement by the SCAs.
2. Availability of adequate State Government/Bank Guarantee.
3. Acceptance of Letter of Intent by the authorised official.
4. Satisfactory level of utilisation of funds released to the SCAs as per (Annexure-I).
5. Repayment of NSFDC dues.
6. Submission of List of Selected Beneficiaries as per (Annexure-2 to Annexure- I).
7. Availability of Subsidy, Margin Money Loan and Promoter's Contribution as per the Means of Finance sanctioned.
8. Identification of assets and suppliers as per beneficiary's choice and in conformity of the terms and conditions of sanction.

BUSINESS OPPORTUNITIES

Agricultural & Allied Sector			
1.	Agricultural Land Purchase	11.	Duckery
2.	Irrigation Bore wells/Minor Irrigation	12.	Goatery
3.	Horticulture	13.	Sheep Farming
4.	Sericulture	14.	Fisheries
5.	Poultry	15.	Ornamental Fish Rearing
6.	Dairy	16.	Tractors
7.	Piggery	17.	Power Tillers etc.
8.	Bullock/Camel Cart	18.	Cultivation and Processing of Medicinal Plants

Agricultural and Allied Sector			
9	Floriculture	19.	Honey Bee Cultivation
10	Hatcheries	20.	Agricultural Implements
Small Industries Sector			
1.	Bricks Making	26.	Printing Press
2.	Readymade Garments Manufacturing	27.	Furniture Making
3.	Handlooms/Power looms	28.	Flour Mill
4.	Handicrafts Making	29.	Soft Toys making
5.	Footwear Manufacturing	30.	Embroidery/Knitting
6.	Silver Ornaments making	31.	Woollen Garments/Shawls making etc.
7.	Bakery	32.	Hosiery Units
8.	Bamboo Furniture Making	33.	Jute Fabrics/Bags
9.	Battery Making	34.	Leather Garments
10.	Bicycle Repairing Shops	35.	Leather Processing
11.	Bicycle Seat Cover Making	36.	Leatherand Rexine Articles
12	Bio-gas Plant	37.	Lime Kilns
13.	Candles Manufacturing	38.	Plastic Bags Manufacturing
14.	Car Upholstery and Seat Making	39.	Potteries
15.	Cement Solid Blocks	40.	Pouch Making
16.	Coir Industry	41.	Power looms
17.	Carpet Manufacturing	42.	Prawn Culture
18.	Copperware/Utensils Manufacturing	43.	Rubber Industry
19.	Exercise Books and Registers Making	44.	Shoe/Chappal Manufacturing
20.	Ginger and Turmeric Processing	45.	Umbrella Making
21.	Granite Tiles	46.	Fiber Glass Manufacturing
22.	Handmade Papers	47.	Mineral Water Bottling Plant
23.	Ornaments Polishing Units	48.	Oil mills
24.	Stone Crushing	49.	Saw Mills
25.	Supari Manufacturing	50.	Soft/Stuffed Toys Making
Service and Transport Sector			
1.	Departmental Stores	42.	Dhabas/Mini Hotels

Service and Transport Sector			
2.	Stationery Shops	43.	Tourist Lodge
3.	Photography/Videography	44.	Automobile Repairs
4.	Chemist Shops	45.	Electrical Items Shop
5.	Kiryana Store	46.	Hardware Shop
6.	Bangle/Cosmetic Shop	47.	Electrical Winding
7.	Garments Shop	48.	Welding and Refrigeration
8.	Commercial Centre (STD/Photocopier/Scanner)	49.	Vegetable vending
9.	Internet Cafe	50.	Watch Repair/Sales Shop
10.	Cable TV	51.	Digital Mixing Lab
11.	Tent House	52.	Seeds/Fertilizers/Pesticides Shops
12.	Beautician	53.	Auto rickshaws/Auto Load Carrier
13.	Band Party	54.	Light Commercial Vehicles/Mini Buses
14.	Fish/Meat Shops	55.	Jeeps/Car/Taxies
15.	Petty Shops	56.	Earth Movers (JCB) etc.
16.	Bicycle Repairing Shops	57.	Laundry/Dry-cleaning Shops
17.	Blood Bank	58.	Machine Shops
18.	Book Binding/Book Shops	59.	Marble Polishing
19.	Cards Shop	60.	Milk Chilling Centres/Booths
20.	Clinical Labs	61.	Mobile Crane
21.	Cloth Merchant	62.	Nursing Home/Hospitals
22.	Computer Centres	63.	Nursery School
23.	Computer Hardware and Servicing	64.	Passenger/Fishing Boats
24.	Dental Clinics	65.	Public Address System
25.	Desk Top Printing	66.	Pump set/Minor Irrigation
26.	Driving School	67.	Rabbit Rearing
27.	Eye Clinics	68.	Ropeway
28.	Food Processing	69.	Sales and Servicing of Electric Items
29.	Gas Agency	70.	Saw Mills
30.	Gem Stone Cutting and	71.	Supplying Unit

Service and Transport Sector			
31.	Shopping Complex	72.	Seeds and Pesticides Shops
32.	Shuttering	73.	Sericulture Development
33.	Spice Grinding	74.	Tannery
34.	Spray Painting	75.	Tent House/Decorators
35.	Silk Weaving	76.	Transport Vehicles (Autos , Taxies, LCVs, Buses, Trucks)
36.	Spray Painting Unit	77.	Travel Agency
37.	Steel Fabrication	78.	T.V./Audio-Video/Refrigerator/A.C. Repair
38.	Sweet Shop	79.	Typing School
39.	Tailoring	80.	Tyre Retreading
40.	Water Sports Equipments	81.	Tyre Servicing and Vulcanising
41.	Wooden/Steel Furniture	82.	Xerox/Fax/Typing/Lamination Centre

2. TAMIL NADU ADI-DRAVIDAR HOUSING and DEVELOPMENT CORPORATION (TAHDCO)

TAHDCO is a state level organisation on the line of NSFDC to implement the SC/ST development programme in Tamil Nadu. TAHDCO was incorporated in 1974 under the Companies Act, 1956. The Government of Tamil Nadu and the Government of India contribute to the Share Capital of the Corporation. At present the Authorised Share Capital of the Corporation is Rs 100 Crore and paid up share capital is Rs 95.12 Crore. The State Government and the Central Government contribute the share capital in the ratio of 51:49.

Though the corporation was initially started as a construction company in 1974, the activities of the corporation was extended to enable it to undertake a wide spectrum of economic development schemes for income generation, skill development training for Scheduled Castes and Scheduled Tribes in the State.

Main Activities of TAHDCO

- To implement economic development schemes for the welfare of SC/ST in the State.
- To provide skill development training to youth belonging to Scheduled Castes and Scheduled Tribes for job/self-employment.
- To undertake construction activities entrusted by the government.

Schemes

1. Land Purchase Scheme
2. Financial assistance for individuals
3. Financial Assistance for Self-help Groups
4. Discretionary Fund
   (a) Managing Director's/Collector's Discretionary Fund
   (b) Managing Director's Discretionary Fund
5. Self Employment Programme for Youth
6. Special Economic Projects.

Training Programmes

1. Free Vocational Training
2. Employment Enhancement Training
3. Training Courses Organised in GOI Agencies by TAHDCO

National Schemes

1. NSFDC
2. NSTFDC

3. NSKFDC
4. NSLRS

SCHEMES IMPLEMENTED THROUGH SPECIAL CENTRAL ASSISTANCE

For the economic development of Scheduled Caste, the TAHDCO has been implementing many programmes / schemes with financial assistance from Special Central Assistance. The Corporation receives approximately Rs 50.00 Crore annually under SCA.

Following schemes are implemented:

1. Land Purchase and Land Development Scheme.
2. Entrepreneur Development Programme.
3. Self Employment Programme for Youth (SEPY).
4. Revolving Fund to Self Help Groups.
5. Economic Assistance to Self Help Groups.
6. Skill development training to SHG members.
7. Welfare Fund.
8. Fast Track Power Supply (Electricity Board Deposit).
9. Financial Assistance to Civil Services Preliminary Examination passed candidates.
10. Financial Assistance to Law Graduates to set up their profession.

Land Purchase and Land Development Scheme

The aim of the schemes is to improve the land holding of Schedule Castes and to enhance their socio-economic status in the state. The government have issued orders for the exemption of 100 per cent stamp duty for the registration of the land purchased under the scheme.

Eligibility

- The applicant shall be a Scheduled Caste Women.
- The applicant should be in the age group of 18-55.
- The annual family income of the applicant should not exceed Rs 1.00 lakh.
- The applicant should not own any agricultural land.
- The occupation of the applicant should be agriculture.
- Applicants and their family members should not have availed any subsidy so far.

Conditions

- Applicants themselves should select the land to be purchased.
- The lands have to be purchased from the land owners who do not belong to Schedule Caste.
- The land purchased shall be registered only in the name of applicant.
- The land purchased shall not be sold out within twenty years.
- The applicant who has the land registered in their name can alone take up land development activities.
- The land development activities of digging of open well, bore well and electrification of pump sets shall be taken up as per the NABARD guidelines.
- The feasibility certificate shall be obtained from geologist in respect of digging of open well/bore well.
- The applicant and the family members should not have sold/transferred their lands to others in the last five years.

Entrepreneur Development Programme

Objective

- Financial Assistance to income generating activity
- Age limit 18–55 years

Scheme Assistance

- Subsidy - 30 per cent of Unit Cost or Rs 2.25 Lakh whichever is less.
- Bank loan - Balance Amount.
- The subsidy will be a Back End Subsidy.

Eligibility

- The applicant should have prior experience/desire and knowledge in the trade applied.
- The applicant and their family members should not have availed any subsidy so far.
- Revolving Fund and Economic Activities to Self Help

Groups

The salient feature

1. Rs 10,000 per Self Help Group will be released as a Back End Subsidy for revolving fund.
2. 50 per cent of the project cost or Rs 2.50 lakhs whichever is lower. The subsidy will be a Back End Subsidy for economic assistance.

Eligibility

- The members of the Self help groups shall belong to Scheduled Caste.
- The annual family income of the self help group members should not exceed Rs 1.00 lakh each.
- The self help group should have qualified in the first rating for revolving fund.

- The self help group should have qualified in second rating for economic assistance.
- The member of self help group and their family members should not have availed any subsidy so far.

Discretionary Fund

(a) Managing Director's/District Collector's Discretionary Fund

The programme is designed to give immediate financial assistance to the persons who could not avail relief benefit under any TAHDCO/other scheme. Preference is given to differently-abled, destitute widows, children who don't have parents/guardians, Aravanies and unmarried women above 40 years. A maximum of Rs 20,000 per beneficiary is given as one time grant.

(b) Managing Director's Discretionary Fund

Under this scheme financial assistance is provided to the selected candidates those who are desire to have a special coaching/training related to ICWA/CA through the reputed training institutes. The selection of candidates/institutions/course fee etc. will be decided by the Managing Director, TAHDCO.

3.2.5. Self-employment Programme for Youth (SEPY)

Youth in the age group of 18-35 are trained and escorted in obtaining financial assistance to commence ventures sustainable over a period of time.

The Salient Feature

- 30 per cent of the project cost or Rs 2.25 lakhs whichever is lower. The subsidy will be a Back End Subsidy.

Eligibility

- The applicant should belong to Scheduled Caste.

- The annual family income of the applicant should not exceed Rs 1.00 lakh.
- The applicant should be in the age group of 18-35.
- The applicant should have prior experience in the trade applied.
- The applicant and their family members should not have availed any subsidy so far.
- The applicant should posses eligibility certificate issued by recognised institutions.

Conditions

- Applicants themselves can select the trade.
- The assets created under the scheme shall be registered only in the name of the applicant.
- The applicant shall carryout the business in the district where subsidy is sanctioned.

Special Economic Schemes

1. Setting up of Petrol/Diesel/Gas retail outlet.

Objective

1. To increase the entrepreneurs in the community.
2. To ensure an equitable participation of Adi-Dravidars in the process of industrialisation. This special scheme is introduced for setting up of petrol/diesel outlet.

Eligibility

- The applicant should reside in the district.
- The applicant should have passed 12th Standard.
- Annual family income should not exceed Rs 3.00 Lakh.
- The applicant should posses eligibility prescribed by the oil companies for appointment as agency.

2. Setting up of Clinic

- Financial Assistance to the young Doctors for setting up to own a Clinic
- Increase medical facilities in rural/semi-urban areas

Eligibility

- To establish clinic, the applicant should have MBBS/ BSMS/BDS degree.
- The applicant and their family members should not have availed any subsidy under TAHDCO schemes.
- The applicant should register his/her name in the Indian Medical Council.

3. Financial Assistance to Civil Services (Preliminary) Examination Passed Candidates

To encourage the SC youth to join Civil Services, a financial assistance of Rs 50,000 will be given per candidate, who has passed Civil Services (Preliminary) Examination to prepare for Civil Services (Main) Examination. Rs 50,000 is for meeting purchase of books and incidental expenses.

Eligibility

- The applicant should belong to Scheduled Caste.
- The annual family income of the applicant should not exceed Rs 2.00 lakh.

Conditions

- Applicant should have passed the Civil Service Preliminary Examination.
- Applicant should have applied for Main Examination.
- The Applicant should not be a permanent/temporary employee of Central or State Government.

4. Financial Assistance to Law Graduates to set up their Profession

To encourage the young Law Graduates to set up their profession, a financial assistance of Rs 50,000 is given. The financial assistance released through the Commissioner, Adi Dravidar Welfare.

Eligibility

The candidates:

- Should belongs Scheduled Castes
- Should be a Law Graduate
- Should be a member in Bar Council
- Annual Family income should not exceed of Rs 1,00,000.

5. Fast Track Power Supply (E.B. Deposit) Scheme

Objective

SC farmers are encouraged to put their land for productive use by giving them priority power supply. Under this programme, Rs 10,000 is remitted to Tamil Nadu Electricity Board to enable them to effect service connections on priority basis.

Eligibility

The annual family income of the applicant should not exceed Rs 1.00 lakh.

Conditions

- The applicant should own the land and patta shall be in the name of applicant.
- Either an open well or a bore well should have been dug, in the land.

Training

1. Vocational Training Programme for SC/ST Youth.

- Free Vocational Training Programmes are organised for youth in the age group of 18-35 years in reputed and recognised training institutions in all districts through the TAHDCO District Vocational Training Programme Committee headed by the District Collector.
- Courses having high employment potential such as Nursing, Hotel Management and Catering, Apparel Design and Manufacturing, Computer Software Programming, IT-enabled services, Electrical/ Electronics repair and maintenance, etc. are organised to enable the SC/ST youth to seek gainful employment in the private sector.
- The entire course fee is borne by TAHDCO and also stipend of Rs 400 per month is provided to these students.

2. Employability Enhancement Training Programmes of TAHDCO

Policy

To enable the Scheduled Caste and Scheduled Tribe Youth of Tamil Nadu to obtain immediate job employment at all levels, by significantly upgrading their employability status, through job-oriented skill training programmes and also to enable them to start self-employment ventures.

Organising the Training Programmes

TAHDCO's Vocational Training Programmes are organised in all the 30 Districts of Tamil Nadu through the TAHDCO District Manager's office in each district. Every year, Vocational Training Committee under the Chairmanship of the District Collector selects job oriented courses in accordance with the potential in the district. Only such training institutions which are recognised by Government of Tamil Nadu or Government of India or highly reputed private organisations are selected by this committee to conduct the courses. After extensive publicity through newspaper advertisements, candidates are selected through interviews by the committee for various courses as per eligible and merit.

Features of the Training Programmes

- Entire cost of training payable to the training institutions is borne by TAHDCO.
- Stipend of Rs 400 per month is given to the candidates to support them during training.
- Course duration ranges from three months to two years.
- Training is organised only in such institutions which have valid recognition of the Department of Employment and Training or Department of Technical Education or Department of Medical Education of Government of Tamil Nadu or of Government of India. Training highly reputed private institutions are organised, in exceptional cases only.
- On passing the examinations conducted by the Government, certificates are issued by the respective government department.
- Candidates are assisted in getting job placements.
- Candidates who are able and willing are given financial assistance under TAHDCO schemes, for starting self-employment ventures, after a short duration Entrepreneurship Development Programme.

3. Training Courses Organised in Government of India Agencies by TAHDCO

1. National Institute of Fashion Technology (NIFT), Chennai

- One year Programme in Fashion and Clothing Technology.

- One year Programme in Fashion Knitwear and Production Technology.
- One year Programme in Clothing Production Technology.
- Six months Programme in Industrial Pattern Making.

2. Central Institute of Plastic Engineering and Technology (CIPET), Chennai

- Six months course in CAM/CNC
- Three months course in Plastics Mould Design with AUTOCAD.
- Six month course in Plastic Processing Technology.
- Six month course in Plastic Processing Machine Operator.
- Three months course in CAD/CAM.

3. National Film Development Corporation (NFDC), Chennai

Three weeks course in Non-Linear Editing.

4. Apparel Training and Design Centre (ATDC), Chennai

1. One year course in Apparel Manufacturing Technology.
2. Six months course in Pattern Cutting Master's Course.
3. Three months course in Sewing Machine Operator.
4. Six months course in Production Supervisor and Quality. Controller Course.

5. Indian Institute of Hotel Management and Catering Technology (IIHM), Chennai

(a) Six months course in Catering and House Keeping Supervisor.

b. Six months course in Food Production.

c. Six months course in Bakery and Confectionery.

d. Six months course in House Keeping.

e. Six months course in Front Office Operation.

f. Six months course in Food and Beverage Service.

Other Agencies Including State Controlled in Tamil Nadu

1. Confederation of Indian Industries (CII)

Focus Areas

- Affirmative Action
- Climate Change
- CSR and Community Development
- Disaster Management
- Education
- Environment
- Industry – NGO Partnerships
- Public Health
- Rural Development
- Skill Development
- Social Development
- Special Abilities
- Sports
- Women Empowerment.

Affirmative Action

Affirmative Action for the Scheduled Castes and Scheduled Tribes is a voluntary commitment by Indian companies to help the government and civil society in the national endeavour to ensure equal opportunity to members of the Scheduled Castes and Scheduled Tribes. CII has been leading Indian Industry's efforts on affirmative action agenda since 2006. Attempts have contributed in building positive and favourable ecosystem for affirmative action in the country. CII continuously interacts with stakeholders through the National committee/ Subcommittee/ Panel meetings and report back on the initiatives to the government on the quarterly basis. CII has formulated the Code of Conduct on affirmative action. Four focus areas, the 4E's have been identified for concrete steps - Education, Employability, Entrepreneurship and Employment.

2. Federation of Indian Chambers of Commerce and Industry (FICCI)

Established in 1927, FICCI is the largest and oldest apex business organisation in India.

A non-government, not-for-profit organisation, FICCI is the voice of India's business and industry.

FICCI involved in many sectors viz. agriculture, disaster management, education, HRD, culture, labour and employment, manufacturing, MSME, skill development, etc.

Skill Development

FICCI recognises that skills development for achieving India's ambitious growth targets. It is committed to working with the stakeholders, especially the industry, government and academia to create sustainable and scalable skills propositions which will benefit the youth of the country from all sections of society. With this in mind, FICCI through its skills Development activities is pursuing the following vision:

FICCI would act as a "skills development aggregator" to complement Government of India's ambition of training 500 million people by 2022.

FICCI shall offer support and facilitation services through Policy Advocacy, Industry Intervention and International Collaboration so that the youth can acquire skills to meaningfully participate in and contribute to the economy.

Skills Development Forum

The FICCI Skills Development Forum (SDF) was launched in 2008 to supplement the government initiatives with industry interventions. The forum has since start discussed and critically examined the skill development policies in the country. Members of the forum in the leadership of the Chairman have interacted with various government departments and the National Skills Development Corporation (NSDC) to stimulate meaningful discussions.

3. Confederation of Women Entrepreneurs (COWE), Hyderabad

Confederation of Women Entrepreneurs is an NGO/social organisation engaged in the social and economic upliftment of women through entrepreneurship. COWE stands for *"Of the women, for the women and by the women"*.

Entrepreneurs from varied fields and those dedicated to the promotion of entrepreneurship among women, got together and formed COWE. This organisation has been working un-relentlessly towards providing opportunities for women in Industry, Trade, Retail, Franchising and Service Sectors. Traditional professions are also encouraged and hand holding support is given wherever required. The expertise and experience of seniors in the field is sought and passed on to the members.

COWE was inaugurated on 22nd November, 2004 and has emerged as a well organised and established organisation working towards their goal of liberating women by making them financially independent and vibrant. COWE has in a short span, achieved recognition with Government, Bankers and Industrial Associations and Bodies.

From 20 members as on the date of commencement, today the membership is over 500. Altruism or selfless concern for the well being of women prompted the founders to come together and start the organisation.

4. Associated Chambers of Commerce and Industry of India (ASSOCHAM)

ASSOCHAM is a non-profit organisation, facilitating reach of India to all businesses around the globe, for wanting to do business with India.

Evolution of Value Creator

ASSOCHAM initiated its endeavour of value creation for Indian industry in 1920. Having in its fold more than 400 Chambers and Trade Associations, and serving more than 4,50,000 members from all over India. It has witnessed upswings as well as upheavals of Indian Economy, and contributed significantly by playing a catalytic role in shaping up the Trade, Commerce and Industrial environment of the country.

Today, ASSOCHAM has emerged as the fountainhead of Knowledge for Indian industry, which is all set to redefine the dynamics of growth and development in the technology driven cyber age of 'Knowledge Based Economy'. ASSOCHAM is seen as a forceful, proactive, forward looking institution equipping itself to meet the aspirations of corporate India in the new world of business. ASSOCHAM is working towards creating a conducive environment of India business to compete globally.

ASSOCHAM derives its strength from its Promoter Chambers and other Industry/Regional Chambers/ Associations spread all over the country.

Vision

Empower Indian enterprise by inculcating knowledge that will be the catalyst of growth in the barrierless technology driven global market and help them upscale, align and emerge as formidable player in respective business segments.

Mission

As a representative organ of Corporate India, ASSOCHAM articulates the genuine, legitimate needs and interests of its members. Its mission is to impact the policy and legislative environment so as to foster balanced economic, industrial and social development. ASSOCHAM believes education, IT, BT, Health, Corporate Social responsibility and environment to be the critical success factors.

Services to Members include

- **Close interaction** with ASSOCHAM's renowned Members, Central and State Governments, international agencies and academia.
- **Assistance to trade and industry** in becoming competitive in national and international markets.
- **Promotion of international trade** through meetings with visiting foreign business delegations, participation in Trade Fairs/Exhibitions and business delegations abroad.
- **Expert advice** on diverse subjects such as industrial growth, monetary and fiscal policy, exchange rate policy, economic planning, taxation and corporate laws.
- **Regular and timely information** on latest national and international policies, Government legislations and technical developments.
- **Generating awareness** and gathering public support regarding specific aspects of business for overall business development.
- **Analysis of legislation:** Helping policy-makers, foreign investors and trade and industry.

- **Platform to interact** and gain professional knowledge through seminars, workshops and round table meetings.
- **Total Quality Management Cell (TQMC):** Organises seminars/workshops/training programmes on TQM, ISO 9000, ISO 14000, TPM and related topics. Provides guidance in adoption of lean operation practices including ISO 9000, ISO 14000. Networks with other operational bodies towards promoting new concepts of management.
- **Participate in the Expert Committees/Task Forces of ASSOCHAM:** ASSOCHAM has more than 100 National Councils which regularly take up the issues of its Members interest in various fields with the Policy Makers.
- **Redressal of general/common problems** of Members at Central/State Government levels and other Institutions.
- **Networking with** Indian missions and counterpart organisations across the globe.
- **Assist identifying joint venture** partners at various national and international events organised by ASSOCHAM.
- **Web Services**: Information on important events organised by ASSOCHAM and other activities, press releases, membership, etc.
- **Quick Mail Service**: QMS (Weekly) makes available to members government notifications, circulars, reports, etc.
- **Opportunity to gain mileage** by becoming a sponsor/co-sponsor of ASSOCHAM events.
- **Access to ASSOCHAM periodicals/publications:** Assocham Bulletin, Overseas Business Contacts, Parliamentary Digest, News and Views Weekly etc.

- **Access to library, study reports and data.**
- **Access to use Conference and Meeting Room facilities of Centrally located at** concessional rates at Centrally Air-conditioned ASSOCHAM House, New Delhi.

5. Tata Affirmative Action Programme (TAAP)

Under TAAP, the company is trying to ensure all round development of Scheduled Caste and Scheduled Tribe communities of India under different initiatives aligned with Employment, Education, Employability and Entrepreneurship. As a matter of policy, the company positively discriminates against SC/ST candidates and all other things being equal gives preference to SC/ST candidates in employment. As regards education, like earlier years, during the year 2012-13 too, two high value scholarships of Rs 70 thousand each were provided to SC/ST students for higher technical education through Foundation for Academic Excellence and Access. 1021 Scheduled Caste (SC) and 1599 Scheduled Tribe (ST) students were benefited directly or indirectly through various interventions in 34 schools across India. Five hundred SC/ST candidates were provided skill development training in various constructions-related and vocational trades during the year 2012-13. More than half of them have already been gainfully employed/started their enterprises/income level enhanced. At least one SC entrepreneur has done business worth more than INR 10 million with the Company during the year 2012-13. Tata Housing has been providing entrepreneurship development training to potential youths in partnership with Entrepreneurship Development Institute of India, Ahmedabad too.

6. Dalit Indian Chamber of Commerce and Industry (DICCI)

'Be job givers instead of job seekers'.

DICCI is actively involved in creating business opportunities for its members and empowering them through information and knowledge exchange. A variety of seminars, workshops, personality development programmes and interaction with industry and government experts, help to educate members on the latest trends, developments and opportunities in the field. More than 1000 entrepreneurs as well as professionals are currently members of the DICCI and have benefited from its activities.

DICCI was established on 14th April 2005 by Pune-based Milind Kamble, a Civil Engineer and entrepreneur. While Mr Kamble is currently the Chairman, the organisation has grown with the help of new state chapters. Its membership base is rapidly expanding as more Dalit entrepreneurs become aware of its activities and what it can offer them.

The activities of its members are quite diversified ranging from manufacturing (sectors such as chemicals, agri-products, frozen foods, plastics, textiles, pest control, metals and metallurgy, marine engineering, solar energy, sugar refining), construction and services (healthcare, hospitality industries, education and international trade).

Vision

To instill the spirit of entrepreneurship among Dalit youth to develop business leadership, thus empowering them to walk in step with the world.

Mission

To motivate Dalit youth to enter the business and industry sector as entrepreneurs and to carve their own niche; to encourage them to contribute to the nation's economy through wealth creation and to spread the spirit of enterprise to other fellow members. DICCI mission is to encourage Dalit entrepreneurs and support them in their ventures.

DICCI's Representation

1. Planning Commission (Government of India), Ministry of Social Justice and Empowerment
2. CII- National Council
3. CII – Affirmative Action Council
4. National Skill Development Council – BFSI Segment
5. Directorate General of Supplies and Disposals (P and C - Planning Directorate)
6. Delhi - Mumbai Industrial Corridor Development Corporation Limited (DMICD)

SERVICES

1. Mentoring
2. Business Networking
3. Financial and Tax Management and Assistance
4. Industry Linkages
5. Quality Management Services (QMS) certification Guidance
6. Training
7. Business Trade Fair
8. Conferences and Seminars
9. Awards and Recognitions
10. Updates by Email Notification.

7. Directorate of Industries and Commerce, Government of Tamil Nadu.

The primary objective of the department is to promote Micro, Small and Medium Enterprises, Cottage and Handicrafts Industries. At present, this Department implements a variety of programmes as given below:

1. Implementing Micro, Small and Medium Enterprises Development (MSMED) Act 2006.
2. Registration of Industrial Co-operative Societies.

3. Testing Facilities.
4. Training Facilities.
5. Implementation of Prime Minister's Employment Generation Programme (PMEGP).
6. Creating awareness for the development of Industries through Seminars and Dissemination Meets.
7. Providing escort services to entrepreneurs.
8. Conducting of Techno Economic Surveys and Sample/ Comprehensive Survey.
9. Identification, declaration and assistance to sick units.
10. Providing Incubator facilities to deserving entrepreneurs.
11. Sanction of incentives to Micro, Small and Medium Enterprises.

These programmes are implemented with an accent on development and modernisation of industries, upgradation of technology and quality control. The packages of services offered by the Directorate of Industries and Commerce is Multidimensional and need based so that industrial growth is facilitated.

Functions

1. Small Industries Cluster Development Programme
2. Export Guidance Cell
3. Market Development Assistance
4. Nucleus Cell
5. Entrepreneurship Development Institute
6. Common Facility Centre
7. Sago Service
8. Indcoserve
9. Tea serve.

SCHEMES

- The New Entrepreneurship–cum-enterprise Development Scheme (NEEDS)
- Back Ended Interest Subsidy to Small Scale Industries
- Electrical and Electronic Industrial Estate
- Electrical and Electronic Testing Laboratories
- Ceramic Institute Estate
- Cooperative Industrial Estate
- Chemical Testing Laboratories.

Conclusion

The work-force engaged in self-employment in agriculture and non-agriculture has increased among all social groups, and the rate of increase was high among the SCs as compared to other social groups in India. While there was a decline in the work-force engaged as agricultural workers among all social groups. Entrepreneurs development institutes have been established both at the national and state levels including private sectors have benefitted SCs and STs including the poor sections of the society. The economic development programmes including the entrepreneur development programmes implemented by NSFDC and TAHDCO benefitted the SCs and STs exclusively. The role played by other agencies viz. state controlled and private agencies in providing skills and training to the beneficiaries is immense.

Entrepreneurship among SCs, no doubt improves not only the family of the Entrepreneurs but also the wealth of the nation as a whole. SCs youth are willing to give up the jobs that were polluting in nature and are willing take up activities that were once considered to the upper caste persons only. SCs entrepreneurs must be molded properly with entrepreneurial traits and skills to meet the changes in trends, challenges global markets and also be competent enough to sustain and strive for excellence in the entrepreneurial arena.

References

1. Economic Survey, Government of India – 2013-14.
2. Employment and unemployment among social groups in India, 1999-2000, NSSO, 55th Round, Department of Statistics, Government of India, New Delhi, 2001.
3. Employment and unemployment among social groups in India, 2004-05, NSSO, 61st Round, Department of Statistics, Government of India, New Delhi, 2006.
4. World Bank study/survey report, as quoted in The Hindu, 21st January 2015, (Chennai edition) .
5. (http://www.businessdictionary.com/definition/entrepreneur.html).

5

Educational Status in Tamil Nadu*

Introduction

Tamil Nadu is one of the educationally developed states in India and this is amply reflected in its HDI. Educational advancement of Tamil Nadu has been contributed by the government and benevolent institutions, as these institutions have contributed immensely to the educational development of the state. In this chapter, an attempt is made to map out the constitutional privileges, impact of noon meal scheme, educational programmes, public expenditure on education, and the number of private management schools, teachers, students by both gender, the enrolment rates, dropout rates, completion rates, repetition rates and attendance rates.

---

*This chapter was drawn from "Educational Status of the Scheduled Castes in Tamil Nadu: Attainment and Challenges", Department of Economics, University of Madras, October 2014. The project report was sponsored by the ICSSR, New Delhi and the author of the report was the Project Director.

Reservation

Indian Constitution provides reservation to the Scheduled Castes (SCs) and Scheduled Tribes (STs). There are three types of reservation given to the SCs and STs. They are: (1) reservation in admission to the educational institutions, (2) reservation in employment in government and the public sector undertakings and various economic development programmes to improve their livelihood opportunities, and (3) reservation/nomination to the elected offices as people's representatives, viz., Members in the Parliament, Legislative Assembly and Presidents and Members in the Panchayat Raj Institutions.

Controversy over reservation

However, the problem as to whether the concessions should be provided to the people belonging to the Scheduled Castes itself has been controversial. Three points of view have been by and large put forth in this regard. 1. Some people argue that giving concessions to a particular section is unjust, because, in this way only one section will be favoured at the cost of other sections. Their argument is that all people should be treated equally by the government without discrimination. 2. Another group of people strongly feel that the concessions should be provided to the people belonging to Scheduled Castes especially on the basis of caste, rather than economic status, because they hold that by and large the persons belonging to SCs have been deprived of economic benefits and social equality down the ages. 3. The last viewpoint is that concessions should be extended to all those who are economically backward rather than being based on caste to which a person belongs.

Objectives

1. To examine the current status of education of children by social groups through secondary data.

2. To find out the level of inequalities in education by gender and social groups.

Sources of data

Secondary data have been collected regarding the literacy rates by social groups from Census of India 1991, 2001, 2011. The data regarding enrolment in primary and upper primary School Education by social groups were collected from the District Information System for Education (DISE), Cohort Study and Elementary Education Register (EER), Government of Tamil Nadu for the year from 1990-91 to 2007-08. Data were also collected from Annual Reports of the Department of School Education and Literacy and Department of Higher Education, Ministry of Human Resource Development (MHRD), Government of India, regarding secondary education and different levels of school education by various social groups for different years.

Impact of noon meal scheme

The issue of admission to schools and retention of attendance at schools was addressed as a fallout of noon meal scheme. Tamil Nadu is in a leading position in the rate of literacy in India. Children from poor and underprivileged families were attracted to attend the corporation schools because of one square meal (lunch) provided under the noon meal scheme as early as 1922 in Chennai by the Justice Party in Tamil Nadu under the leadership of Pitti Theogarayar, the then Mayor of Chennai City. The noon meal scheme was further extended in 1956, by Mr. K. Kamaraj, then Chief Minister of Tamil Nadu. He introduced the noon meal scheme in many of the state-run schools. Later in 1982, M. G. Ramachandran, the then Chief Minister of Tamil Nadu, has brought all primary and upper primary schools run by the Government of Tamil Nadu into its ambit. Implementation of noon meal scheme has paid rich dividends by way of improving enrolment and retention in elementary schools.

It has also addressed the problem of child malnutrition and child labour. Now, noon meal scheme has become a popular scheme and is being implemented not only in Tamil Nadu, but also in all states of India.

Problems in School Education for SCs

The experience in the implementation of various educational programmes by the government to improve the access of education by the downtrodden sections, especially the Scheduled Castes, revealed that though enrolment has increased substantially, it has failed to retain the children in the system. The reasons attributed for this phenomena are largely due to the prevailing socio-economic conditions, social environment and teaching-and-learning environment in the schools. In other words, participation of children in schools depends on the above parameters and also pushes them out of schools due to unpleasant environment experienced and prevailing in the school environment. This clearly shows that there is interdependence between their rate of participation, social environment, teaching and learning environment and the social background of the children.

Population

For proper and efficient planning, population is an important parameter to decide the allocation of funds for future development. More specifically, special provisions have to be earmarked for the weaker section among the total population. Educational planners have to make provisions based on district level data on literacy, enrolment, gross enrolment ratio, drop out, etc.

Sarva Shiksha Abhiyan (SSA)

The Scheme of SSA, a national flagship programme, is being implemented and the aim of SSA is to provide useful and relevant elementary education for all children in the 6-14 age groups by 2010. The scheme of SSA was launched in 2001.

Table 5.1: Distribution of population by region, gender and social groups (per cent)

Social groups	*SC*			*ST*			*Non-SC/ST*		
Tamil Nadu	*1991*	*2001*	*2011*	*1991*	*2001*	*2011*	*1991*	*2001*	*2011*
Rural (R)									
Male	22.94	23.72	25.35	1.39	1.59	1.78	75.67	74.69	72.86
Female	22.89	23.86	25.55	1.36	1.57	1.76	75.75	74.57	72.69
Total	**22.91**	**23.79**	**25.45**	**1.37**	**1.58**	**1.77**	**75.71**	**74.63**	**72.78**
Urban (U)									
Male	11.87	12.79	14.14	0.36	0.36	0.38	87.77	86.85	85.47
Female	12.08	13.04	14.29	0.36	0.37	0.39	87.56	86.60	85.33
Total	**11.97**	**12.91**	**14.21**	**0.36**	**0.36**	**0.38**	**87.67**	**86.72**	**85.40**
Both (R+U)									
Male	19.13	18.89	19.94	1.04	1.05	1.11	79.83	80.06	78.82
Female	19.22	19.11	20.09	1.02	1.04	1.09	79.76	79.85	78.95
Total	**19.18**	**19.00**	**20.01**	**1.03**	**1.04**	**1.10**	**79.79**	**79.96**	**78.89**

Source: Census of India, 1991, 2001 and 2011, Primary Census Abstract, General Population, Scheduled Castes and Scheduled Tribes.

The goals of SSA are as follows:

- All the 6-14 age group of children admitted in School/ Education Guarantte Scheme (EGS) Centre/Bridge Course by 2005.
- Bridge all gender and social category gaps at primary stage by 2007 and at elementary education level by 2010.
- Universal retention by 2010.
- Focus on elementary education of satisfactory quality with emphasis on education for life.

The assistance under the Sarva Shiksha Abhiyan was on a 85:15 sharing arrangement during the Ninth Plan, 75:25 sharing arrangement during the Tenth Plan, and 50:50 sharing thereafter between the Central Government and the State Government for all major states.

The programme covers the entire country with special focus on the educational needs of girls, SCs/STs and other children in difficult circumstances. The programme seeks to open new schools in those places, which do not have schooling facilities and strengthen existing school infrastructure through provision of additional class rooms, toilets, drinking water, maintenance grants and school improvement grants. The SSA has a special focus on girls and children of weaker sections. A number of initiatives, including distribution of scholarship, free uniforms and textbooks for children under the programme.[1]

Tamil Nadu has been successfully implementing *Sarva Shiksha Abhiyan (SSA)* Mission since its inception. The State has gained a lot in the process of planning and implementing the Mission. Over the years, the State has achieved several milestones in terms of quantity.

Constitutional Arrangement

The Constitution of India guarantees Right to Equality under Article 14 and imposes a prohibition on the State under Article 15(1) that it shall not discriminate against any citizen on grounds only of religion, race, caste, sex, place of birth or any of them. However, exception is made in favour of women, children, socially and educationally backward classes and Scheduled Castes and Scheduled Tribes.

Article 29 (2) provides that no citizen shall be denied admission into any educational institution maintained by the State or receiving aid out of State funds on grounds of religion, race, caste, language or any of them. Even though it is a general clause, Article 29 limits its operation to 'protection of interests of minorities'.

To protect their interests, Article 30 (2) imposes a restriction on the State not to make any discrimination against any educational institution in granting aid on the grounds that it is under the management of Minority, whether based on religion or language.

In order to promote the educational interests of the weaker sections of people and in particular the Scheduled Castes and Scheduled Tribes, Article 46 enjoins upon the State an obligation to take 'special care' in case of such classes of people. Primary education was now given a place under the list of principles fundamental to the governance of the country.

Article 45 makes provisions that 'the state shall endeavor to provide, with in a period of ten years from the commencement of this Constitution, free and compulsory education for all children until they complete the age of fourteen years'.

Status of school education by social groups in Tamil Nadu

After Independence, education for all children was a prime goal of our Indian democracy. Free, compulsory and universal education to the children of the age group 6-14 years was to fulfill the constitutional obligation. However, more than 25 million primary school age children are not in schools now. Two out of five first-grade students do not complete the primary cycles of 4th to 5th standards, and therefore the learning achievement of those graduating is low.

The Planning Commission of India in its Approach Paper for the Eleventh Plan (2006) explicitly states that large parts of our population are still to experience a decisive improvement in their standard of living. It also emphasizes that the need to ensure access of education services to the vulnerable sections of the society. The vulnerability traditionally is linked to social criteria and hence with the Scheduled Castes/Tribes. As these sections of our society were traditionally and historically deprived of their basic rights, education was far away from their reach due to unequal opportunities and discrimination.[2]

Literacy rates among social groups in Tamil Nadu and India

The rate of literacy indicates the level of socio-economic development. A country or region with a high literacy rate is expected to have better human development index (HDI). HDI is a measure of wellbeing (life expectancy, literacy, education and standard of living) of people in a country. The data as given in Table 5.2 provide information relating to literates of Scheduled Castes (SCs), Scheduled Tribes (STs) non-SCs/STs and total population in India and Tamil Nadu. Literacy rate for Tamil Nadu was 62.54 per cent and for all India was 52.20 per cent in 1991. The literacy rate of Tamil Nadu has substantially increased to 71.85 per cent and for

Table 5.2: Literacy rates by social groups: 1991, 2001 and 2011

India/	*SCs*			*STs*			*Non-SC/ST*			*Total*		
Tamil Nadu	1991	2001	2011	1991	2001	2011	1991	2001	2011	1991	2001	2011
All India	37.41	54.69	56.49	29.6	47.1	49.51	47.69	64.84	66.09	52.2	64.8	63.07
Gap between SCs/STs to Non-SCs/STs	10.28	10.15	9.60	18.09	17.1	16.58	-	-	-	-	-	-
Tamil Nadu	46.74	63.19	65.18	27.89	41.53	47.23	58.27	76.2	73.89	62.54	73.5	71.85
Gap between SCs/STs to Non-SCs/STs	11.27	10.26	8.70	30.38	31.92	26.65	-	-	-	-	-	-

Source: Census of India –1991, 2001 and 2011, Primary Census Abstract.

Table 5.3: Literacy rates by sex and by social groups in Tamil Nadu and India – 1991, 2001 and 2011

Social Groups	*SCs*			*STs*			*Non-SC/ST*			*Total*		
Year	1991	2001	2011	1991	2001	2011	1991	2001	2011	1991	2001	2011
All India	37.41	54.69	56.49	29.60	47.10	49.51	47.69	64.84	66.09	52.20	64.80	63.07
Males	49.91	66.64	64.21	40.65	59.17	57.36	57.59	75.26	72.38	64.13	75.30	69.76
Females	23.76	41.90	48.33	18.19	34.76	41.59	36.98	53.67	59.39	39.28	53.70	55.97
Tamil Nadu	46.74	63.19	65.18	27.89	41.53	47.23	58.27	73.45	73.89	62.54	73.50	71.85
Males	58.36	73.41	71.81	35.25	50.15	53.46	67.62	82.42	79.39	73.75	82.40	77.59
Females	34.89	53.01	58.58	20.23	32.78	40.88	48.57	64.43	68.35	51.33	64.40	66.09

Source: Census of India, 1991, 2001 and 2011, Primary Census Abstract

all India to 63.07 per cent in 2011. The literacy rate among SCs in Tamil Nadu has gone up from 46.74 per cent in 1991 to 65.18 per cent in 2011; whereas the literacy rate at all India for SCs has increased from 37.41 per cent in 1991 to 56.49 per cent in 2011 which indicates the literacy rate for SCs was high in Tamil Nadu as compared to that of All-India level.

Literacy rate by Gender

Women are mostly excluded in decision-making and accessing livelihood opportunities in India. Gender parity is linked to economic development. Education is an important instrument to achieve gender equality in which women and men enjoy equal opportunities and rights in all spheres of life. Discrimination based on gender is peculiar to the Indian situation and needs attention. Male children are preferred and abundant family support is given to them. Female children are neglected. Male child preference is attributed to the social and cultural milieus adopted in India.

The data as given in Table 5.3 show that there is a wide disparity between the education of males and females. The data further show that there is a wide "disparity" of educational development between the advanced classes and the Backward Classes, viz., the Scheduled Castes and Scheduled Tribes as compared to non-SCs/STs. It is essential to make special efforts to equalise educational opportunities between these groups, viz., males and females and between the SCs/STs and non-SCs/STs.

Expenditure on Education

In India, education is provided by the government and also by private sector. Expenditure on education in the private sector is, by and large, met by the parents themselves. The volume of expenditure on education by government is huge as compared to that of the private sector. Kothari Commission (1966) recommended that six per cent of GDP for expenditure on education to achieve quality education. There is no official estimate of educational expenditure in the private sector and educational institutions under the control of private management has been increasing in number day-by-day, as privatisation is going on unabatedly in India. The data as given in Table 5.4 depict expenditure on education in Tamil Nadu during the period 2001-02 to 2005-06. The Gross State Domestic Product (GSDP) of Tamil Nadu has increased from Rs 1,49,074 crores in 2001-02 to Rs 2,23,528 crores in 2005-06. The expenditure on education has also gone up from Rs 5019.27 crores in 2001-02 to Rs 5826.80 crore in 2005-06. But the expenditure on Education as a percentage of GSDP has declined from 3.37 per cent in 2001-02 to 2.61 per cent in 2005-06.

The decline in the public expenditure in education would result in poor quality of education and also access to education by the poor and underprivileged section would be severely hampered.

Table 5.4: Public expenditure on education in Tamil Nadu: (Rs in crores)

Year	*Gross State Domestic Product (GSDP)*	*Expenditure on Education*	*Expenditure on Education as percentage of GSDP*
2001-02	149074	5019. 27	3.37
2002-03	158370	4713. 64	2.98
2003-04	175897	4953. 73	2.82
2004-05	200781	5506. 89	2.74
2005-06	223528	5826. 80	2.61

Source: State Profile, Selected Educational Statistics, MHRD, 2005-06.

Educational institutions

Data on number of schools under the categories of Primary, Upper Primary, Secondary and Higher Secondary

Schools in Tamil Nadu from 2001 to 2005 is given in Table 5.5. There was 31,488 Primary Schools, 5,809 Upper Primary Schools, 4,903 Secondary Schools and 3,608 Higher Secondary Schools in Tamil Nadu in 2001. The data clearly show that there is a substantial increase in all schools in 2005, when compared to 2001.

Table 5.5: Number of school education institutions in Tamil Nadu: (Figures in numbers)

Years	*Primary*	*Upper*	*Secondary*	*Hr. Secondary*
2001	31488	5809	4903	3608
2002	33394	6544	4356	4065
2003	32242	6825	4859	4136
2004	33470	7111	5004	4230
2005	34208	8017	5046	4536

Source: State Profile, Selected Educational Statistics, MHRD, 2005-06.

Distribution of educational institutions by colleges, polytechnics and engineering colleges as given in Table 5.6 clearly shows that there was an increase in the educational institutions under the control of private management, i.e. self-financing institutions and there is no change in the educational institutions controlled by the government and government-aided institutions.

The number of educational institutions under the control of state board in high and higher secondary schools as given in Table 5.7 shows that 148 HS/HSS are under the control of Adi-Dravidar Welfare Department, 30 HS/HSS are under the control of Tribal Welfare Department and 51schools under the control of Department of Backward Classes, Most Backward Classes and Minorities (Kallar Reclamation schools). In all Tribal schools, hostels are attached.

Table 5.6: Number of educational institutions (Technical) in Tamil Nadu

	Colleges				*Polytechnics*					*Engineering colleges*				
Year	*Govt*	*Govt Aided*	*Self-financing*	*Total*	*Govt*	*Govt Aided*	*Affiliated Institute*	*Self–financing*	*Total*	*Govt*	*Govt Aided*	*Anna Univ*	*Self–financing*	*Total*
2006-07	67	162	441	670	22	34	5	153	214	6	3	4	235	248
2007-08	74	162	567	803	22	34	3	166	225	6	3	4	238	251
2008-09	76	162	622	860	22	34	3	205	264	6	3	-	263	272
2009-10	77	162	902	1141	22	34	3	258	317	6	3	11	336	356
2010-11	78	162	1014	1254	22	34	3	307	366	6	3	16	431	456
2011-12	93	162	1063	1318	30	34	3	365	432	6	3	18	464	491

Source: Policy Note on Higher Education, Government of Tamil Nadu, years from 2006-07 to 2011-12.

Table 5.7: Number of state board high and higher secondary schools in Tamil Nadu by managements as on 30.09.2011 (Rural and Urban)

HS/HSS	*HS*			*HSS*			*Grand Total*
Rural /Urban	*Rural*	*Urban*	*Total*	*Rural*	*Urban*	*Total*	
Government	2808	108	2916	1935	292	2227	5143
Corporation		61	61		68	68	129
Municipality	3	72	75	6	49	55	130
Railway	1	4	5		3	3	8
Aranilayam	4		4	3	5	8	12
Army	4		0	1	1	2	2
Adi-Dravidar	71	5	76	59	13	72	148
Tribal	14	3	17	13		13	30
Kallar	26	1	27	22	2	24	51
Fully aided	187	108	295	299	471	770	1065
Aided - SW	6	5	11	4	5	9	20
Partly Aided	216	120	336	201	144	345	681
Un-aided	193	38	231	155	48	203	434
Forest	1		1	2		2	3
SW-Govt.	3	5	8	3	9	12	20
SW - Pvt.	9	7	16	5	3	8	24
Rubber Board	1		1			0	1
Grand total	**3543**	**537**	**4080**	**2708**	**1113**	**3821**	**7901**

Source: Educational Statistics of Tamil Nadu, Hand Book 2011-12, Directorate of School Education, Chennai.

Enrolment

Enrolment is a process of initiating attendance to a school and is considered as a means to promote over all literacy rates. School enrolment helps to eradicate child labour and promotes literacy rate. The data presented in Table 5.8 expound the percentage of enrolment in primary, middle, high and higher secondary schools by social groups for two points of time, viz., 2005-06 and 2009-10. There was an increase in enrolment for SCs and STs from 2005-06 to 2009-10 in all types of schools, such as primary, middle, high and higher secondary. The increase in enrolment by the deprived sections, viz., SCs and STs may be attributed to the various welfare measures implemented by the government for increasing their education status.

Table 5.8: Percentage of enrolment by social groups in school education 2005-06 and 2009-10

Level of Education	*Years*	*Percentage of Enrolment*		
		SC	*ST*	*Non-SC/ST*
Primary	2005-06	21.79	1.65	76.57
	2009-10	24.65	1.73	73.62
Middle	2005-06	23.54	1.05	75.41
	2009-10	25.11	1.11	73.78
High	2005-06	23.41	0.76	75.83
	2009-10	26.53	1.47	72.00
Hr. Secondary	2005-06	20.93	0.58	78.48
	2009-10	23.95	0.80	75.25
All	**2005-06**	**22.44**	**1.26**	**76.30**
	2009-10	**24.99**	**1.43**	**73.58**

Source: Computed from the Selected Educational Statistics: 2005-06 and 2009-10, MHRD, Government of India.

Enrolment in Higher Education

As regards the enrolment in higher education, the data presented in Table 5.9 clearly explicate that there was an increase in enrolment for the SCs and STs and the percentage of enrolment has declined among the non-SCs/STs in all types of higher education. It is significant to note that the rate of enrolment declines when the education level goes up among the Scheduled Castes i.e. they move in opposite direction showing the negative relationship. As regards the enrollment at Ph.D. level, the per cent of enrolment has increased among the STs and non-SCs/STs and the enrollment rate has declined among the SCs.

Table 5.9: Percentage of enrolment by social groups in higher education

Level of education	*Years*	*Percentage of Enrolment*		
		SC	*ST*	*Non-SC/ST*
Under Graduate (UG)	2005-06	14.95	0.28	84.76
	2009-10	19.70	0.75	79.55
Post Graduate (PG)	2005-06	12.94	0.44	86.62
	2009-10	15.05	0.89	84.06
Ph.D	2005-06	12.20	0.86	86.94
	2009-10	10.72	1.52	87.76
All	**2005-06**	**14.66**	**0.31**	**85.03**
	2009-10	**18.73**	**0.79**	**80.47**

Source: Computed from the Selected Educational Statistics: 2005-06 and 2009-10, MHRD, Government of India.

Schools, Enrolment and Teachers

Data as presented in Table 5.10 reveal the number of schools, enrolment and the number of teachers by districts in Tamil Nadu for 2005-06. The average number of schools per district was 1140 primary schools, 267 middle schools and 319 High/Higher secondary schools in 2005-06. On the other hand, The Nilgiris district has recorded the lowest percentage in terms of number of schools with 1.24 per cent and 1.12 per cent respectively for primary and middle schools, and 1.12 per cent and 1.03 per cent in terms of teachers in primary and middle schools. But in the case of High/Higher secondary schools, the number of schools was lowest in Karur district with 1.52 per cent and number of high schools with 1.28 per cent. The data further show that the proportion of schools and teachers was high in Coimbatore, Thiruvallur, Vellore and Villuppuram districts, as compared to other districts in Tamil Nadu.

Table 5.10: Number of schools, enrolment and teachers by districts in 2005-06 (in numbers)

Sl.No	*District Name*	*No. of schools*			*Enrolment*			*Teachers*		
		Primary school	*Middle school*	*HSC*	*Primary school*	*Middle school*	*HSC*	*Primary school*	*Middle school*	*HSC*
1	Chennai	708 (2.07)	187 (2.33)	743 (7.75)	248193 (3.89)	138718 (3.82)	246366 (8.19)	3642 (3.15)	1698 (2.73)	25056 (11.05)
2	Coimbatore	1567 (4.58)	420 (5.24)	625 (6.52)	392357 (6.15)	323382 (8.90)	212322 (7.06)	5752 (4.98)	3522 (5.67)	15084 (6.65)
3	Cuddalore	1241 (3.63	307 (3.83)	318 (3.32)	251794 (3.95)	225767 (6.21)	117396 (3.90)	4049 (3.50)	2197 (3.53)	7040 (3.10)
4	Dharmapuri	954) (2.79)	245 (3.06)	202 (2.11)	169086 (2.65)	65062 (1.79)	56394 (1.87)	2886 (2.50)	1451 (2.33)	3842 (1.69)
5	Dindigul	1276 (3.73)	233 (2.91)	263 (2.74)	221186 (3.47)	113548 (3.12)	78087 (2.60)	4107 (3.55)	2142 (3.45)	5563 (2.45)
6	Erode	1562 (4.57)	270 (3.37)	365 (3.81)	203276 (3.19)	82880 (2.28)	105124 (3.49)	4529 (3.92)	2016 (3.24)	7704 (3.40)
7	Kancheepuram	1260 (3.68)	327 (4.08)	520 (5.43)	233121 (3.65)	166275 (4.58)	139059 (4.62)	4692 (4.06)	2717 (4.37)	9113 (4.02)
8	Karur	688 (2.01)	121 (1.51)	146 (1.52)	102138 (1.60)	38152 (1.05)	38032 (1.26)	1948 (1.69)	861 (1.39)	2913 (1.28)
9	Krishnagiri	1242 (3.63)	269 (3.36)	223 (2.33)	184255 (2.89)	104825 (2.88)	125049 (4.16)	3822 (3.31)	1369 (2.20)	4692 (2.07)

contd...

Sl.No	District Name	No. of schools			Enrolment			Teachers		
		Primary school	Middle school	HSC	Primary school	Middle school	HSC	Primary school	Middle school	HSC
10	Madurai	1254 (3.67)	319 (3.98)	391 (4.08)	149322 (2.34)	63333 (1.74)	100782 (3.35)	5048 (4.37)	3544 (5.70)	13708 (6.05)
11	Nagapattinam	920 (2.69)	257 (3.21)	194 (2.02)	188349 (2.95)	117469 (3.23)	65876 (2.19)	3146 (2.72)	2137 (3.44)	4105 (1.81)
12	Nagercoil	526 (1.54)	154 (1.92)	383 (4.00)	143084 (2.24)	69508 (1.91)	84784 (2.82)	2683 (2.32)	991 (1.59)	7473 (3.30)
13	Namakkal	823 (2.41)	171 (2.13)	257 (2.68)	68164 (1.07)	33106 (0.91)	36784 (1.22)	2581 (2.23)	1248 (2.01)	8374 (3.69)
14	Nilgiris	424 (1.24)	90 (1.12)	181 (1.89)	140978 (2.21)	75017 (2.06)	51601 (1.72)	1299 (1.12)	641 (1.03)	3770 (1.66)
15	Peramballur	734 (2.15)	183 (2.28)	197 (2.06)	163707 (2.57)	102840 (2.83)	57934 (1.93)	2490 2.15)	1299 (2.09)	3569 (1.57)
16	Pudukottai	1236 (3.61)	314 (3.92)	235 (2.45)	162512 (2.55)	74378 (2.05)	52167 (1.73)	3483 (3.01)	1843 (2.97)	3851 (1.70)
17	Ramnad	1045 (3.05)	216 (2.69)	179 (1.87)	363800 (5.70)	99725 (2.74)	147729 (4.91)	3430 (2.97)	1493 (2.40)	3655 (1.61)
18	Salem	1427 (4.17)	279 (3.48)	402 (4.20)	136315 (2.14)	72618 (2.00)	59929 (1.99)	6147 (5.32)	1338 (2.15)	9978 (4.40)

contd...

Sl.No	District Name	No. of schools			Enrolment			Teachers		
		Primary school	Middle school	HSC	Primary school	Middle school	HSC	Primary school	Middle school	HSC
19	Sivaganga	1015 (2.97)	222 (2.77)	203 (2.12)	224523 (3.52)	129992 (3.58)	106218 (3.53)	2842 (2.46)	1602 (2.58)	3972 (1.75)
20	Thanjavur	1292 (3.78)	298 (3.72)	314 (3.28)	123317 (1.93)	91791 (2.53)	49903 (1.66)	4273 (3.70)	2355 (3.79)	6649 (2.93)
21	Theni	493 (1.44)	155 (1.93)	171 (1.78)	131379 (2.06)	87742 (2.41)	50521 (1.68)	2132 (1.84)	1730 (2.78)	3855 (1.70)
22	Thiruvarur	820 (2.40)	190 (2.37)	160 (1.67)	329125 (5.16)	216820 (5.97)	94067 (3.13)	3963 (3.43)	3011 (4.84)	8562 (3.78)
23	Tirunelveli	1752 (5.12)	416 (5.19)	404 (4.22)	219870 (3.45)	177531 (4.89)	151273 (5.03)	5967 (5.16)	3555 (5.72)	13016 (5.74)
24	Tiruvallur	1138 (3.33)	295 (3.68)	484 (5.05)	243059 (3.81)	134199 (3.69)	111158 (3.70)	3744 (3.24)	2040 (3.28)	3085 (1.36)
25	Tiruvannamalai	1505 (4.40)	360 (4.49)	318 (3.32)	225319 (3.53)	161059 (4.43)	147897 (4.92)	2594 (2.24)	1586 (2.55)	8795 (3.88)
26	Trichy	1268 (3.71)	322 (4.02)	339 (3.54)	169269 (2.65)	115251 (3.17)	65130 (2.17)	4522 (3.91)	2719 (4.37)	8420 (3.71)
27	Tuticorin	1179 (3.45)	291 (3.63)	251 (2.62)	402958 (6.32)	177556 (4.89)	192019 (6.38)	3655 (3.16)	2312 (3.72)	5072 (2.24)

contd...

Sl.No	District Name	No. of schools			Enrolment			Teachers		
		Primary school	Middle school	HSC	Primary school	Middle school	HSC	Primary school	Middle school	HSC
28	Vellore	1986 (5.81)	441 (5.50)	488 (5.09)	351922 (5.52)	204964 (5.64)	124457 (4.14)	6918 (5.99)	3231 (5.20)	8367 (3.69)
29	Villupuram	1725 (5.04)	467 (5.83)	398 (4.15)	228062 (3.58)	103749 (2.86)	71072 (2.36)	5311 (4.60)	3694 (5.94)	12240 (5.40)
30	Virudhunagar	1148 (3.36)	198 (2.47)	228 (2.38)	207879 (3.26)	66359 (1.83)	69142 (2.30)	3913 (3.39)	1814 (2.92)	5219 (2.30)
Tamil Nadu		**34208 (100)**	**8017 (100)**	**9582 (100)**	**6378319 (100)**	**3633616 (100)**	**3008272 (100)**	**115568 (100)**	**62156 (100)**	**226742 (100)**

Note: HSC - Hr. Secondary Schools.
Figures in parenthesis show percentages to their respective column totals.
Source: State Profile, Selected Educational Statistics, MHRD, 2005-06.

Gross Enrolment Ratio (GER)

GER is a statistical measure used in the education sector to determine the number of students enrolled in school at different grade levels (like elementary, middle school and high school). It is used to analyse the ratio of the number of students who live in the country to those who qualify for the particular grade level. The data presented in Table 5.11 exhibit that the GER is high among under-graduates as compared to post-graduate and doctoral candidates. GER declines when educational level goes up, showing the negative relationship between the GER and the level of education and the GER has been increasing over the years from 2005-06 to 2009-10.

Enrolment in Technical Education

Enrolment in technical education by types of technical institutions as given in Tables 5.12 and 5.13 clearly shows that the rate of enrolment was low in engineering among SCs as compared to the enrolment in polytechnics. The enrolment in engineering colleges was high among the non-SC/ST as compared to that of polytechnics. The data also shows that students admitted into self financing institution was high among the non-SC/ST as compared to the SCs.

GER in Technical Education

Polytechnic colleges and engineering colleges offer job oriented technical courses. They differ in terms of both in contents and the number years for completion. It is easy for the poor and the underprivileged section of the people to complete the polytechnic courses as compared to engineering subjects. The data presented in Table 5.14 show that the GER is high in polytechnic students as compared to the engineering students among all social groups. The data further show that the GER is high among the students of self-financing colleges as compared to government colleges among all social groups. The GER was high among non-SC/ST with 4.976 as compared to SCs with 4.962 in both Engineering and Polytechnics education in 2010-11.

Table 5.11: Gross enrolment ratio (GER) by social groups in general higher education: 2005-06 to 2009-10

Year	Under graduate				Post graduate				Ph.D/D.SC/D.Phill				Total			
	SCSC	ST	Non-SC/ST	All	SC	ST	Non-SC/ST	All	SC	ST	Non-SC/ST	All	SC	ST	Non-SC/ST	All
2005-06	4.177	1.494	5.463	5.185	0.565	0.361	0.873	0.811	0.028	0.038	0.047	0.043	4.771	1.893	6.383	6.039
2006-07	8.484	3.319	11.327	10.716	1.148	0.803	1.810	1.675	0.058	0.083	0.097	0.089	9.689	4.206	13.233	12.481
2007-08	13.922	10.991	15.723	15.336	2.167	2.957	3.251	3.042	0.276	0.761	0.565	0.512	16.365	14.709	19.539	18.890
2008-09	14.355	12.602	15.853	15.537	2.182	2.850	3.083	2.909	0.303	0.889	0.594	0.541	16.840	16.342	19.529	18.987
2009-10	17.000	13.255	16.330	16.429	2.473	3.000	3.287	3.129	0.309	0.900	0.601	0.548	19.781	17.155	20.218	20.107

Source: Computed from the Selected Educational Statistics: 2005-06 and 2009-10, MHRD, Government of India.

Table 5.12: Number of enrolment by social groups in technical education: 2006-07 to 2010-11

Year	*Institution*	*Engineering*				*Polytechnics*				*Both*			
		SC	*ST*	*Non-SC*	*All*	*SC*	*ST*	*Non-SC*	*All*	*SC*	*ST*	*Non-SC*	*All*
2006-07	Govt	319	17	1538	1874	1085	85	3856	5026	1404	102	5394	6900
	Govt. Aid	255	14	1519	1788	1695	55	9378	11128	1950	69	10897	12916
	Affiliated	N.A	N.A	N.A	N.A	29	N.A	107	136	29	N.A	107	136
	Self financing	6368	121	63656	70145	5624	115	44185	49924	11992	236	107841	120069
	Total	**6942**	**152**	**66713**	**73807**	**8433**	**255**	**57526**	**66214**	**15375**	**407**	**124239**	**140021**
2007-08	Govt	339	17	1577	1933	1159	84	3788	5031	1498	101	5365	6964
	Govt. Aid	320	18	1871	2209	1953	80	10285	12318	2273	98	12156	14527
	Affiliated	N.A	N.A	N.A	N.A	36	1	90	127	36	1	90	127
	Self financing	8373	169	81443	89985	7266	117	56672	64055	15639	286	138115	154040
	Total	**9032**	**204**	**84891**	**94127**	**10414**	**282**	**70835**	**81531**	**19446**	**486**	**155726**	**175658**
2008-09	Govt	335	18	1513	1866	1164	65	4518	5747	1499	83	6031	7613
	Govt. Aid	339	19	2071	2429	1754	59	10801	12614	2093	78	12872	15043
	Affiliated	787	50	3529	4366	43	N.A	96	139	830	50	3625	4505
	Self financing	11014	182	103074	114270	10287	209	71981	82477	21301	391	175055	196747
	Total	**12475**	**269**	**110187**	**122931**	**13248**	**333**	**87396**	**100977**	**25723**	**602**	**197583**	**223908**

contd...

Year	Institution	Engineering				Polytechnics				Both			
		SC	*ST*	*Non-SC*	*All*	*SC*	*ST*	*Non-SC*	*All*	*SC*	*ST*	*Non-SC*	*All*
2009-10	Govt	426	23	2043	2492	1264	75	4453	5792	1690	98	6496	8284
	Govt. Aid	317	17	2060	2394	2060	78	9887	12025	2377	95	11947	14419
	Affiliated	963	56	4537	5556	47	N.A	99	146	1010	56	4636	5702
	Self financing	10962	188	98482	109632	11355	241	73986	85582	22317	429	172468	195214
	Total	**12668**	**284**	**107122**	**120074**	**14726**	**394**	**88425**	**103545**	**27394**	**678**	**195547**	**223619**
2010-11*	Govt	418	24	1983	2425	1867	97	5416	7380	2285	121	7399	9805
	Govt. Aid	328	15	2162	2505	2259	54	9800	12113	2587	69	11962	14618
	Affiliated	1347	75	5886	7308	39	N.A	126	165	1386	75	6012	7473
	Self financing	15595	289	134108	149992	13615	338	80125	94078	29210	627	214233	244070
	Total	**17688**	**403**	**144139**	**162230**	**17780**	**489**	**95467**	**113736**	**35468**	**892**	**239606**	**275966**

Source: Policy Note on Higher Education, Government of Tamil Nadu, various years from 2006-07 to 2011-12.

NA – Not Available, * Provisional

Table 5.13: Percentage of enrolment by social groups in technical education: 2006-07 to 2010-11

Year	*Institution*	*Engineering*				*Polytechnics*				*Both*			
		SC	*ST*	*Non-SC/ST*	*All*	*SC*	*ST*	*Non-SC/ST*	*All*	*SC*	*ST*	*Non-SC/ST*	*All*
2006-07	Govt	17.00	0.91	82.10	100.00	21.60	1.69	76.70	100.00	20.30	1.48	78.20	100.00
		4.60	11.20	2.31	2.54	12.90	33.30	6.70	7.59	9.13	25.10	4.34	4.93
	Govt. Aid	14.30	0.78	85.00	100.00	15.20	0.49	84.30	100.00	15.10	0.53	84.40	100.00
		3.67	9.21	2.28	2.42	20.10	21.60	16.30	16.80	12.70	17.00	8.77	9.22
	Affiliated	N.A	N.A	N.A	N.A	21.30	0.00	78.70	100.00	21.30	0.00	78.70	100.00
		0.00	0.00	0.00	0.00	0.34	0.00	0.19	0.21	0.19	0.00	0.09	0.10
	Self-financing	9.08	0.17	90.70	100.00	11.30	0.23	88.50	100.00	9.99	0.20	89.80	100.00
		91.70	79.60	95.40	95.00	66.70	45.10	76.80	75.40	78.00	58.00	86.80	85.80
	Total	**9.41**	**0.21**	**90.40**	**100.00**	**12.70**	**0.39**	**86.90**	**100.00**	**11.00**	**0.29**	**88.70**	**100.00**
		100.00	**100.00**	**100.00**	**100.00**	**100.00**	**100.00**	**100.00**	**100.00**	**100.00**	**100.00**	**100.00**	**100.00**

contd...

Year	Institution	Engineering				Polytechnics				Both			
		SC	ST	Non-SC/ST	All	SC	ST	Non-SC/ST	All	SC	ST	Non-SC/ST	All
2007-08	Govt	17.50	0.88	81.60	100.00	23.00	1.67	75.30	100.00	21.50	1.45	77.00	100.00
		3.75	8.33	1.86	2.05	11.10	29.80	5.35	6.17	7.70	20.80	3.45	3.96
	Govt. Aid	14.50	0.81	84.70	100.00	15.90	0.65	83.50	100.00	15.60	0.67	83.70	100.00
		3.54	8.82	2.20	2.35	18.80	28.40	14.50	15.10	11.70	20.20	7.81	8.27
	Affiliated	N.A	N.A	N.A	N.A	28.30	0.79	70.90	100.00	28.30	0.79	70.90	100.00
		0.00	0.00	0.00	0.00	0.35	0.35	0.13	0.16	0.19	0.21	0.06	0.07
	Self financing	9.30	0.19	90.50	100.00	11.30	0.18	88.50	100.00	10.20	0.19	89.70	100.00
		92.70	82.80	95.90	95.60	69.80	41.50	80.00	78.60	80.40	58.80	88.70	87.70
	Total	**9.60**	**0.22**	**90.20**	**100.00**	**12.80**	**0.35**	**86.90**	**100.00**	**11.10**	**0.28**	**88.70**	**100.00**
		100.00	**100.00**	**100.00**	**100.00**	**100.00**	**100.00**	**100.00**	**100.00**	**100.00**	**100.00**	**100.00**	**100.00**

contd...

Year	*Institution*	*Engineering*				*Polytechnics*				*Both*			
		SC	*ST*	*Non-SC/ST*	*All*	*SC*	*ST*	*Non-SC/ST*	*All*	*SC*	*ST*	*Non-SC/ST*	*All*
2007-08		17.50	0.88	81.60	100.00	23.00	1.67	75.30	100.00	21.50	1.45	77.00	100.00
	Govt	3.75	8.33	1.86	2.05	11.10	29.80	5.35	6.17	7.70	20.80	3.45	3.96
		14.50	0.81	84.70	100.00	15.90	0.65	83.50	100.00	15.60	0.67	83.70	100.00
	Govt. Aid	3.54	8.82	2.20	2.35	18.80	28.40	14.50	15.10	11.70	20.20	7.81	8.27
		N.A	N.A	N.A	N.A	28.30	0.79	70.90	100.00	28.30	0.79	70.90	100.00
	Affiliated	0.00	0.00	0.00	0.00	0.35	0.35	0.13	0.16	0.19	0.21	0.06	0.07
		9.30	0.19	90.50	100.00	11.30	0.18	88.50	100.00	10.20	0.19	89.70	100.00
	Self financing	92.70	82.80	95.90	95.60	69.80	41.50	80.00	78.60	80.40	58.80	88.70	87.70
		9.60	**0.22**	**90.20**	**100.00**	**12.80**	**0.35**	**86.90**	**100.00**	**11.10**	**0.28**	**88.70**	**100.00**
	Total	**100.00**	**100.00**	**100.00**	**100.00**	**100.00**	**100.00**	**100.00**	**100.00**	**100.00**	**100.00**	**100.00**	**100.00**

contd...

Year	*Institution*	*Engineering*				*Polytechnics*				*Both*			
		SC	*ST*	*Non-SC/ST*	*All*	*SC*	*ST*	*Non-SC/ST*	*All*	*SC*	*ST*	*Non-SC/ST*	*All*
2008-09	Govt	13.00	0.96	81.10	100.00	20.30	1.13	78.60	100.00	19.70	1.09	79.20	100.00
		2.69	6.69	1.37	1.52	8.79	19.50	5.17	5.69	5.83	13.80	3.05	3.40
	Govt. Aid	14.00	0.78	85.30	100.00	13.90	0.47	85.60	100.00	13.90	0.52	85.60	100.00
		2.72	7.06	1.88	1.98	13.20	17.70	12.40	12.50	8.14	13.00	6.51	6.72
	Affiliated	18.00	1.15	80.80	100.00	30.90	0.00	69.10	100.00	18.40	1.11	80.50	100.00
		6.31	18.60	3.20	3.55	0.32	0.00	0.11	0.14	3.23	8.31	1.83	2.01
	Self financing	9.64	0.16	90.20	100.00	12.50	0.25	87.30	100.00	10.80	0.20	89.00	100.00
		88.30	67.70	93.50	93.00	77.60	62.80	82.40	81.70	82.80	65.00	88.60	87.90
	Total	**10.10**	**0.22**	**89.60**	**100.00**	**13.10**	**0.33**	**86.60**	**100.00**	**11.50**	**0.27**	**88.20**	**100.00**
		100.00	**100.00**	**100.00**	**100.00**	**100.00**	**100.00**	**100.00**	**100.00**	**100.00**	**100.00**	**100.00**	**100.00**

contd...

Year	Institution	Engineering				Polytechnics				Both			
		SC	*ST*	*Non-SC/ST*	*All*	*SC*	*ST*	*Non-SC/ST*	*All*	*SC*	*ST*	*Non-SC/ST*	*All*
2009-10	Govt	17.10	0.92	82.00	100.00	21.80	1.29	76.90	100.00	20.40	1.18	78.40	100.00
		3.36	8.10	1.91	2.08	8.58	19.00	5.04	5.59	6.17	14.50	3.32	3.70
	Govt. Aid	13.20	0.71	86.00	100.00	17.10	0.65	82.20	100.00	16.50	0.66	82.90	100.00
		2.50	5.99	1.92	1.99	14.00	19.80	11.20	11.60	8.68	14.00	6.11	6.45
	Affiliated	17.30	1.01	81.70	100.00	32.20	0.00	67.80	100.00	17.70	0.98	81.30	100.00
		7.60	19.70	4.24	4.63	0.32	0.00	0.11	0.14	3.69	8.26	2.37	2.55
	Self financing	10.00	0.17	89.80	100.00	13.30	0.28	86.50	100.00	11.40	0.22	88.30	100.00
		86.50	66.20	91.90	91.30	77.10	61.20	83.70	82.70	81.50	63.30	88.20	87.30
	Total	**10.60**	**0.24**	**89.20**	**100.00**	**14.20**	**0.38**	**85.40**	**100.00**	**12.30**	**0.30**	**87.40**	**100.00**
		100.00	**100.00**	**100.00**	**100.00**	**100.00**	**100.00**	**100.00**	**100.00**	**100.00**	**100.00**	**100.00**	**100.00**

contd...

Year	Institution	Engineering				Polytechnics				Both			
		SC	ST	Non-SC/ST	All	SC	ST	Non-SC/ST	All	SC	ST	Non-SC/ST	All
2010-11*		17.20	0.99	81.80	100.00	25.30	1.31	73.40	100.00	25.30	1.31	73.40	100.00
	Govt	2.36	5.96	1.38	1.49	10.50	19.80	5.67	6.49	6.44	13.60	3.09	3.55
		13.10	0.60	86.30	100.00	18.60	0.45	80.90	100.00	18.60	0.45	80.90	100.00
	Govt. Aid	1.85	3.72	1.50	1.54	12.70	11.00	10.30	10.70	7.29	7.74	4.99	5.30
		18.40	1.03	80.50	100.00	23.60	0.00	76.40	100.00	23.60	0.00	76.40	100.00
	Affiliated	7.62	18.60	4.08	4.50	0.22	0.00	0.13	0.15	3.91	8.41	2.51	2.71
		10.40	0.19	89.40	100.00	14.50	0.36	85.20	100.00	14.50	0.36	85.20	100.00
	Self financing	88.20	71.70	93.00	92.50	76.60	69.10	83.90	82.70	82.40	70.30	89.40	88.40
		10.90	**0.25**	**88.80**	**100.00**	**15.60**	**0.43**	**83.90**	**100.00**	**15.60**	**0.43**	**83.90**	**100.00**
	Total	**100.00**	**100.00**	**100.00**	**100.00**	**100.00**	**100.00**	**100.00**	**100.00**	**100.00**	**100.00**	**100.00**	**100.00**

Source: Calculated from Table 4.14.

NA – Not Available, * Provisional

Table 5.14: Gross enrolment ratio (GER) by social groups in technical education: 2006-07 to 2010-11

Year	Institution	Engineering				Polytechnics				Both			
		SC	*ST*	*Non-SC/T*	*All*	*SC*	*ST*	*Non-SC/T*	*All*	*SC*	*ST*	*Non-SC/T*	*All*
2006-07	Govt	0.043	0.047	0.049	0.048	0.147	0.236	0.123	0.128	0.190	0.283	0.172	0.176
	Govt. aid	0.034	0.039	0.048	0.046	0.229	0.153	0.298	0.284	0.264	0.164	0.347	0.330
	Affiliated	NA	NA	NA	NA	0.004	0.000	0.003	0.003	0.004	0.000	0.003	0.003
	Self financing	0.861	0.336	2.026	1.790	0.760	0.319	1.406	1.274	1.621	0.562	3.432	3.065
	Total	**0.938**	**0.422**	**2.123**	**1.884**	**1.140**	**0.708**	**1.831**	**1.690**	**2.078**	**0.969**	**3.954**	**3.574**
2007-08	Govt	0.048	0.050	0.054	0.053	0.166	0.247	0.129	0.137	0.214	0.297	0.183	0.190
	Govt. aid	0.046	0.053	0.064	0.060	0.279	0.235	0.350	0.335	0.325	0.262	0.414	0.396
	Affiliated	NA	NA	NA	NA	0.005	0.003	0.003	0.003	0.005	0.003	0.003	0.003
	Self financing	1.198	0.496	2.772	2.451	1.039	0.344	1.929	1.745	2.237	0.764	4.700	4.196
	Total	**1.292**	**0.599**	**2.889**	**2.564**	**1.490**	**0.828**	**2.411**	**2.221**	**2.781**	**1.298**	**5.300**	**4.784**
2008-09	Govt	0.048	0.052	0.051	0.050	0.165	0.189	0.153	0.155	0.213	0.242	0.204	0.206
	Govt. aid	0.048	0.055	0.070	0.066	0.249	0.172	0.365	0.341	0.297	0.208	0.435	0.407
	Affiliated	0.112	0.146	0.119	0.118	0.006	0.000	0.003	0.004	0.118	0.133	0.122	0.122
	Self financing	1.564	0.530	3.482	3.089	1.460	0.609	2.431	2.230	3.024	1.043	5.913	5.319
	Total	**1.771**	**0.784**	**3.722**	**3.323**	**1.881**	**0.971**	**2.952**	**2.730**	**3.652**	**1.606**	**6.674**	**6.053**

contd...

Year	*Institution*	*Engineering*				*Polytechnics*				*Both*			
		SC	*ST*	*Non-SC/T*	*All*	*SC*	*ST*	*Non-SC/T*	*All*	*SC*	*ST*	*Non-SC/T*	*All*
2009-10	Govt	0.060	0.067	0.069	0.067	0.178	0.217	0.149	0.155	0.238	0.284	0.218	0.222
	Govt. aid	0.045	0.049	0.069	0.064	0.290	0.226	0.332	0.323	0.335	0.252	0.401	0.387
	Affiliated	0.136	0.162	0.152	0.149	0.007	0.000	0.003	0.004	0.142	0.148	0.155	0.153
	Self financing	1.545	0.544	3.302	2.942	1.600	0.697	2.481	2.297	3.145	1.137	5.784	5.239
	Total	**1.785**	**0.822**	**3.592**	**3.222**	**2.075**	**1.140**	**2.965**	**2.779**	**3.861**	**1.796**	**6.557**	**6.001**
2010-11*	Govt	0.058	0.069	0.066	0.065	0.261	0.279	0.180	0.197	0.320	0.348	0.246	0.261
	Govt. aid	0.046	0.043	0.072	0.067	0.316	0.155	0.326	0.323	0.362	0.182	0.398	0.389
	Affiliated	0.188	0.215	0.196	0.195	0.005	0.000	0.004	0.004	0.194	0.198	0.200	0.199
	Self financing	2.182	0.830	4.464	3.996	1.905	0.971	2.667	2.506	4.087	1.654	7.131	6.502
	Total	**2.475**	**1.157**	**4.798**	**4.322**	**2.487**	**1.404**	**3.178**	**3.030**	**4.962**	**2.353**	**7.976**	**7.352**

Source: Computed from Policy Note on Higher Education, Government of Tamil Nadu, various years from 2006-07 to 2011-12.

Note: NA – Not Available, * Provisional

Number of Schools by Managements

The distribution of number of schools by management as given in Table 5.15 clearly illustrates that the number of government schools (Government, Municipal and Panchayat Union) was the highest as compared to private management schools (private, nursery, Anglo Indian, and Matriculation). The data also show that enrolment of SCs/STs was high in the government schools as compared to that of private management.

Table 5.15: Number of schools and enrolment in management schools in Tamil Nadu: 2005-06

Type of schools	*Management-wise*	*Number of institutions*	*Enrolment in lakhs*
Primary schools	Government	1529	1.73
	Municipal/corporation	896	1.34
	Panchayat union	21906	19.75
	Private	5255	10.97
	Nursery & primary schools	4622	5.03
	Total	**34208**	**38.82**
Middle schools	Government	390	0.92
	Municipal/corporation	453	1.46
	Panchayat union	5458	13.13
	Private	1716	7.97
	Total	**8017**	**23.48**
	Total (primary+ middle)	**42225**	**62.30**
High schools	Government	2016	8.33
	Municipal/corporation	110	0.50
	Aided	613	3.12
	Unaided	179	0.43
	Anglo Indian (high school)	12	0.10
	Matriculation (high school)	2053	6.17
	Central board (high school)	63	0.51
	Total for all high schools	**5046**	**19.16**

contd...

Type of schools	*Management-wise*	*Number of institutions*	*Enrolment in lakhs*
Hr. Sec. Schools	Government	1696	18.89
	Municipal/corporation	93	1.33
	Aided	1062	14.77
	Unaided	139	0.75
	Total(state board)	2990	35.74
	Anglo Indian (Hr. Sec.)	29	0.42
	Matriculation (Hr. Sec.)	1421	11.26
	Central board (Hr. Sec.)	96	1.32
	Total for all Hr. Sec. schools	**4536**	**48.74**
Total Schools	Government	5631	29.87
	Municipal/corporation	1552	4.63
	Panchayat union	27364	32.88
	Private	8964	38.01
	Nursery & primary schools	4622	5.03
	Anglo Indian	41	0.52
	Matriculation	3474	17.43
	Central board	159	1.83
	Grand Total	**51807**	**130.20**

Source: Department of school education, government of Tamil Nadu.

Drop-outs

Students who withdraw from education before completing the class or course are known as the drop-outs due to number of reasons. The data as presented in Tables 5.16 and 5.17 show the drop-out rates by districts in Tamil Nadu for primary schools and upper primary schools by social groups. These data clearly indicate that the rate of dropouts has come down for all population and also for Scheduled Castes and Scheduled Tribes from 2001 to 2005 for primary and upper primary schools. The data further show that the drop-out was high among SCs as compared to all social groups for primary and upper primary schools.

Table 5.16: Drop-out rates by districts – Primary Schools

Sl. No	*Districts*	*All*					*SCs*					*STs*				
		2001	*2002*	*2003*	*2004*	*2005*	*2001*	*2002*	*2003*	*2004*	*2005*	*2001*	*2002*	*2003*	*2004*	*2005*
1.	Chennai	11	34	18	8.86	6.75	38	32	19	9.42	5.17	51	12	10	11.00	5.85
2.	Coimbatore	20	12	11	6.29	6.00	24	13	11	7.00	5.58	36	22	13	11.56	6.71
3.	Cuddalore	7	7	4	2.64	1.88	8	10	8	2.63	2.09	8	14	10	5.90	5.25
4.	Dharmapuri	15	13	12	9.09	2.49	15	15	11	8.12	3.40	28	26	24	19.64	6.54
5.	Dindigul	19	14	11	1.53	4.73	26	14	8	1.65	5.24	25	12	10	5.53	10.94
6.	Erode	19	18	14	7.00	4.38	25	20	19	8.89	4.64	23	17	16	10.07	14.02
7.	Kancheepuram	13	13	7	6.54	3.61	15	10	7	5.36	2.90	31	23	15	12.73	5.13
8.	Kanyakumari	14	2	2	1.61	1.92	15	1	1	1.20	3.32	14	2	2	2.33	11.61
9.	Karur	21	14	8	6.76	6.22	28	13	9	4.67	5.98	0	25	20	0.00	13.33
10.	Krishnagiri	NA	13	10	8.59	6.03	NA	11	10	7.59	5.94	NA	19	24	22.43	26.02
11.	Madurai	13	10	9	7.00	2.69	15	9	9	8.00	2.82	10	7	9	7.02	4.23
12.	Nagapattinam	10	8	8	5.96	2.62	11	13	11	8.83	2.23	11	0	10	8.82	16.92
13.	Namakkal	17	14	9	6.10	7.25	24	16	15	6.45	6.01	17	16	16	1.76	6.76
14.	Perambalur	13	9	4	3.26	2.54	16	9	5	4.11	2.29	12	10	7	7.20	6.05
15.	Pudukkottai	11	9	5	4.00	2.76	12	9	5	3.99	2.45	0	0	0	0.00	0.00
16.	Ramanathapuram	9	6	3	3.00	1.86	10	8	3	3.00	2.15	0	0	13	12.50	0.00
17.	Salem	25	19	16	13.8	5.10	26	18	13	13.77	5.85	13	13	13	18.83	14.88

contd...

Sl. No	Districts	ALL					SCs					STs				
		2001	2002	2003	2004	2005	2001	2002	2003	2004	2005	2001	2002	2003	2004	2005
18.	Sivagangai	16	19	7	2.53	2.60	16	12	11	3.50	3.34	0	0	0	0.00	0.00
19.	Thanjavur	17	14	6	4.02	1.98	19	20	6	5.50	1.37	0	23	13	15.79	5.97
20.	The Nilgiris	20	8	5	1.38	3.81	22	34	28	2.14	2.91	36	55	44	7.34	14.14
21.	Theni	27	11	10	9.91	3.52	28	12	10	10.45	5.61	0	45	39	18.75	18.75
22.	Thiruchirappalli	15	7	7	5.23	3.94	25	17	17	6.34	4.30	27	38	37	7.71	6.04
23.	Thiruunelveli	22	13	12	3.00	1.34	15	12	10	3.52	1.32	0	20	18	8.15	6.21
24.	Thiruvallur	10	8	7	6.56	7.43	28	19	15	10.70	5.94	27	26	24	16.37	22.23
25.	Thiruvannamalai	15	9	7	5.29	5.02	9	9	5	4.93	4.02	28	30	25	18.99	24.06
26.	Thirurvarur	25	14	5	3.00	2.74	16	6	10	4.00	2.52	34	9	9	1.33	20.45
27.	Thoothukudi	9	8	4	3.56	3.33	14	12	5	3.31	2.45	0	1	1	4.00	2.50
28.	Vellore	15	15	9	6.23	3.64	14	13	9	4.41	3.11	26	25	23	8.06	10.44
29.	Villupuram	14	10	6	4.87	3.30	16	10	6	4.62	3.37	18	10	7	7.57	7.03
30.	Viruthunagar	24	17	9	8.49	2.80	25	20	16	10.06	3.71	23	19	25	2.50	30.88
	Tamil Nadu	**16**	**12**	**8**	**5.79**	**3.81**	**19**	**14**	**10**	**6.23**	**3.73**	**22**	**19**	**16**	**11.42**	**11.14**

Source: 1. DISE 2001 and DISE 2002 SSA, State consolidated annual work plan and budget 2003 – 2004. p..42

2. Cohort Study, SSA, Tamil Nadu State Annual Work Plan and Budget. 2006-2007 p.80.

Note: NA – Not available

Table 5.17: Drop-out rate by districts – Upper Primary Schools

Sl. No	Districts	All					SCs					STs				
		2001	2002	2003	2004	2005	2001	2002	2003	2004	2005	2001	2002	2003	2004	2005
1.	Chennai	19	15	11	8.65	6.02	32	32	14	10.4	8.21	46	26	10	5.56	5.83
2.	Coimbatore	18	11	11	10.2	10.41	17	13	13	13.2	11.87	29	16	11	9.25	18.71
3.	Cuddalore	11	10	8	8.45	7.64	7	10	9	9.58	9.29	0	16	15	16.19	12.34
4.	Dharmapuri	12	15	16	6.8	13.17	5	12	17	5.9	11.58	3	41	16	9.88	12.75
5.	Dindigul	22	18	13	1.66	7.19	29	14	12	1.78	9.15	46	22	15	6.94	8.42
6.	Erode	22	18	14	10	8.25	14	12	12	10.6	11.49	27	20	19	8.58	29.27
7.	Kancheepuram	16	16	8	8.48	7.04	16	12	9	7.89	7.43	30	31	17	11.09	12.98
8.	Kanyakumari	14	1	1	1.31	2.29	19	16	15	5.01	2.11	0	15	13	4.88	8.82
9.	Karur	23	16	12	11.7	12.79	28	14	13	14.9	15.13	0	0	0	0	5.56
10.	Krishnagiri	NA	15	15	13.4	10.98	NA	27	15	15.4	13.95	NA	18	20	16.06	48.18
11.	Madurai	16	11	10	8.52	6.28	15	9	10	8.5	8.26	7	5	5	5.19	3.14
12.	Nagapattinam	5	4	3	3.1	6.51	4	13	7	7.1	7.21	4	0	3	7.46	6.41
13.	Namakkal	22	11	10	6.49	10.87	19	16	16	11.6	13.75	16	17	14	2.24	14.55
14.	Perambalur	12	11	11	9.65	9.94	10	9	9	8.54	11.88	10	10	10	27.7	14.29

contd...

Sl. No	Districts	All					SCs					STs				
		2001	2002	2003	2004	2005	2001	2002	2003	2004	2005	2001	2002	2003	2004	2005
15.	Pudukkottai	10	12	12	8	5.39	10	9	7	7.01	5.59	0	0	0	0	9.09
16.	Ramanathapuram	16	13	10	11	7.48	18	8	13	11	6.04	1	9	0	0	6.67
17.	Salem	22	20	14	12.6	5.82	22	18	17	14.6	6.79	14	15	15	13.68	12.29
18.	Sivagangai	17	17	6	4	6.72	13	12	10	4.53	6.57	0	0	0	0	0.00
19.	Thanjavur	21	19	11	4.02	6.21	22	20	11	6.04	7.87	0	23	4	18.8	14.77
20.	The Nilgiris	26	8	6	3.49	4.14	26	34	29	3.52	4.15	10	39	33	9.65	13.97
21.	Theni	22	9	11	13.7	2.21	32	12	12	11.6	2.32	0	6	16	0	0.00
22.	Thiruchirappalli	15	9	9	8.99	7.69	27	17	17	9.86	9.04	29	41	41	17	7.97
23.	Thiruunelveli	20	19	8	7	4.35	18	12	10	7.5	4.70	0	25	23	8.35	8.96
24.	Thiruvallur	11	9	8	7.53	8.02	22	19	18	10	8.21	11	22	20	12.24	16.52
25.	Thiruvannamalai	14	12	13	12.1	10.87	8	9	8	13.2	11.96	17	18	17	14.21	17.85
26.	Thirurvarur	20	17	10	8.11	8.17	17	6	12	9	9.04	13	7	10	10.83	9.68
27.	Thoothukudi	10	13	12	10.1	7.70	12	12	11	9.9	9.16	0	7	7	5.77	7.25
28.	Vellore	11	13	12	11.5	10.05	13	13	13	11.3	10.88	13	13	15	12.02	20.47
29.	Villupuram	11	14	12	11.5	8.91	10	10	12	12.5	11.15	14	17	15	14.29	14.31
30.	Viruthunagar	20	9	9	9.62	4.33	19	20	13	12	5.85	23	20	12	6.58	17.65
	Tamil Nadu	**16**	**13**	**10**	**8.64**	**7.58**	**18**	**15**	**13**	**9.75**	**8.69**	**20**	**17**	**14**	**11.24**	**13.53**

Source 1: DISE 2001 and DISE 2002, SSA, State consolidated annual work plan and budget 2003 – 2004, p. 43.
2: Cohort Study, SSA, Tamil Nadu State Annual Work Plan and Budget. 2006-2007, p. 86.
Note: NA – Not available

Completion Rate

Completion rate is a measure showing the percentage of students completing the schooling minus repeaters in that grade". Completion rate (CR) of all social groups at primary level was at 77.57 per cent at the state level. The CR was above the state average in 15 districts. The CR was the highest in Chennai with 87.33 per cent and the lowest in Nagapattinam with 67.68 per cent. The State-level completion rate for SCs was at 74.35 per cent and for STs was 67.50 per cent. The completion rate for girls was high as compared to boys for all social groups, SCs and STs (Tables 5.18, 5.19 and 5.20).

Completion rates of all social groups at upper primary level was 82.02 per cent at the state level. The CR was the highest in Kanyakumari with 91.57 per cent and the lowest in Karur District with 73.45. The State-level CR for SC was at 78.31 per cent. The CR for SCs was the highest in The Nilgiris with 89.62 per cent and the lowest in Karur with 66.03 per cent. The State-level CR for ST was at 76.90 per cent and the CR of ST was the lowest in Erode District with 60.98 per cent. The CR was high among girls as compared to boys for all social groups, SCs and STs.

Repetition Rate

Repetition rate is simply the division of number of repeaters in a grade to the enrolment in the previous year, but in the same grade. Repetition Rate (RR) of all social groups at primary level was at 18.62 per cent. The lowest RR was reported in Chennai district with 5.91 per cent and the highest was reported in Nagappattinam district with 29.71 per cent. The RR for SC was at 21.92 per cent and for STs with 21.37 per cent (Table 5. 21). The repetition rate was high among boys as compared to girls for all social groups, SCs and STs.

Table 5.18: Completion rate by districts – Primary Schools (2004-05)

Sl.No	Districts	All			SC			ST		
		Boys	Girls	Total	Boys	Girls	Total	Boys	Girls	Total
1	Chennai	88.22	86.51	87.33	86.70	87.26	86.99	85.66	84.35	85.04
2	Coimbatore	82.53	85.20	83.83	76.73	80.12	78.40	76.74	76.96	76.85
3	Cuddalore	79.81	81.87	80.86	77.48	79.13	78.31	67.53	81.46	74.43
4	Dharmapuri	69.91	74.94	72.26	68.94	73.38	71.04	63.38	63.35	63.37
5	Dindigul	69.74	73.93	71.76	63.14	69.83	66.39	70.59	53.33	62.50
6	Erode	79.83	83.92	81.82	74.70	78.83	76.71	68.26	65.32	66.74
7	Kancheepuram	77.54	81.93	79.74	76.23	80.30	78.25	65.09	68.44	66.74
8	Kanyakumari	83.67	87.34	85.48	76.67	82.85	79.75	69.23	90.38	78.63
9	Karur	70.52	73.64	72.06	65.60	67.12	66.36	100.00	66.67	80.00
10	Krishnagiri	70.40	72.98	71.66	70.89	72.23	71.58	38.94	43.37	40.82
11	Madurai	81.12	83.97	82.55	76.06	79.25	77.63	79.49	90.63	84.51
12	Nagapattinam	65.25	70.17	67.68	58.83	64.55	61.62	32.26	58.82	46.15
13	Namakkal	71.25	74.80	72.98	68.32	72.10	70.16	76.07	73.27	74.68
14	Perambalur	82.17	82.59	82.37	79.45	80.79	80.10	76.32	73.13	74.6.0
15	Pudukottai	86.30	87.58	86.93	86.57	87.36	86.95	100.00	100.00	100.00
16	Ramanathapuram	73.98	77.08	75.49	71.79	72.67	72.23	80.00	66.67	72.73
17	Salem	75.97	79.45	77.58	73.91	76.10	74.96	67.68	73.86	70.43

contd...

Sl.No	Districts	All			SC			ST		
		Boys	Girls	Total	Boys	Girls	Total	Boys	Girls	Total
18	Sivagangai	70.31	73.95	72.11	69.32	69.64	69.47	0	0	0
19	Thanjavur	74.94	77.10	76.00	69.23	68.68	68.96	70.00	62.16	65.67
20	Nilgiris	84.53	85.10	84.81	81.44	81.86	81.64	64.29	78.29	70.37
21	Theni	71.86	72.07	71.96	64.96	68.99	66.89	0	33.33	18.75
22	Thiruchirappalli	71.02	75.69	73.30	68.72	72.29	70.50	70.33	75.16	72.40
23	Thirunelveli	75.66	79.66	77.64	73.55	77.02	75.25	72.13	72.62	72.41
24	Thiruvallur	74.00	77.93	75.99	74.15	78.30	76.20	56.72	64.35	60.45
25	Thiruvannamalai	79.77	82.10	80.90	78.24	80.40	79.27	60.50	62.22	61.26
26	Thiruvarur	66.85	71.30	69.08	60.81	64.25	62.61	60.00	54.17	56.82
27	Thoothukudi	76.96	81.31	79.09	73.68	80.45	77.00	72.73	70.21	71.25
28	Vellore	72.31	75.91	74.08	71.82	75.24	73.53	57.36	58.65	57.95
29	Villupuram	82.63	83.96	83.29	80.51	82.18	81.34	75.56	79.73	77.43
30	Virudhunagar	75.09	78.22	76.60	68.54	72.34	70.38	48.48	60.00	54.41
	Total	**76.14**	**79.07**	**77.57**	**72.90**	**75.86**	**74.35**	**66.39**	**69.99**	**67.50**

Source: Village education registrar, Cohort study, SSA 2004 and 2005.

Table 5.19: Completion rate by districts - Upper Primary Schools (2004-2005)

Sl No	*Districts*	*All*			*SC*			*ST*		
		Boys	*Girls*	*Total*	*Boys*	*Girls*	*Total*	*Boys*	*Girls*	*Total*
1	Chennai	88.65	89.32	89.01	86.48	85.23	85.8	86.85	87.74	87.26
2	Coimbatore	77.81	82.79	80.33	70.48	78.55	74.47	71.24	72.58	71.93
3	Cuddalore	83.41	84.38	83.88	80.45	80.69	80.57	78.47	77.91	78.16
4	Dharmapuri	71.51	77.15	74.00	72.65	73.37	72.98	68.21	73.14	70.11
5	Dindigul	79.46	83.66	81.45	73.66	77.47	75.52	79.17	89.36	84.21
6	Erode	72.99	81.16	76.77	64.63	73.64	68.97	56.47	65.82	60.98
7	Kancheepuram	77.82	83.52	80.68	74.3	80.48	77.39	68.86	75.70	72.14
8	Kanyakumari	88.68	94.54	91.57	84.84	93.19	89.03	75.93	75.00	75.49
9	Karur	69.20	78.11	73.45	61.51	71.19	66.03	100.00	87.50	94.44
10	Krishnagiri	73.84	78.81	76.17	71.23	75.18	73.13	31.51	78.38	47.27
11	Madurai	82.74	88.08	85.37	77.40	81.33	79.36	92.31	91.84	92.05
12	Nagapattinam	74.03	79.54	76.77	69.21	73.3	71.25	72.41	71.43	71.79
13	Namakkal	81.85	86.89	84.17	77.20	81.23	79.06	75.43	85.11	79.63
14	Perambalur	78.27	82.06	80.16	74.82	77.34	76.09	79.82	62.77	71.92

contd...

Sl No	*Districts*	*ALL*			*SC*			*ST*		
		Boys	*Girls*	*Total*	*Boys*	*Girls*	*Total*	*Boys*	*Girls*	*Total*
15	Pudukottai	86.59	88.45	87.52	85.48	86.98	86.24	88.89	100.00	90.91
16	Ramanathapuram	76.16	80.32	78.24	77.80	81.73	79.72	81.82	100.00	86.67
17	Salem	85.27	86.59	85.88	80.80	82.42	81.57	73.20	79.94	76.18
18	Sivagangai	83.21	86.21	84.71	83.65	85.85	84.75	0	0	0
19	Thanjavur	81.19	85.99	83.57	77.43	81.37	79.37	70.00	79.31	76.14
20	Nilgiris	89.24	91.96	90.58	87.95	91.25	89.62	75.74	83.01	79.41
21	Theni	83.67	86.66	84.92	79.85	83.20	81.33	0	0	0
22	Thiruchirappalli	77.95	84.39	81.10	73.14	79.97	76.58	86.70	90.86	88.69
23	Thirunelveli	81.83	87.46	84.58	78.55	84.51	81.53	75.36	80.00	77.61
24	Thiruvallur	80.40	83.55	81.96	78.34	81.49	79.88	71.03	72.28	71.63
25	Thiruvannamalai	79.64	79.62	79.63	77.08	76.30	76.71	74.87	75.14	74.97
26	Thiruvarur	72.56	81.99	77.17	67.68	76.81	72.06	45.71	85.19	62.9
27	Thoothukudi	82.69	89.02	85.8	79.62	86.16	82.80	86.49	90.63	88.41
28	Vellore	73.78	77.54	75.65	71.27	74.92	73.11	63.06	62.31	62.73
29	Villupuram	83.20	84.32	83.74	79.97	79.86	79.92	81.08	78.27	79.75
30	Virudhunagar	79.57	83.85	81.69	71.23	78.15	74.46	65.00	100.00	79.41
	Total	**79.91**	**84.26**	**82.02**	**76.29**	**80.44**	**78.31**	**74.13**	**81.12**	**76.99**

Source: Village education registrar, Cohort study, SSA 2004 and 2005.

Table 5.20: Completion rate: Primary and Upper Primary Schools (2002-2010)

Year	*Completion Rate*					
	PRIMARY			*UPPER PRIMARY*		
	All	*SC*	*ST*	*All*	*SC*	*ST*
2002	64	61	58	68	62	59
2003	69	66	61	74	68	67
2004	75	73	72	79	74	76
2005	78	74	68	82	78	77
2006	86.55	84.40	83.40	88.57	85.85	84.48
2007	92.46	89.88	87.10	91.29	88.89	87.73
2008	93.94	91.18	88.16	92.7	90.15	89.07
2009	97.03	96.59	91.95	93.04	90.24	89.40
2010	97.36	96.84	92.08	93.35	90.67	89.74

Source: District information system for education, Cohort study, SSA, 2002-10.

Repetition Rate (RR) for all social groups at upper primary level was at 10.41 per cent. The RR was the lowest in Namakkal district with 4.96 per cent and the RR was the highest in Nagapattinam district with 16.71 per cent. The RR of SCs was at 13.00 per cent. The RR of SC was the highest in Nagapattinam district with 21.53 per cent and the lowest in Chennai district with 5.90 per cent and for STs, it was at 9.57 per cent at the state level. There was no repeater recorded in Karur, Pudukkottai and Sivagangai (Table 5.22). The RR was high among boys as compared to that of girls for all social groups including SCs and STs.

Transition Rate

Transition Rate (TR) for V standard to VI standard indicates number of children who passed the V standard from Primary School and the number of children who joined VI standard in the Upper Primary Sections. The data presented in Table 4.24 furnishes district-wise and gender-wise transition rate of V to VI standard in the year 2005-2006. Transition Rate (TR) for V to VI standard stood at 98.25 for all social groups at the state level. TR for boys and girls remained almost the same with 98 per cent among all social groups, 97 per cent among the SCs and 91 per cent among the STs (Table 5.24).

Attendance rate – primary and upper primary schools

The attendance rate (AR) at primary level was 96 per cent for all social groups at the state level. The AR was the highest in Nagapattinam District with 99 per cent. The AR for SC children was at 93 per cent at the state level. Ramanathapuram district has recorded the highest AR with 98 per cent and The Nilgiris district has registered the lowest AR with 85 per cent. The AR for the ST children was at 90 per cent at the state level. The highest AR was registered in two districts viz. Karur and Ramanathapuram with 97 per cent and The Nilgiris district has registered the lowest with 71 per cent (Table 5.25).

Table 5.21: Repetition rate by districts - Primary Schools (2004-2005)

Sl. No.	*Districts*	*ALL*			*SC*			*ST*		
		Boys	*Girls*	*Total*	*Boys*	*Girls*	*Total*	*Boys*	*Girls*	*Total*
1	Chennai	5.46	6.33	5.91	8.30	7.42	7.84	8.51	9.78	9.11
2	Coimbatore	11.38	8.90	10.17	17.97	14.00	16.02	20.00	12.90	16.44
3	Cuddalore	18.09	16.47	17.26	20.23	18.98	19.60	25.32	15.23	20.33
4	Dharmapuri	27.87	22.25	25.25	28.01	22.82	25.55	31.08	28.91	30.09
5	Dindigul	25.33	21.57	23.51	31.16	25.43	28.37	20.59	33.33	26.56
6	Erode	15.51	11.99	13.80	20.15	17.07	18.65	17.83	20.56	19.25
7	Kancheepuram	18.57	14.73	16.64	20.54	17.14	18.85	23.20	20.04	21.65
8	Kanyakumari	14.23	10.92	12.6	19.41	14.43	16.93	26.15	3.85	16.24
9	Karur	23.02	20 38	21.72	28.81	26.51	27.67	0	11.11	6.67
10	Krishnagiri	23.56	20.99	22.31	22.68	22.26	22.47	39.82	24.10	33.16
11	Madurai	16.15	13.37	14.75	21.06	18.00	19.56	15.38	6.25	11.27
12	Nagapattinam	32.02	27.32	29.71	38.76	33.4	36.15	41.94	32.35	36.92
13	Namakkal	21.73	17.72	19.78	26.17	21.36	23.83	18.04	19.09	18.56
14	Perambalur	15.87	14.24	15.08	18.75	16.40	17.61	20.18	18.66	19.35
15	Pudukottai	11.02	9.58	10.31	11.18	9.97	10.59	0	0	0

contd...

Sl. No.	*Districts*	*ALL*			*SC*			*ST*		
		Boys	*Girls*	*Total*	*Boys*	*Girls*	*Total*	*Boys*	*Girls*	*Total*
16	Ramanathapuram	24.00	21.22	22.65	25.77	25.48	25.62	20.00	33.33	27.27
17	Salem	19.03	15.33	17.32	21.00	17.24	19.19	15.37	13.83	14.68
18	Sivagangai	27.19	23.35	25.29	27.75	26.60	27.19	0	0	0
19	Thanjavur	23.18	20.81	22.02	29.64	29.70	29.67	30.00	27.03	28.36
20	Nilgiris	11.85	10.89	11.39	15.87	15.00	15.44	17.26	13.18	15.49
21	Theni	24.45	24.6	24.52	29.38	25.45	27.50	85.71	44.44	62.50
22	Thiruchirappalli	25.04	20.37	22.76	27.29	23.11	25.20	23.92	18.47	21.58
23	Thirunelveli	23.03	18.97	21.02	25.26	21.53	23.43	19.67	22.62	21.38
24	Thiruvallur	18.05	15.10	16.59	19.50	16.17	17.86	17.80	16.82	17.32
25	Thiruvannamalai	14.98	13.14	14.08	17.50	15.85	16.71	14.15	15.33	14.67
26	Thiruvarur	30.31	26.06	28.18	36.60	33.11	34.87	20.00	25.00	22.73
27	Thoothukudi	19.41	15.69	17.58	23.42	17.56	20.55	27.27	25.53	26.25
28	Vellore	23.82	20.68	22.28	24.95	21.77	23.36	31.63	31.58	31.60
29	Villupuram	14.02	12.79	13.41	16.13	14.44	15.29	16.43	14.43	15.53
30	Virudhunagar	22.05	19.04	20.60	27.86	23.84	25.91	18.18	11.43	14.71
	Total	**20.01**	**17.16**	**18.62**	**23.37**	**20.40**	**21.92**	**22.95**	**19.63**	**21.37**

Source: District information system for education, Cohort study, SSA, 2002-10.

Table 5.22: Repetition rate by districts - Upper Primary Schools (2004-2005)

Sl.No.	Districts	All			SC			ST		
		Boys	*Girls*	*Total*	*Boys*	*Girls*	*Total*	*Boys*	*Girls*	*Total*
1	Chennai	4.84	5.09	4.97	5.95	6.03	5.99	5.98	7.55	6.70
2	Coimbatore	11.22	7.34	9.26	16.00	11.27	13.66	12.88	6.05	9.36
3	Cuddalore	9.36	7.57	8.48	10.72	9.49	10.14	9.72	9.30	9.49
4	Dharmapuri	14.35	10.92	12.84	17.09	13.44	15.45	17.5	16.57	17.14
5	Dindigul	13.58	8.89	11.36	17.43	13.13	15.32	8.33	6.38	7.37
6	Erode	13.22	11.21	14.98	23.42	15.38	19.54	14.12	5.06	9.76
7	Kancheepuram	14.22	10.36	12.28	17.50	12.86	15.18	15.02	14.74	14.89
8	Kanyakumari	8.28	3.95	6.15	13.29	4.45	8.86	18.52	12.50	15.69
9	Karur	16.51	10.75	13.76	22.30	14.89	18.84	0	0	0
10	Krishnagiri	14.01	11.55	12.86	12.96	12.87	12.92	4.11	5.41	4.55
11	Madurai	10.18	6.58	8.41	13.55	11.19	12.38	5.13	4.08	4.55
12	Nagapattinam	18.50	14.9	16.71	22.41	20.66	21.53	17.24	24.49	21.79

contd...

Sl.No.	*Districts*	*All*			*SC*			*ST*		
		Boys	*Girls*	*Total*	*Boys*	*Girls*	*Total*	*Boys*	*Girls*	*Total*
13	Namakkal	5.91	3.85	4.96	7.91	6.36	7.19	8.19	2.73	5.82
14	Perambalur	11.78	8.02	9.90	13.53	10.54	12.03	11.01	17.02	13.79
15	Pudukottai	8.04	6.14	7.08	9.16	7.21	8.18	0	0	0
16	Ramanathapuram	15.91	12.65	14.28	16.26	12.13	14.24	9.09	0	6.67
17	Salem	9.08	7.41	8.31	12.14	11.08	11.64	12.77	9.96	11.53
18	Sivagangai	10.02	7.13	8.57	10.35	7.03	8.68	0	0	0
19	Thanjavur	12.06	8.35	10.22	14.60	10.87	12.76	13.33	6.90	9.09
20	Nilgiris	6.23	4.31	5.28	7.07	5.40	6.23	8.42	4.85	6.62
21	Theni	14.30	10.88	12.87	18.00	14.26	16.35	0	0	0
22	Thiruchirappalli	13.19	9.15	11.21	16.43	12.36	14.38	3.94	2.69	3.34
23	Thirunelveli	13.56	8.53	11.07	16.08	11.47	13.78	13.04	13.85	13.43
24	Thiruvallur	11.63	8.38	10.02	13.43	10.33	11.92	11.03	12.73	11.85

contd...

Sl. No.	Districts	All			SC			ST		
		Boys	*Girls*	*Total*	*Boys*	*Girls*	*Total*	*Boys*	*Girls*	*Total*
25	Thiruvannamalai	10.15	8.80	9.51	11.88	10.71	11.33	7.18	7.18	7.18
26	Thiruvarur	17.71	11.45	14.66	21.82	15.73	18.90	40.00	11.11	27.42
27	Thoothukudi	8.50	4.43	6.51	10.64	5.30	8.04	8.11	0	4.35
28	Vellore	15.55	13.05	14.31	16.86	15.16	16.00	18.35	14.84	16.80
29	Villupuram	8.11	6.53	7.35	9.14	8.69	8.93	5.68	6.25	5.95
30	Virudhunagar	16.20	11.72	13.98	23.57	15.24	19.69	5.00	0	2.94
	Total	**12.04**	**8.66**	**10.41**	**14.72**	**11.18**	**13.00**	**10.85**	**7.94**	**9.57**

Source: District information system for education, Cohort study, SSA, 2002-10.

Table 5.23: Repetition rate for primary and upper primary schools (2002-2010)

Year	*Repetition Rate*					
	PRIMARY			*UPPER PRIMARY*		
	All	*SC*	*ST*	*All*	*SC*	*ST*
2002	24	25	23	19	23	19
2003	23	24	23	16	19	19
2004	19	21	16	12	16	13
2005	19	22	21	10	13	10
2006	11.54	13.64	13.10	7.35	9.37	10.49
2007	6.14	8.90	11.06	6.67	8.78	9.86
2008	4.84	7.69	10.43	5.41	7.64	8.66
2009	1.95	2.47	6.69	5.08	7.57	8.49
2010	1.65	2.25	6.59	4.85	7.34	8.28

Source: District information system for education, Cohort study, SSA, 2002-10..

Table 5.24: Transition rate by districts (2004-2005)

Sl. No.	Districts	All			SC			ST		
		Boys	Girls	Total	Boys	Girls	Total	Boys	Girls	Total
1	Chennai	97.00	97.20	97.00	95.00	95.00	95.00	93.20	92.00	92.30
2	Coimbatore	97.97	97.24	97.11	97.10	96.75	96.93	94.06	92.88	95.47
3	Cuddalore	99.01	98.65	98.63	87.34	89.14	88.21	83.97	83.71	83.83
4	Dharmapuri	99.32	99.96	99.6	98.87	98.49	98.69	96.76	97.21	96.97
5	Dindigul	98.71	98.47	98.59	98.81	98.60	98.71	98.00	97.00	96.80
6	Erode	98.61	98.28	98.45	93.3	92.98	93.14	87.66	87.04	87.15
7	Kancheepuram	99.07	99.79	98.59	98.52	98.24	98.71	95.81	94.78	95.31
8	Kanyakumari	99.68	99.79	99.73	99.55	99.81	99.67	99.20	99.50	99.40
9	Karur	99.19	99.19	99.19	99.12	99.14	98.25	98.40	98.00	96.80
10	Krishnagiri	98.84	97.63	98.34	99.31	97.27	98.79	95.29	96.87	96.08
11	Madurai	98.50	98.67	98.58	98.12	97.66	97.89	95.45	94.12	94.74
12	Nagapattinam	97.75	97.58	97.87	97.61	97.18	97.38	90.00	90.00	90.25
13	Namakkal	98.15	97.60	98.84	98.29	97.77	98.23	99.56	96.99	98.27

contd...

Sl. No.	Districts	All			SC			ST		
		Boys	Girls	Total	Boys	Girls	Total	Boys	Girls	Total
14	Perambalur	98.93	98.15	98.29	98.54	97.45	98.00	90.58	89.76	90.19
15	Pudukkottai	99.18	99.10	99.14	97.67	97.77	99.12	98.00	98.15	98.30
16	Ramanathapuram	98.35	98.71	98.53	97.41	98.04	97.72	97.67	98.40	98.33
17	Salem	97.52	96.98	97.27	96.87	96.46	96.67	93.65	93.44	93.55
18	Sivagangai	99.15	98.10	98.63	97.51	99.42	99.17	0	0	0
19	Thanjavur	96.90	98.30	97.06	98.24	98.21	98.23	98.69	96.20	96.44
20	Nilgiris	98.78	99.04	98.91	98.41	99.00	98.69	97.67	98.20	97.92
21	Theni	99.10	99.00	99.00	99.00	92.00	90.00	96.00	94.30	95.00
22	Thiruchirappalli	99.54	99.58	97.16	99.52	99.43	99.47	99.19	99.12	99.35
23	Thirunelveli	98.85	99.00	98.92	97.51	99.10	98.30	98.59	92.96	95.77
24	Thiruvallur	95.40	96.00	95.50	94.00	94.00	94.00	90.63	88.76	89.71
25	Thiruvannamalai	98.24	98.05	98.15	97.38	97.95	97.66	93.37	94.52	93.91
26	Thiruvarur	98.45	98.68	98.57	98.86	98.59	98.72	91.67	90.40	96.00

contd...

Sl. No.	*Districts*	*All*			*SC*			*ST*		
		Boys	*Girls*	*Total*	*Boys*	*Girls*	*Total*	*Boys*	*Girls*	*Total*
27	Thoothukudi	99.10	98.20	98.66	98.47	97.24	97.87	98.59	97.06	97.84
28	Vellore	98.69	98.53	98.61	99.00	98.95	99.00	94.56	93.61	94.13
29	Villupuram	97.65	97.80	97.72	97.77	98.01	97.89	93.31	92.67	93.01
30	Virudhunagar	97.23	97.18	96.75	96.49	95.84	96.17	96.00	95.08	94.87
	Tamil Nadu	**98.43**	**98.36**	**98.25**	**97.45**	**97.18**	**97.21**	**91.85**	**91.09**	**91.59**

Source: District information system for education, Cohort study, SSA, 2002-10.

Table 5.25: Attendance rate by districts (2005-2006)

Sl. No	*Districts*	*Primary*			*Upper Primary*		
		All	*SC*	*ST*	*All*	*SC*	*ST*
1	Chennai	97	95	90	95	94	89
2	Coimbatore	96	91	91	95	92	99
3	Cuddalore	94	93	85	88	85	81
4	Dharmapuri	96	96	93	92	91	88
5	Dindigul	95	92	94	94	94	92
6	Erode	96	96	90	93	92	91
7	Kancheepuram	95	90	90	93	89	95
8	Kanyakumari	97	93	91	95	91	90
9	Karur	98	96	97	97	95	95
10	Krishnagiri	95	89	85	96	83	89
11	Madurai	96	88	91	95	91	91
12	Nagapattinam	99	87	85	85	81	77
13	Namakkal	98	96	95	96	94	93
14	Perambalur	97	92	84	92	89	84
15	Pudukkottai	96	94	92	95	93	91
16	Ramanathapuram	98	98	97	94	96	97
17	Salem	98	97	96	93	97	96

contd...

Sl. No	*Districts*	*Primary*			*Upper Primary*		
		All	*SC*	*ST*	*All*	*SC*	*ST*
18	Sivagangai	97	95	0	97	92	0
19	Thanjavur	96	93	93	95	92	93
20	Nilgiris	95	85	71	94	84	79
21	Theni	95	92	92	95	92	91
22	Thiruchirappalli	93	94	91	89	90	90
23	Thirunelveli	96	95	90	96	93	93
24	Thiruvallur	94	91	87	92	89	86
25	Thiruvannamalai	95	92	90	94	91	93
26	Thiruvarur	95	91	89	93	91	87
27	Thoothukudi	96	95	93	96	93	94
28	Vellore	94	92	90	90	89	84
29	Villupuram	93	92	89	98	91	82
30	Virudhunagar	95	93	90	97	93	92
	Tamil Nadu	**96**	**93**	**90**	**94**	**91**	**90**

Source: District information system for education, Cohort study, SSA, 2002-10.

The attendance rate (AR) at upper primary level was at 94 per cent for all social groups at the state level. The AR was the highest in Villuppuram district with 98 per cent. The AR for SCs children was at 91 per cent at the state level. Salem district has recorded the highest AR with 97 per cent and Krishnagiri district has registered the lowest AR with 83 per cent. The AR for the STs children was at 90 per cent at the state level. The highest AR was registered in Coimbatore district with 97 per cent and Cuddalore district has registered the lowest with 71 per cent at the state level (Table 5.25).

Universalisation of Elementary Education

In order to achieve universalisation of elementary education and for the benefit of students, the following welfare programmes are being implemented by the Government of Tamil Nadu.

1. Supply of Nutritious Noon Meal for the Standard 1 to 10.
2. Supply of Free Slates for I Standard.
3. Supply of Free Bus Pass for all students going to school.
4. Supply of Free Text Books for all students from Standard 1 to Standard 12.
5. Supply of uniforms for students from Standards 1 to 8.
6. Teaching-Learning Materials through Operation Blackboard Scheme in elementary and middle schools.
7. Provision of infrastructural facilities under Operation Black Board Scheme, under Eleventh Finance Commission, Prime Minister's Gramadoya Yojana Programme, Area Intensive Programme and Educational Technology Scheme.

8. Provision of Computer Education in 1197 Higher Secondary Schools by which students from Standards IX to XII are benefited.
9. Provision of Vocational Education at Higher Secondary Level.
10. Provision of free cycles to all students studying in +1 and +2 standards.
11. Total Literacy and Post-Literacy Campaigns and Continuing Education Scheme for adults.
12. Non-formal Education for dropouts.
13. State Open Schools for those who completed 8th Standard.
14. Shramik Vidya Peeth (at 3 places).
15. Diploma in Teacher Education through Teacher Training Institutes (83 Institutions)
16. National Bank for Agricultural and Rural Development Assistance Scheme for provision of infrastructure facilities such as buildings, drinking water, toilet facilities in high and higher secondary schools.

Conclusion

Analysis of the literacy rates by social groups clearly reveals that the rate of literacy has gone up substantially for all social groups in 2011 as compared to 1991 in Tamil Nadu. The rate of literacy was high among the non-SC/ST as compared to SCs and STs in Tamil Nadu. There was a fluctuation in the rates of literacy by districts in Tamil Nadu. The rate of enrolment has gone up in the recent past, but the proportion of enrolment is still low among the Scheduled Castes and Scheduled Tribes in Tamil Nadu. The rate of drop outs has come down for all population, Scheduled Castes and Scheduled Tribes in 2005 as compared to 2001. The schools run by the government have enrolled more students as compared to the schools under private management.

The study also clearly indicates that the enrolment both at the UG and PG levels in colleges have increased among the SCs, whereas the percentage of enrolment at the Ph.D level has decreased among the SCs. Percentage of enrolment among the non-SC/STs has increased at all levels of education from UG to Ph.D levels, but the rate of enrolment has declined among the SCs during the same period.

The result of the study clearly shows that attendance rate, completion rate and transition rate were low among the SC as compared to non-SC/ST. The data relating to repetition rate was high among the SCs as compared to non-SC/ST at the school levels.

Analysis of data by gender shows that repetition rate was high among the boys, completion rate was high among the girls and the transition rate remains more or less the same for both the boys and girls.

The real solution to these problems lies in the formation of a universal education policy where children of all social groups, irrespective of their social and economic background, have to be admitted to the same kind of educational institutions with adequate boarding and lodging facilities.

Notes

1. Uma, S. Hiremath, *Asian Journal of Home Science,* Volume 8, No. 1, June 2013, pp. 20-23.
2. Wankhede, G.G., "Educational Inequalities among Scheduled Castes in Maharashtra", *Economic and Political Weekly,* May 5th 2001, Vol. 36, No. 18, p. 1553.

References

1. Balaji Pandey, Educational Development among Scheduled Castes, *Social Scientist,* Vol. 14, No. 2/3 (Feb. - Mar. 1986). pp. 59-68.

2. Chalam, K.S, "Caste Reservations and Equality of Opportunity in Education" *Economic and Political Weekly,* Vol: 41.13, No. 25, October-1990, pp. 2333-39.
3. Dholakia, R and Iyenkar, S, "Access of Poor Household to Primary Education in Rural India", *Journal of Educational Planning and Administration,* Vol. XXII, No. 3, July 2008, pp. 255-271.
4. Ghosh, A.K., "The Gender Gap in Literacy and Education among the Scheduled Tribes in Jharkhand and West Bengal" *Sociological Bulletin,* Vol. 56 (1), Jan-Apr 2007, pp. 109-125
5. Jariwal, C.M., Constitution and Education, *Encyclopedia of Indian education,* Vol. I, pp. 355.
6. Nambian, G., "Equity in Education? Schooling of Dalit Children in India", *Economic and Political Weekly,* Vol. XXXI, No. 16 and 17, April 20-27, 1996, pp. 1011-1024.
7. Nambissan, G., "Exclusion, Inclusion and Education; Perspectives and Experiences of Dalit Children", National Conference on Social Exclusion and Inclusive Policies, organised by *Indian Institute of Dalit Studies,* on 26-27- Oct-2007, pp. 95-126.
8. Ratna and Nageswara, "Primary Education: Progress and Constraints", *Economic and Political Weekly,* Vol. XXXVIII, No. 12 and 13, March 22-29, 2003, pp. 1242-1251.
9. Rubina, K., "Regional Returns to Education, Child Labour and Schooling in India", *Journal of Development Studies,* Vol. 44, No. 2, February-2008, pp. 233-257.
10. Velaskar, P."Education, Caste, Gender: Dalit Girls' Access to Schooling in Maharashtra" *Journal of Educational Planning and Administration,* Vol. XIX, No. 4, October 2005, pp. 459-482.
11 Vendatanarayana, "Child Schooling in Community in Transition: A Case of Scheduled Tribe Community in Andhra Pradesh", *Journal of Educational Planning and Administration,* Vol. XX, No. 1, January 2006, pp. 1-25.
12. Annual Report, Sarva Shiksha Abhiyan, Tamil Nadu, 2009-10
13. Annual Report, *Selected Educational Statistics,* Ministry of Human Resource Development, 1990-91 to 2007-08.
14. Seventh Educational Survey 2002, NCERT.
15. Census of India: 1991, 2001 and 2011 *Primary Census Abstract,* Series 23, Tamil Nadu, Volume-I.
16. http://india.gov.in/sectors/education.sarva_shiksha.php

6

Health and Consumption Expenditure in Tamil Nadu

Health in India/Tamil Nadu has positively correlated with the family income. Poor people tend to have more health problem than their rich counterparts, as the poor can't offer to meet the ever increasing and costly health expenditure. Poverty is the root cause for ill health for the poor people. It is an established fact that the people belonging to the SCs are poor, as they are assetless and engaged as landless wage labour. Health of the SC-people depends upon their household income. Access to healthcare including the paid and free health services largely depends upon educational level of the members of the household. United Nations International Millennium Development Goals (MDGs) lays emphasise on improving health of the people. Of the eight international Millennium Development Goals (MDGs), goal one deals with the eradication of poverty and hunger; goal four outlines the reduction of child mortality; goal five discusses about the maternal healthcare and goal six addresses the issues relating to HIV and related diseases.

Consumption expenditure is also depends upon household income. The relation between income and household expenditure is known as consumption function or consumption schedule. Consumption will go up when disposable income increases. The consumption may exceed disposable income for poor people. There is an inverse relation between the disposable income and the propensity to consume/consumption expenditure.

Objectives of the Study

An attempt has been made in this chapter to:

1. Discuss mortality rates (infants and child) and morbidity rates (prevalence of certain diseases and immunisation of child by social groups viz. SCs, STs, OBCs and Others); and
2. Examine the level of consumption expenditure by social groups.

Sources of Data and Data Analysis

Health related data on mortality and morbidity were collected from the report on National Health and Family Welfare (Tamil Nadu Reports) for two points of time viz. 1998-99 and 2005-06 and data on consumption expenditure were collected from 1. Differences in level of consumption among socio-economic groups 1993-94, NSS 42nd Report, July 1993-June 1994 and 2.Employment and unemployment situation among social groups in India -2004-05, NSS Report. Part one of the paper deals with health status and in part two an attempt is made to delineate the per capita consumption expenditure. Important issues addressed to this section are : 1. Health status, 2. Access to healthcare, 3. Women food consumption. 4. Prevalence of anemia among women and children, 5. Vaccination and 6. Consumption expenditure.

Social/Disparity gap is used for analysing the disparity between the social groups. The disparity can be measured as simple gap, i.e., a gap between the social groups.

6.1 Child Mortality

Infant mortality rates reflect the quality of life and health status of the country. Neonatal mortality refers to the probability of dying in the first month of life. Post-neonatal mortality indicates the probability of dying after the first month of life but before the first birth day. Infant mortality refers to the probability of dying before the first birth day. Child mortality indicates the probability of dying between first and fifth birth days. Under-five mortality refers to the probability of dying before the fifth birth day. Neonatal mortality, post-neonatal mortality, infant mortality, child mortality and child under-five mortality as shown in Table 6.1A clearly indicate that the possibility of dying in early childhood has declined for all social groups in Tamil Nadu in 2005-06. There is a variation in the child mortality between these two social groups.

Table 6.1A: Infant and child mortality by background characteristics in Tamil Nadu

Background characteristic	*Neonatal mortality*	*Post neonatal mortality*	*Infant mortality*	*Child mortality*	*Under-five mortality*
1998-99					
SCs	29.2	12.6	41.8	22.5	63.3
OBCs	37.1	15.5	52.7	10.9	63.0
2005-06					
SCs	25.2	12.1	37.4	11.3	48.3
OBCs	26.7	11.5	38.2	6.6	44.6

Source:

1. National Family Health Survey India, 1998-99: Tamil Nadu, International Institute of Population Studies, Mumbai, India, 2001.
2. National Family Health Survey India, 2005-06: Tamil Nadu, International Institute of Population Studies, Mumbai, India, 2008.

Social gaps i.e. difference between the OBCs and SCs as shown in the Table 6.1B clearly explicate that there was a considerable decline in the social gaps in 2005-06 as compared to 1998-99 in Tamil Nadu.

Table 6.1 B: Social Gaps in Infant and Childhood Mortality Indicators

Background characteristic	*Neonatal mortality*	*Post neonatal mortality*	*Infant mortality*	*Child mortality*	*Under-five mortality*
1998-99					
OBCs-SCs	7.9	2.9	10.9	-11.6	-0,3
2005-06					
OBCs -SCs	1.5	-0.6	0.8	-4.7	-3,7

Source:

1. National Family Health Survey India, 1998-99: Tamil Nadu, International Institute of Population Studies, Mumbai, India, 2001.
2. National Family Health Survey India, 2005-06: Tamil Nadu, International Institute of Population Studies, Mumbai, India, 2008.

6.2. Access to Healthcare

Vitamin Supplementation

Vitamin A deficiency is one of the most common nutritional problems in India. The national programmes on prevention of blindness targets children less than five years and administers oral doses of vitamin A every six months starting from nine months after birth of a child. The percentage of children aged 12 – 35 months who received at least one dose of vitamin A and those who received at least one dose within past six months preceding the survey was low among the SCs (Table 6.2). Main reason for low

Table 6.2: Vitamin A supplementation for children (12-35 months): 1998-99

Background characteristic		
	At least one dose	*At least one dose within past six months*
SCs	11.6	7.4
OBCs	17.8	10.7

Source: National Family Health Survey India, 1998-99: Tamil Nadu, International Institute of Population Studies, Mumbai, India, 2001.

vitamin A supplementation for SCs may be attributed to illiteracy and low standard of living. Other reason may be attributed to the lack of vitamin supplementation that women belonging to SCs unable to get the vitamin A dose, as they have to go for wage employment to supplement the family income.

Antenatal care

Antenatal care refers to pregnancy related healthcare provided by a doctor or health worker. 'The safe motherhood initiative proclaims that pregnant women must have access to basic antenatal care. The reproductive and healthcare programme recommends that as part of antenatal care, women receive two of tetanus toxoid vaccine, adequate amount of iron and folic acid tablets to prevent anaemia and at least three antenatal check-ups to detect pregnancy-related complications. The percentage of women who have received antenatal care was low among SCs women in 2005-06 (Table 6.3).

Table 6.3 : percentage of women availed antenatal care: 2005-06

	Doctor	*ANM/Nurse/Midwife/LHW*	*Anganwadi/ICDS worker*	*None*
SCs	77.9	18.3	1.9	2.0
STs	-	-	-	-
OBCs	85.3	13.2	0.7	0.8

Source: National Family Health Survey India, 2005-06: Tamil Nadu, International Institute of Population Studies, Mumbai, India, 2008.

Delivery care

An important thrust of the reproductive and child health programme is to encourage deliveries under the supervision of the trained health professionals. The data presented in Table 6.4 shows that nearly 69 per cent of the delivery in Tamil Nadu took place in health facility/Institutions among SCs. About 83 per cent of the deliveries took place in health facility/Institutions among OBCs. About 21 per cent of the deliveries among SCs and 17 per cent of the deliveries among OBCs took place at home (own home and parents' home).

Table 6.4: Percentage distribution of delivery care (place of birth): 1998-99

	Place of birth					
	Health facility/Institution			*Home*		*Other*
	Public	*NGO/Trust*	*Private*	*Own home*	*Parents' home*	
SCs	42.9	0.8	25.0	18.5	11.7	1.1
OBCs	36.7	1.3	44.8	11.1	5.6	0.5

Source: National Family Health Survey India, 1998-99: Tamil Nadu, International Institute of Population Studies, Mumbai, India, 2001.

Delivery assistance

The data presented in Table 6.5 provide information on assistance during delivery. The data show that there was a variation among SCs and OBCs with regard to deliveries assisted. The proportion of births attended by doctors was higher among women belonging to OBCs. About 65 per cent of the delivery was assisted by doctors among OBCs, while only 46 per cent of the deliveries were assisted by doctors among SCs.

Table 6.5: Percentage distribution of birth assistance: 1998-99

	Attendant assisting during delivery				
	Doctor	*ANM/Nurse/Midwife/LHW*	*Other health professional*	*Dai (TBA)*	*Other*
SCs	45.9	27.0	1.8	16.1	9.2
OBCs	64.9	20.7	1.3	8.1	5.0

Source: National Family Health Survey India, 1998-99: Tamil Nadu, International Institute of Population Studies, Mumbai, India, 2001.

6.3. Women's Food Consumption

Consumption of a variety of nutritious foods is an important and basic necessity for women's health. Women should consume adequate quantity of a well balanced diet. Consumption of food items as presented in Table 6.6 clearly indicate that the percentage of food consumption viz. milk/ curd, green leafy vegetables and fruits by women was low among SCs as compared to OBCs and Other. It is striking to note that the consumption for Others with regard to vegetarian food was high and low in non-vegetarian food.

Table 6.6: Percentage of ever married women's food consumption: 1998-99

	Milk/curd	*Pulses/ beans*	*Green, leafy veget- ables*	*Other vegetables*	*Fruits*	*Eggs*	*Chicken, Meat or fish*
SCs	51.1	94.6	70.8	98.6	33.5	45.5	53.1
OBCs	71.2	94.6	79.4	98.9	49.4	55.7	53.2
Others	94.0	97.8	95.1	100.0	88.6	34.6	26.4

Source: National Family Health Survey India, 1998-99: Tamil Nadu, International Institute of Population Studies, Mumbai, India, 2001.

6.4. Prevalence of Anemia among Women and Children

Anemia is a major health problem in Tamil Nadu/India. Women and children suffer more dur anemia. Anemia is characterised by low level of haemoglobin/decrease in healthy red blood cells in the blood. It is necessary for transporting oxygen from lungs to other organs of the body. Nutritional deficiencies viz. iron, folate, vitamin B_{12} and some other deficiency results in anemia. These nutrients are provided to pregnant women to prevent anemia during pregnancy. The data presented in Table 6.7 clearly explicate the prevalence of anemia is much higher among women belonging to SCs. The data further shows that the occurrence of anemia has declined among all social groups in 2005-06. The data presented in Table 6.7A clearly indicate that the gap between the social groups have come down 2005-06.

Table 6.7: Percentage of women with anemia

	Percentage of women with			
	Mild anemia	*Moderate anemia*	*Severe anemia*	*Any anemia*
	1998-99			
SCs	41.4	18.9	3.9	64.2
OBCs	35.2	15.0	4.0	54.2
Others	35.7	13.3	0.4	49.4
	2005-06			
SCs	39.6	16.0	3.1	58.7
OBCs	17.1	13.1	1.9	52.0
Others	30.3	7.4	0.7	38.4

Sources

1. National Family Health Survey India, 1998-99: Tamil Nadu, International Institute of Population Studies, Mumbai, India, 2001.
2. National Family Health Survey India, 2005-06: Tamil Nadu, International Institute of Population Studies, Mumbai, India, 2008.

Table 6.7A: Social gap in percentage of women with anemia

Background characteristic	*Mild anemia*	*Moderate anemia*	*Severe anemia*	*Any anemia*
1998-99				
OBCs-SCs	-6.2	-3.9	0.1	-10
Others-SCs	-5.7	-5.6	-3.5	-14.8
2005-06				
OBCs -SCs	-22.5	-2.9	-1.2	-6.7
Others-SCs	-9.3	-8.6	-2.4	-20.3

Anemia is a serious problem for young children also, as it can damage the cognitive performance and physical development. Anemia would result in risk of child mortality. The percentage of children suffer from anemia has come down moderate and severe anemia in 2005-06 for both the

SCs and OBCs; while there was an increase in the case of mild anemia for both the SCs and OBCs (Table 6.8). The data presented in Table 6.7A clearly indicate that the gap between the social groups have come down in 2005-06.

Table 6.8: Percentage of children with anemia

	Percentage of women with			
	Mild anemia	*Moderate anemia*	*Severe anemia*	*Any anemia*
	1998-99			
SCs	22.3	43.2	7.8	73.3
OBCs	21.7	39.2	6.8	67.7
	2005-06			
SCs	29.6	36.8	4.3	70.7
OBCs	26.0	33.6	1.9	61.4

Sources

1. National Family Health Survey India, 1998-99: Tamil Nadu, International Institute of Population Studies, Mumbai, India, 2001.
2. National Family Health Survey India, 2005-06: Tamil Nadu, International Institute of Population Studies, Mumbai, India, 2008.

Table 6.8A: Social gap in percentage of children with anemia

Background characteristic	*Mild anemia*	*Moderate anemia*	*Severe anemia*	*Any anemia*
	1998-99			
OBCs-SCs	-0.6	-4	-1	-5.6
	2005-06			
OBCs -SCs	-3.6	-3.2	-2.4	-9.3

Prevalence of acute respiratory infection, fever and diarrhea

Acute respiratory infection (ARI) is a major cause of illness and childhood mortality among children in India. The percentage of children with cough by fast breathing ARI, fever, and diarrhea during the two weeks preceding the survey and percentage with ARI who were taken to a health facility or provider as shown in Table 6.9 clearly indicate that the prevalence of ARI was slightly high among the children belonging to SCs as compared to OBCs in Tamil Nadu.

Table 6.9: Percentage of children under age three with acute respiratory infection fever and diarrhea during two weeks before the survey : 1998-99

	Cough accompanied by fast breathing (ARI)	*Fever*	*Diarrhea*		*% with ARI taken to health facility or provider*
			Any diarrhea	*Diarrhea with blood*	
SCs	11.8	22.7	12.2	0.7	75.5
OBCs	9.9	22.0	15.3	2.1	86.7

Source: National Family Health Survey India, 1998-99: Tamil Nadu, International Institute of Population Studies, Mumbai, India, 2001.

6.5. Vaccination

The vaccination of children against six serious but preventable diseases viz. tuberculosis, diphtheria, pertusis, tetanus, poliomyelitis and measles has been an important step taken up for the child healthcare in India as a part of national health policy. This step has been taken upon a priority basis to reduce morbidity, mortality and disabilities arising from six diseases. As per immunisation schedule, all primary vaccinations including measles have to be completed when child attains 12 months. The data presented in Table 6.10 clearly indicate that the percentage of all children received vaccination was low among the SCs children in both 1998-99 and 2005-06 as compared to MBCs. The data further show that the percentage of children received all vaccinations have declined in 2005-06 as compared to 1998-99 for both the SCs and OBCs. The data presented in Table 6.10A clearly indicate that there is a gap between the social groups between 1998-99 and 2005-06.

Table 6.10: Percentage of children received vaccination - 12-35 months

	BCG	*DPT*			*Polio*				*Measles*	*All*
		1 dose	*2 dose*	*3 dose*	*0 dose*	*1 dose*	*2 dose*	*3 dose*		
	1998-99									
SCs	99.0	99.0	99.0	97.0	77.9	100.0	100.0	99.0	85.2	84.2
OBCs	98.8	98.8	99.0	97.0	88.8	99.6	99.2	98.0	92.2	90.6
	2005-06									
SCs	100.0	98.7	95.6	89.0	94.3	100.0	99.9	83.1	88.9	72.3
OBCs	99.8	98.9	98.6	98.4	95.0	100.0	95.1	90.1	94.2	84.6

Source:

1. National Family Health Survey India, 1998-99: Tamil Nadu, International Institute of Population Studies, Mumbai, India, 2001.
2. National Family Health Survey India, 2005-06: Tamil Nadu, International Institute of Population Studies, Mumbai, India, 2008.

Table 6.10A: Social gap in children received vaccination - 12-35 months

	BCG	*DPT*			*Polio*				*Measles*	*All*
		1	*2*	*3*	*0*	*1*	*2*	*3*		
	1998-99									
OBCs - SCs	-0.2	-0.2	0	0	10.9	-0.4	-0.8	-1	7	6.4
	2005-06									
OBCs - SCs	-0.2	0.2	3	9.4	0.7	0	-4.8	7	5.3	12.3

Source: Computed from Table 6.10.

II. CONSUMPTION EXPENDITURE

Monthly Per Capita Consumption Expenditure (MPCE) is an index which measures the standard of the living of the people. "Household monthly consumer expenditure could serve as a proxy for household monthly income and is taken to reflect the standard of living of the members of a household" (NSS Report No. 516, p. 26).

Table 6.11A: Monthly per capita consumer expenditure of households by social groups in 1993-94: Rural (in Rs)

	<120	*120-140*	*140-165*	*165-190*	*190-210*	*210-235*	*235-265*	*265-300*	*300-355*	*355-455*	*455-560*	*560>*	*Total*
STs	53	91	131	142	83	51	59	163	108	61	27	31	1000
SCs	62	82	129	138	93	126	107	68	81	58	35	21	1000
All	**53**	**48**	**82**	**113**	**85**	**104**	**113**	**99**	**103**	**88**	**51**	**61**	**1000**

Source: Differences in level of consumption among socio-economic groups 1993-94, NSS Report No. 422, July 1993-June 1994, Ministry of Statistics and Programme Implementation, Government of India, August 1997.

Table 6.11B: Monthly per capita consumer expenditure of households by social groups in 2004-05: Rural (in Rs)

	<235	235-270	270-320	320-365	365-410	410-455	455-510	510-580	580-690	690-890	890-1150	1150>	Total
STs	98	0	98	0	153	282	36	43	0	82	188	20	1000
SCs	43	34	77	107	119	105	99	121	110	124	32	29	1000
OBCs	17	19	55	57	84	89	102	134	167	143	77	56	1000
Others	5	43	0	6	104	33	79	67	147	204	119	193	1000
All	**24**	**23**	**61**	**69**	**94**	**93**	**101**	**129**	**151**	**138**	**66**	**50**	**1000**

Source: Employment and unemployment situation among social groups in India -2004-05, NSS Report No. 516, July 2004-June 2005, Ministry of Statistics and Programme Implementation, Government of India, October 2006

Rural Areas

Data on per capita consumer expenditure is presented for rural areas in Table 6.11A. The data as given in Table 6.11A indicate that the percentage of households in each of the six lower MPCE classes i.e. up to Rs 235 was high among the SCs with 63.0 per cent followed by STs with 55.1 per cent and All with 48.5. While in the monthly per capita consumer expenditure above Rs 560 was high among All with 6.1 per cent followed by STs with 3.1 per cent and SCs with 2.1 per cent in rural areas in 1993-94.

The data as presented in Table 6.11B show that the percentage of households in each of the six lower MPCE classes i.e. up to Rs 455 was high among the STs with 63.1 per cent followed by SCs with 48.5 per cent, MBCs with 32.1 per cent and Others with 19.1 per cent. While in the monthly per capita consumer expenditure above Rs 1150 was high among Others with 19.3 per cent followed by OBCs with 5.6 per cent SCs with 2.9 per cent and STs with only 2.0 per cent in rural areas in 2004-05.

Table 6.11C: Social gap in Monthly per capita consumer expenditure of households by social groups: Rural Areas

	Up to 1st six consumer expenditure class of MPCE	*Highest level of MPCE*
	1993-94	
SCs-STs	79 (630-551)	-1 (21-31)
SCs -All	145 (630-485)	-4.1 (61)
	2004-05	
SCs-STs	-146 (485-631)	0.9 (29-20)
SCs -All	121 (485-364)	-21 (29-50)

Source: Computed from Tables 6.11A and 6.11B.

Social gaps i.e. difference in the first six per capita consumer expenditure classes (up to Rs 455 in 2004-05 and Rs 235 in 1993-94), between SCs and STs and also SCs and All as shown in the Table 6.11C clearly explicate that there was a considerable decline in the social gaps in between SCs and STs and increase between the SCs and All in 2005-06 in rural areas, Tamil Nadu. There was a marginal increase in highest level of MPCE between SCs and STs and decline between the SCs and All in 2004-05.

Urban Areas

A similar observation could be made in the urban areas as in the case of rural areas. The data as given in Table 6.12A clearly shows that the percentage of households at the lower level of monthly per capita consumer expenditure up to Rs 355 was high among SCs with 7.34 per cent, while the percentage of per capita monthly expenditure at the higher level of per capita expenditure above Rs 1055 was among All with 4.2 per cent in urban areas in 1993-94.

A similar observation could be made in the urban areas as in the case of rural areas. The data as presented in Table 6.12B clearly explicate that the percentage of households at the lower level of monthly per capita consumer expenditure up to Rs 790 was high among SCs, while the percentage of per capita monthly expenditure at the higher level of per capita expenditure abouve Rs 2540 was among Others in urban areas in 2004-05.

Social gaps i.e. difference in the first six classes of per capita consumer expenditure between SCs and STs and also SCs and All as shown in the Table 6.12C clearly explicate that there was a considerable decline in the social gaps in between SCs and STs and SCs and All in Urban Areas, Tamil Nadu. There was a fall in social gap in highest level of MPCE between SCs and STs and SCs and All in 2004-05 in urban areas.

Table 6.12A: Monthly per capita consumer expenditure of households by social groups in 1993-94: Urban (in Rs)

	<160	*160-190*	*190-230*	*230-265*	*265-310*	*310-355*	*355-410*	*410-490*	*490-605*	*605-825*	*825-1055*	*1055>*	*Total*
STs	0	9	155	78	64	185	63	52	63	20	257	34	1000
SCs	118	95	157	143	145	76	99	71	26	37	16	17	1000
All	46	54	107	100	129	99	104	114	79	86	40	42	1000

Source: Differences in level of consumption among socio-economic groups 1993-94, NSS 42nd Report, July 1993-June 1994, Ministry of Statistics and Programme Implementation, Government of India, August 1997.

Table 6.12B: Monthly per capita consumer expenditure of households by social groups in 2004-05: Urban (in Rs)

	<335	*335-395*	*395-485*	*485-580*	*580-675*	*675-790*	*790-930*	*930-1100*	*1100-1380*	*1380-1880*	*1880-2540*	*2540>*	*Total*
STs	279	5	69	45	90	15	46	71	246	0	34	80	1000
SCs	88	36	106	153	138	93	103	83	89	86	12	13	1000
OBCs	18	20	56	107	127	111	92	105	103	137	66	58	1000
Others	1	2	10	33	26	27	44	45	83	162	253	314	1000
All	28	20	59	105	118	99	88	95	100	131	77	77	1000

Source: Employment and unemployment situation among social groups in India -2004-05, NSS 61st Report, July 2004-June 2005, Ministry of Statistics and Programme Implementation, Government of India, October 2006.

Table 6.12C: Social gap in Monthly per capita consumer expenditure of households by social groups: Urban areas

	Up to 1st six consumer expenditure class of MPCE	*Highest level of MPCE*
	1993-94	
SCs-STs	243 (734-491)	-17 (17-34)
SCs -All	199 (734-535)	-25 (17-42)
	2004-05	
SCs-STs	111 (614-503)	-67 (13-80)
SCs -All	185 (614-429)	-64 (13-77)

Source: Computed from Tables 6.12A and 6.12B.

Conclusion

The mortality rates among children belonging to all social groups have declined in Tamil Nadu. The children who received Vitamin A supplementation was low among SCs children. The percentage of women who have received antenatal care was low among SCs women. The delivery assisted by doctors was high among OBCs, as compared to the delivery assisted by doctors among SCs. The food consumption viz. milk/curd, green leafy vegetables and fruits was low among SCs as compared to OBCs and Other. Prevalence of anemia is much higher among women and children belonging to SCs. The prevalence of ARI was slightly high among the children belonging to SCs as compared to OBCs in Tamil Nadu. Percentage of children received vaccination was low among the SCs children in both 1998-99 and 2005-06 as compared to MBCs. The percentage of households at the lower levels of monthly per capita consumer expenditure was high among the SCs and STs, while the percentage of households at the higher levels of monthly per capita consumer expenditure was high among OBCs and Others both in rural and urban areas.

References

Thangaraj, M., Demographic and Occupational Characteristics of the Scheduled Castes and Scheduled Tribes in India, *Madras Institute of Development Studies,* Working paper No. 134, 1995.

Vijay Kumar Baraik and P M Kulkarni, Health Status and Access to Health Care Services – Disparities among Social Groups in India, *Indian Institute of Dalit Studies,* Working Paper Series, New Delhi, Vol. 1, No. 4, 2006.

7

Scheduled Caste Sub-Plan in Tamil Nadu

The SCs, in the past, were socially ostracised, economically exploited. Scheduled Caste people are widely spread all over India. Majority of them are depending on agriculture as landless agricultural workers. They are also engaged in traditional occupations, such as, scavenging, leather work and other menial low income occupations. They are unable to get employment opportunities, in spite of development effort made by the government both at the central and at the state levels.

Colonial government and Christian Missionaries also formulated and implemented several welfare programmes for down-trodden section of the society. Welfare of the poor and oppressed has been the major concern of planners and policy-makers in India, during the post-independence era. Several welfare programmes were drawn up and implemented for the well-being of the disadvantaged groups. After having formulated several Five-Year Plans and spent crores of rupees, there was no significant and perceptible change in the life of the Scheduled Castes (SCs) in India, despite the fact that all Five Year Plans emphasised that the SCs must get their due share from the general sector of the development. The Government of India noticed that the financial allocations were found to be quite inadequate so as to focus on the needs and potentialities of the SCs, as compared to the size of their population. The persistence socio-economic backwardness of the SCs, despite constitutional mandate and development measures necessitated a special scheme for the overall development of the SCs.

The Government of India formulated a new strategy of quantification of funds for the development of the SCs for those States and Union Territories having a large population from the Sixth Five Year Plan onwards and the new strategy was known as the Special Component Plan (SCP) for the Scheduled Castes. The term 'Special Component Plan' has been changed as Scheduled Caste Sub-Plan (SCSP) by the Government of India recently. SCSP is a composite plan consisting of outlays from the state plan flowing for the benefit of the SCs and also specific new schemes undertaken for the economic betterment of the SCs with the Special Central Assistance (SCA) of the Government of India. Besides these allocations, Central Ministries are also required to identify programmes and allocate funds out of central and centrally sponsored schemes. The Government of India is implementing the SC Sub-Plan since (Sixth Five Year Plan) 1980-81 to accelerate the socio-economic and educational development of the SCs in India.

The working groupon the development of SCs (1980-85) recommended that SC Sub-Plan should have the following elements: (i) It should include the effort in every sector by every department and agency, (ii) It should be based on the developmental needs of the Scheduled Castes, (iii) The target group approach, taking into account the occupational categories in which there is a large number of

Scheduled Castes, must be adopted. The important instruments devised for ensuring the economic development of the Scheduled Castes include: (i) SC Sub-Plan for States and Central Ministries; (ii) The Special Central Assistance for the SC-Sub-Plan for the States; (iii) Scheduled Castes Development Corporation in the States (SCDCS) and (iv) Central Assistance to the states for these corporations.

The then Prime Minister of India, Indira Gandhi, wrote to the Chief Ministers of the states in the month of March, 1980 that the objective of the Special Component Plan should enable the families of the SCs in the States to cross the poverty line within a short and specified period of time and if possible at least half of them during the Sixth Plan itself. The state governments were asked to prepare Special Component Plan (SC Sub-Plan (SCSP)) for the SCs. The departments of the central government, institutions under its direct control and state governments were instructed to adopt this policy. The main aim of SCSP is not only to increase the budgetary allocation but also to find out about the utilisation of the funds and to achieve the stated targets successfully. Under this scheme financial allocation has to be made in proportion of the SCs to the total population. The SCSP also envisaged help to increase the living condition of the families of the SCs through the provision of infrastructure facilities, such as, safe drinking water supply, house sites, link roads, etc. It was planned that the Scheduled Castes Development Corporations should be actuated and made effective in implementing the development programmes. Close linkages should be created between the sectoral programmes in the SCSP and the activities of the Scheduled Castes Development Corporation.

The target fixed under SCSP has been disaggregated by districts and by schemes and communicated to all heads of departments and Collectors for effective implementation and monitoring. At the state level, the SC Welfare Department is the coordinating authority. A monitoring and evaluation cell has been set up in the Welfare Department at the Secretariat of the respective states for the purpose of the effective implementation of development programmes. District Collectors are responsible for coordinating the implementation of the SCSP at the district level.

The schemes implemented under SCSP and Tribal Sub-Plan (TSP) are classified into divisible and indivisible schemes. The direct flow of resources to the beneficiaries through income generating programmes for individuals are called divisible schemes and the flow of resources for social services, infrastructure development and other facilities are called indivisible schemes.

Objective of the Study

The objective of the study is to examine the allocation of fund under the Scheduled Caste Sub-Plan (SCSP).

Data Base

Data have been collected from 1. Performance Budget, Adi-Dravidar and Tribal Welfare Department, Government of Tamil Nadu, 2. Special Component Plan for Scheduled Castes: 2000-2001, Tamil Nadu, Adi-Dravidar and Tribal Welfare, Chennai, and 3. Annual Plan: Plan Budget Link.

Population

Out of a total population of 721.47 lakhs in Tamil Nadu in 2011, the Scheduled Castes form 20.01 per cent with 144.3 lakh persons, the Scheduled Tribes constitute 1.10 per cent with 7.95 lakh persons. It is significant to note that the percentage of SC population was more that 30 per cent in four districts viz. Thiruvarur district with 34.08 per cent, the Nilgiris with 32.08 per cent, Nagapattinam district with 31.54 per cent and Perambalur district with 31.01 per cent. It is also significant to note that the proportion of SC population in southern parts of Tamil Nadu is less than the proportion of SC population in Tamil Nadu.

Special Component Plan in Tamil Nadu

The Government of Tamil Nadu is implementing the SCSP since 1980-81 to accelerate the socio-economic and educational development of SCs. When the Government of India releases Special Central Assistance (SCA) every year to the state governments under the SCSP for Scheduled Castes, the amount is released to the Adi-Dravidar Housing and Development Corporation (TAHDCO) which is taking up economic development programmes by its district level branches and other sectoral departments in Tamil Nadu. In addition to the income generating schemes, other schemes, such as, supply of inputs for agricultural development, supply of cross-breed cows, sericulture, rams, goats, training to women for driving autos, Tamil Nadu Adi Deravida Housing, and Development Corporation (TADHCO) and heavy vehicles, nursing course, etc, are being implemented by various departments. Individual entrepreneur development schemes and formation of industrial estates are also being implemented by the TAHDCO in Tamil Nadu.

In order to implement the SCSP, the resources of more than twenty departments are pooled together in Tamil Nadu. Schemes by these departments include in the broad areas to educational, social and economic development of the Scheduled Castes. The state plan outlay, flow to SCSP and expenditure incurred by the departments are furnished by the Adi-Dravidar and Tribal Welfare Department (ADTWD). Data relating to the SCSP expenditure as furnished by the ADTWD are a mix of both actual and notional. The flow to SCSP is also a notional one. Tamil Nadu Peoples Forum for Social Development (TNPFSD) report on social development of Dalits rightly states that 'the SCSP demands strict criteria for working out the schemes under it. Many departments simply claim that due benefits reach Scheduled Castes from their general programmes. Apart from such notional allocations and explanations, they have failed to work out special plans under the Special Component Plan for the Scheduled Castes'.

It is important to note that the flow to SCSP expenditure should reflect in the Plan–Budget Link i.e. if any scheme is implemented under it by the respective departments, the details about the scheme should have been entered in the Plan-Budget Link. The SCSP expenditure based on Plan-Budget Link is the real and actual. Data regarding the expenditure under SCSP based on Plan-Budget Link shows that the SCSP is not implemented seriously in Tamil Nadu. For example, about five per cent of the total plan outlay was spent in 1999-2000 but actually the amount spent should have been 19 per cent – the percentage of Scheduled Castes population to the total population in 1991 (Table 7.1).

The data furnished by the Adi-Dravidar and Tribal Welfare Department does not correlate to the budget figures in the Plan-Budget Link (Table 7.1). For example, the percentage of SCSP expenditure to the total plan furnished by the Adi-Dravidar and Tribal Welfare Department has gone up from 18.35 per cent in 1991-92, to 23.71 per cent in 2014-2015. The Plan-Budget Link shows that the percentage of SCSP expenditure to the total state plan has gone up from 1.22 in 1991-92 to 11.17 per cent in 2007-08. In fact, these two figures viz. the data furnished by the Adi-Dravidar and Tribal Welfare Department and Plan-Budget Link should tally each other and this being the case the Adi-Dravidar and Tribal Welfare Department continues to publish the notional figures in its official document. It is to be noted that the data furnished by different departments to the Adi-Dravidar and Tribal Welfare Department are compiled without reference to actualities. It is also stated that the implementing departments do not conduct evaluation of SCSP schemes after its completion.

The Tamil Nadu Peoples forum for Social Development's report further states that, "funds allocations have been wrong and inadequate. The basic approach to SCP in the state has been faulty. Implementation of SCP by the departments in Tamil Nadu has been lax and cynical". The report further shows that "In June 1999, at a review meeting with the Chief Secretary and other officials of the state government, Mr. Dileep Singh Bhuria, Chairman of the National Commission for SCs/STs had taken a serious note of the under utilisation of funds by the Tamil Nadu government with regard to the welfare of the SCs/STs".

The funds allotted under this scheme have been inadequate and this has been accepted by the Finance Minister of Tamil Nadu. In his Budget Speech 2001-2002, Finance Minister of Tamil Nadu stated that the government is aware that the allocation for the Scheduled Caste Sub-Plan for Adi-Dravidar is not commensurate with their proportion in total population. We propose to review the progress and achievements under the SCSP on a regular basis. While presenting budget for the year, 2002-2003, the Finance Minister of Tamil Nadu has again stated that the review of the implementation of the SCSP for the welfare of the SCs reveals discrepancies in the actual allocation of funds for the welfare of these people. A high level committee has been constituted to prioritise schemes based on specific requirements of the SCs under the SCSP.

In order to effectively implement the Scheduled Caste Sub-Plan for the SCs, the report of the Commission for the SCs and STs has rightly stated as early as in 1979-80 that SCSP should have adequate inbuilt mechanism of concurrent monitoring and evaluation and separate budget heads. The difficulty in accounting some schemes under the SCSP for the Scheduled Castes, it is stated, is that the outcome of benefits from SCSP will be quantified only from the divisible schemes or plan which directly benefit the SCs and the schemes which are not divisible, cannot be brought into account.

Table 7.1: Expenditure on Special Component Plan in Tamil Nadu (Rs in lakhs)

Year	*Data supplied by Adi-Dravidar and Tribal Welfare Department*				*Data based on Annual Plan Budget Link*	
	State plan Outlay	*Flow to SCP*	*Expenditure incurred*	*% of expenditure to the total state plan*	*Expenditure as shown in the budget link book*	*% of expenditure as shown in the link book to the total state plan outlay*
91-92	160000.44	27267.64	29330.09	18.35	1965.66	1.22
92-93	175135.11	29308.18	30044.39	17.15	3206.02	1.83
93-94	210100.00	35369.87	33518.15	15.95	1622.17	0.77
94-95	275001.52	52306.23	44319.13	16.11	2885.11	1.05
95-96	320000.00	61824.57	48329.96	15.10	3182.74	0.99
96-97	370072.00	65238.75	40854.72	11.03	16792.64	4.54
97-98	405260.00	75223.22	72004.18	17.77	23945.97	5.91
98-99	450009.00	82553.41	81563.12	18.12	27963.94	6.21
99-00	525[illegible]12.00	111024.54	101050.80	19.24	26718.66	5.09
00-01	604000.00	101337.00	70978.00	11.75	NA	NA
01-02	NA	NA	NA	NA	15384.52	NA
02-03	575153.0	110373.6	119279.1	20.74	8709.69	1.51
03-04	700013.2	135370.7	161513.8	23.07	16241.27	2.32
04-05	800108.1	154343.8	158721.7	19.84	56722.05	7.10
05-06	910000.0	210455.0	173684.8	19.09	57338.84	6.30
06-07	1250000.0	311785.4	246303.9	19.70	117646.13	9.41
07-08	1400000.0	335688.8	290361.9	20.74	156334.24	11.17
08-09	1600000.0	417830.9	345335.4	21.58	212612.00*	11.2*
09-10	1750000.0	460268.2	360426.7	20.59	294859.00*	14.4*
10-11	2006300.0	424072.5	421000.5	20.98	416196.00*	15.5*
11-12	2353500.0	500700.0	449196.7	19.09	422909.00*	12.2*
12-13	2800000.0	610860.8	540512.1	21.82	NA	NA
13-14	3700000.0	704199.7	709779.6	20.21	NA	NA

contd...

Year	*Data supplied by Adi-Dravidar and Tribal Welfare Department*				*Data based on Annual Plan Budget Link*	
	State plan Outlay	*Flow to SCP*	*Expenditure incurred*	*% of expenditure to the total state plan*	*Expenditure as shown in the budget link book*	*% of expenditure as shown in the link book to the total state plan outlay*
14-15	4218500.0	1000107.9	906272.2	23.71	NA	NA
15-16	5510000.0	11277416.3	NA	NA	NA	NA

*Report of the Comptroller and Auditor General of India (General and social sector) for the year ended 31 March, 2012, Government of Tamil Nadu, Report No. 3, 2013.

NA = Not Available

Sources:

1. Performance Budget, Adi-Dravidar and Tribal Welfare Department, Government of Tamil Nadu, various years.
2. Special Component Plan for Scheduled Castes: 2000-2001, Tamil Nadu, Adi-Dravidar and Tribal Welfare, Chennai, (various years).
3. Annual Plan: Plan Budget Link@ (various years).

@Tamil Nadu Government have published the expenditure on SCSP with actual expenditure, revised budget expenditure and budget estimate in Annual Plan: Budget Link till 2010. It was good source of information as there was a lot difference between the budget estimate and the actual expenditure. Now Annual Plan: Budget Link provides only budget estimate for the current year and hence, actual expenditure could not be obtained. It is stated the government have deliberated avoided in giving the actual expenditure to prevent the public from getting the actual expenditure of the SCSP.

The government desires to improve the status of the Adi Dravidars through various welfare schemes. The Government of India has also instructed the States that flow of funds from State Annual Plan outlay should be proportionate to the Adi Dravidar population. Scheduled Castes Sub Plan is implemented through 21 Sectoral Departments. The schemes under Scheduled Castes Sub-Plan are classified as divisible and indivisible schemes from Tenth Five Year Plan onwards. The direct flow of resources to the beneficiaries through family oriented and individual income generating programmes are called divisible schemes and the flow of resources through the provision of social services, infrastructure development and other facilities are called indivisible schemes. From 2011-12 to 2012-13, only the divisible head is being followed. Nodal Officers are appointed in all Sectoral Departments to monitor the schemes implemented under Scheduled Castes Sub-Plan. The details of flow (divisible and indivisible) and expenditure (divisible and indivisible) under Scheduled Castes Sub-Plan for the years 2002-03 to 2014-15 are given in Table 7.2. The data shows that the allocation of fund is quite satisfactory in Tamil Nadu. The details regarding the allocation of fund by department given in Table 7.3 clearly indicate that the percentage of flow of funds to SCSP to annual plan outlay and the percentage of expenditure to flow to SCSP are not uniform and vary across department in Tamil Nadu.

The implementation of the SCSP and TSP (Tribal Sub-Plan) is being monitored by an apex empowered committee under the Chairmanship of Member - State Planning Commission dealing the subject with Secretary, Planning and Development, Special Secretary, Finance Department as Members, besides all the Secretaries of the concerned Departments. Secretary, Adi-Dravidar and Tribal Welfare Department is the Member Secretary. The committee's role is to ensure that benefits of the schemes under SCSP and TSP reach the deserving SCs and STs, to finalise the quantum of funds allocated under each scheme and to oversee the implementation, monitoring and evaluation of the schemes, priorities, targets and achievement of output indicators set by the State Government vis-á-vis SCSP and TSP. Though the State Government has fixed the output indicators in every sector for the State, there are no specific SC and ST related targets and indicators, vision document or a long term perspective Plan for guiding the development activities of SCs and STs in the State.

The targets fixed under SCSP and TSP are disaggregated into district and scheme-wise targets and communicated to all sectoral Head of Departments and Collectors for effective implementation. At the State level, the Secretary, Adi-Dravidar and Tribal Welfare Department is the coordinating authority for SCs and STs. He reviews the progress, implementation of schemes with the Head of the Departments and ensures effective and speedy implementation of the schemes by removing bottlenecks with the help of Commissioner, Adi-Dravidar Welfare and Director, Tribal Welfare. The Director, Adi-Dravidar Welfare and Director, Tribal Welfare have been nominated to review and monitor periodically to fulfill the targets. District Collectors are responsible for coordinating and implementing the schemes of SCs and STs through District Managers, Departmental Heads and extension officers every month.

Conclusion

Thus, the foregoing analysis vividly brings out the fact that the SCSP has not been effectively implemented in Tamil Nadu. The funds allotted under the scheme have been inadequate and less than the required allocation of fund from the state plan viz. allocation of fund should be equal to the proportion of the Scheduled Caste population in the State. A suitable law may be enacted for effective implementation SCSP with adequate provision for protection of fund only meant for the Scheduled Castes and the funds

Table 7.2: Scheduled Castes Sub-Plan (SCSP), Flow (Target) and Expenditure (Rs in lakhs)

Year	Annual Plan Outlay	Flow (target)			Expenditure			
		Divisible	Indivisible	Total	Divisible	Indivisible	Total	
2002-03	575153.0	11048.2	99325.35	110373.6	40209.13	79069.95	119279.1	20.74%
2003-04	700013.2	17528.01	117842.6	135370.7	61388.49	100125.3	161513.8	23.07%
2004-05	800108.1	17409.73	136934.1	154343.8	59955.43	98766.25	158721.7	19.84%
2005-06	910000.0	14105.47	196349.5	210455.0	55481.74	118203.1	173684.8	19.09%
2006-07	1250000.0	123869.7	187915.8	311785.4	124368.70	121935.3	246303.9	19.70%
2007-08	1400000.0	164984.4	170704.4	335688.8	168159.10	122202.8	290361.9	20.74%
2008-09	1600000.0	237920.0	179911.0	417830.9	255169.90	90165.53	345335.4	21.58%
2009-10	1750000.0	261544.4	198723.8	460268.2	295978.10	64448.66	360426.7	20.60%
2010-11	2006800.0	382783.5	41289	424072.5	398631.12	22369.39	421000.5	20.98%
2011-12	2353500.0	500700.0	0	500700.0	449196.70	0	449196.7	19.09%
2012-13	2800000.0	610860.8	0	610860.8	540512.10	0	540512.1	19.30%
2013-14	3700000.0	704199.7	43500	704199.7	709780.00	33320.0	709779.6	20.20%
2014-15	4218500.0	760299.7	239808.2	1000107.9	827416.00	78857.0	906273.0	21.48%

Source: Performance budget 2014-15, Adi-Dravidar and Tribal Welfare Department.

Table 7.3: Allocation of fund under Scheduled Castes Sub-Plan (SCSP) 2013-14 (Rs in Lakhs)

Sector / Heads of Development	*Annual Plan Outlay*	*Flow to SCSP*	*Expenditure*	*% of flow to SCSP to annual plan outlay*	*% of expenditure to flow to SCSP*
1. Agriculture Crop Husbandry	123185.20	25681.96	19819.66	20.85	77.17
2. Soil and Water Conservation	5845.03	1264.80	959.94	21.64	75.90
3. Animal Husbandry	34412.58	7391.05	8767.87	21.48	118.63
4. Reg. of Co-Op. Societies	48160.79	4025.00	1999.92	8.36	49.69
5. Rural Development	263901.35	72040.59	81349.56	27.30	112.92
6. Community Development	211518.31	62437.86	40787.34	29.52	65.32
7. Power and Energy	300272.92	57000.00	84545.82	18.98	148.33
8. Industries and Minerals (Handloom & Textiles)	82402.38	8800.00	12228.48	10.68	138.96
9. Transport : Roads and Bridges	332541.44	41375.35	41375.32	12.44	100.00
10. General Education	441398.05	69237.62	55541.36	15.69	80.22
11. Sport and Youth Services	5715.51	119.59	187.45	2.09	156.74
12. Medical and Public Health	239456.04	44242.77	43823.34	18.48	99.05
13. Water Supply and Sanitation	67020.18	18690.00	16764.47	27.89	89.70

contd...

Sector / Heads of Development	*Annual Plan Outlay*	*Flow to SCSP*	*Expenditure*	*% of flow to SCSP to annual plan outlay*	*% of expenditure to flow to SCSP*
14. Housing	15345.89	3253.52	3300.00	21.20	101.43
15. Urban Development	202774.33	5257.18	6164.55	2.59	117.26
16. Welfare of SCs	65100.39	56975.53	78199.14	87.52	137.25
17. Social Security and Welfare	487356.44	109681.05	114103.08	22.51	104.03
18. Nutrition	168401.70	25099.05	28136.20	14.90	112.10
19. Labour and Employment	52154.88	16626.81	12975.83	31.88	78.04
20. Special Programme Implementation	300000.00	75000.00	58750.25	25.00	78.33
21. Others Depts. where no funds earmarked under SCSP	253036.59	-	-		
Total	**3700000.00**	**704199.73**	**709779.58**	**19.03**	**100.79**

Source: http://www.tn.gov.in/deptst/adidravidarandtribalwelfare.pdf (Adi Dravidar and Tribal Welfare Department, Chennai)

provided under the SCSP should be made non-divertible and non-lapsable.

The hope of the deprived section of the people with regard to the effective implementation of the SCSP still remains a distant dream, due to lack of political will on the part of administrative machinery. The SCSP is a landmark provision for SCs, as it mainly deals with the eradication of poverty and other economic problems among SCs. But due to vested interests, the authorities do not genuinely implement this important provision. If this provision were put into practice genuinely, the problem of poverty among SCs would have been vanished long ago.

References

1. Report of the Commissioner for SCs and STs (Various years).
2. Special Component Plan for Scheduled Castes, 2000-2001 Tamil Nadu, Adi Dravidar and Tribal Welfare, Chennai, January 2001.
3. "Social Development of Dalit and Tamil Nadu Government budget: A Critique", Tamil Nadu People's Forum for social Development, Year of the publication is not available.
4. "Tamil Nadu Social Development Report 2000", Tamil Nadu People's Forum for Social Development, 2000.
5. Thangaraj, "Demographic and Occupational Characteristics of the Scheduled Castes and Scheduled Tribes in Tamil Nadu", MIDS Working Paper No. 134, Madras Institute of Development Studies, 1995.

8

Atrocities on Scheduled Castes in Tamil Nadu

The world has entered into the era of new millennium with all modern scientific and technological advancements, it is depressing to note that people of India, particularly the Hindus, are divided on the basis of birth. They have been arranged in hierarchical social order and it is impossible to unite them under one umbrella, as they very often fight for social issues, such as superiority over others, temple entry, social boycotts, economic development of the SCs, participation in democratic institution, etc. These social issues are no doubt human rights violations. Human right violations are going on unabatedly and unashamedly in this country. All human rights violations are not reported in the media and in many cases issues relating to human rights violations may not come to light through and most of the violations are against the Scheduled Castes (SCs) and other weaker sections of the society in India. In fact, no day is passing with perpetrating atrocities on SCs. These atrocities take several forms viz. murder, hurt, rape, looting of/damaging properties, etc by the upper caste people.

Atrocity refers to an extreme form of wicked or cruel act involving physical violence or injury. In India, atrocities are perpetrated on the basis of religion, language and castes. Atrocities committed on Scheduled Castes (SCs) are many and no day is passing such inhuman activities on SCs. The SCs are struggling hard to fight against the non-SCs (caste-Hindus). Indian government is committed to provide welfare of its people in general and of vulnerable sections of society viz. Scheduled Castes (SCs) and Scheduled Tribes (STs) in particular. Equality of opportunity to all citizens is guaranteed by the Constitution of India and no individual shall be discriminated against on the grounds of religion, caste and sex.

Objective of the Study

The objective of the paper is to examine nature and types of atrocities committed on SCs in Tamil Nadu.

Database*

Information relating to the types of atrocities, cases filed and disposed of by police and court at the state level were mainly collected from National Crime Record Bureau (NCRB) and the same information at the district level were collected from the Crimes Review, State Crime Record Office, Chennai for the year 2014 only.

Fundamental Rights

Fundamental rights and other specific provisions, namely, Articles 15, 38, 39 and 46 in the Constitution of India stand

---

* Social Justice Department attached to Director General of Police, Chennai is in charge monitoring and collecting information on atrocities on SCs and STs in Tamil Nadu. The department is headed by an IPS Officer. The Researcher made a request to provide information on atrocities and the working special courts in Tamil Nadu. But the Researcher was informed that such information were not available with the department. Hence, data on atrocities by districts could not be collected from the Social Justice Department.

testimony to the commitment of the Country/State towards its people.

Article 15 of the Indian Constitution deals with prohibition of discrimination on the grounds of religion, race, caste, sex or place of birth. It also guarantees that every citizen shall have equality of status and opportunity.

Article 38 of the Indian Constitution makes provision to secure a social order for the promotion of welfare of the people

(1) The State shall strive to promote the welfare of the people by securing and protecting as effectively as it may a social order in which justice, social, economic and political, shall inform all the institutions of the national life.

(2) The State shall, in particular, strive to minimise the inequalities in income, and endeavour to eliminate inequalities in status, facilities and opportunities, not only among the individuals but also among the groups of people residing in different areas or engaged in different vocations.

Article 39 of the Constitution deals with certain principles of policy to be followed by the State. The State shall, in particular, direct its policy towards securing—

(a) that the citizens, men and women equally, have the right to an adequate means of livelihood;

(b) that the ownership and control of the material resources of the community are so distributed as best to subserve the common good;

(c) that the operation of the economic system does not result in the concentration of wealth and means of production to the common detriment;

(d) that there is equal pay for equal work for both men and women;

(e) that the health and strength of workers, men and women, and the tender age of children are not abused and that citizens are not forced by economic necessity to enter avocations unsuited to their age or strength;

Article 46 of the constitution of India states that the State shall promote the educational and economic development of the weaker sections of the society, in particular of SCs and STs with special care and shall protect them from injustice and all forms of exploitation.

Legal Rights

The major legal enactments to fight against the social inequality at the national level are: (i) Article 15 deals with prohibition of discrimination, (ii) Article 17 of the constitution abolished untouchability and its practice in any form, (ii) Protection of Civil Rights Act, 1955; (iii) Scheduled Caste/ Scheduled Tribe (Prevention of Atrocities) Act, 1989.

Article 15 deals with Prohibition of discrimination on grounds of religion, race, caste, sex or place of birth.

Article 17 deals with the abolition of the Untouchability and its practice in any form is made punishable under the law.

To strengthen further, the constitutional provision in Article 15 and Article 17, the Parliament of India enacted the Untouchability (Offences) Act in 1955. This act was further amended and renamed in 1976 as Protection of Civil Rights Act, 1955. This Act lays down that whatever is open to general public (or Hindus) should be open to the members of the Scheduled Castes. The Scheduled Castes and Scheduled Tribes (Prevention of Atrocities) Act, 1989 was brought into force from 30th January 1990 in order to check and prevent crimes against SCs/STs by persons belonging to other communities. Special Courts have been established in major states for speedy trial of cases registered exclusively under these Acts. This Act was further amended in 2014 by the UPA government and the same was approved by the NDA government.

The atrocities committed on the SCs have been increasing every year. The National Crime Record Bureau 2013 states that "a total of 13,975 cases were reported under this Act during the year 2013 as compared to 12,576 in the year 2012, thus reporting an increase of 11.1 per cent. Bihar has reported 5,584 cases accounting for 39.9 per cent of the total cases reported in the country followed by Uttar Pradesh (13.2 per cent) (1,847 cases), Odisha (12.8 per cent) (1,785 cases), and Karnataka (9.9 per cent) (1,380 cases)".

Caste Deprivation and Discrimination

The Scheduled Castes have been facing deprivation and discriminations even today. They face these deprivation and discriminations from cradle to grave. The discriminations are also political in nature. The SCs are not allowed to vote and not allowed to contest in elections. In many places, elected representatives, in the Panchayat Raj Institutions, were not allowed to function their duties by the non-SCs and STs, due to deep-rooted caste prejudices and practices. An attempt is made to give few examples relating to the atrocities on SC students and other atrocities on SCs.

Atrocities on Students

The Dalits have been barred from wearing footwear on the main roads or even pedal bi-cycle for long. On January 4, a group of caste Hindu youth accosted a Dalit student, Suresh, who was returning home wearing chappals and beat him up severely for allegedly 'violating the local norms' ('Reconciliation between Dalits, caste Hindus at Kavanampatti', *The Hindu,* January 20, 2005). A Dalit student's wrist was slit by his seniors at Sivakasi near Madurai allegedly because he was wearing a watch ('Dalit student's wrist slit 'for wearing watch' in Madurai', *Financial Express,* September 05, 2014).

A Dalit boy was stabbed multiple times on his face in Kumaram village near Madurai for talking to non-Dalit girl by the girl's father, ('Dalit boy stabbed for talking non-dalit girl', *Times of India*, 24-08-2013). Caste Hindus raised objection to admission of Dalit boys in government school. The reason cited was Dalit boys tease our girls and they also have stated that Dalit Boys have to study in Adi-Dravidar welfare school in the same village (A. Marx, 'Kalvikkoodangalil Theendamai', *Makkal Kalam*, July 2012, also in *The Hindu*, 12-06-2012). Several children of Dalit familes in Kurayur village in Madurai district have been allegedly barred from admission to the government school by upper caste people and forced them to join missionary-run government aided school on the outskirts of that village, ('TN school excludes dalit children', *Deccan Herald*, 31-08-2012).

The Hindu (15th November 2015, p. 9) reported that a Dalit from second standard was forced to remove the excreta after a classmate defecated in the municipal middle school, Ramapuram Puthur, Namakkal by the teacher in April 2015. The same newspaper on the same date reported that : 1. In April 2015, SC students were compelled clean the school toilets by the teachers of a government school in Tirunelveli; 2. In 2007, the Tamil teacher of a government middle school in Cuddalore district prevented Dalit students from participating in a dance programme during the Republic Day celebrations; 3. A Mathematics teacher in South Tamil Nadu classified Dalit students as 'minus' and caste Hindu students as 'plus'; 4. An anganwadi staff issued different coloured plates to students to differentiate between Dalit and non-Dalit children. The report further quoted Mr. A. Kathir, Executive Director, Madurai based NGO, Evidence that, "In southern districts of Ramanathapuram, Sivaganga, Viruthunagar, Tirunelveli and Tuticorin, teachers are known for discriminating Dalit students on campuses. These students were used as a tool by the non-Dalit teachers to get menial tasks done, faculty members from Madurai Kamaraj University, who are familiar with instances of caste discrimination".

Other Atrocities

'Way back in 1946, an ex–serviceman named Vadamalai belonging to the Dalit community was tied up to a tree and tortured. His offence was growing a moustache. Then, Dalit men were not allowed to grow moustaches, wear chappals or new dresses. Dalit women were not allowed to cover the upper part of their bodies'. (*Communalism Combat,* July 2000 Dalit Drishti). Tamil Nadu has a long history of brutal violence against dalits, starting from the Kilvenmani massacre of 1969 when 44 landless dalit labourers were burnt alive by upper caste landlord goons because they were demanding better wages. This trend has continued till recent times, with the massacre of the dalit panchayat president and others in Melavalavu in 1997.

In September 2002, at Kaundampatti in Dindigul district, a dalit agricultural worker was forced to drink urine for having lodged a complaint of trespass with the police against a person from a dominant caste. In May 2002, two dalits were forced to eat human excreta in Thinniyam village in Tiruchi district. Such atrocities continue even today, with dalits being severely punished and tortured if they violate the caste codes established by the dominant castes. About 20 years ago, upper caste Hindus in Uthapuram, Madurai district and Periyar Nagar, Coimbatore district, had built "untouchability walls" for prohibiting usage of common passage by dalits in areas inhabited by the upper castes, (Sampath, Progress and Struggle, Experiences of Struggles Against untouchability in Tamil Nadu, Pragothi, 15-05-2010).

Tamil Nadu Untouchability Eradication Front conducted a survey of 1,845 villages in Tamil Nadu, *listed over 80 forms of Untouchability practices in Tamil Nadu. Dalits were 1. Not allowed to speak on the cell phone in the presence of caste Hindus, 2. Not allowed to keep male dogs. (Why? They might breed with female dogs from upper caste neighbourhoods.) 3. Separate* *work timings under the National Rural Employment Guarantee Scheme. (anti-caste, June 12, 2010,* www.anti-caste.org*)*

Nagaraj documents the deprivations and discriminations in terms of livelihood issues: Dalits are denied access to land; their legitimate and traditional fishing rights in ponds are taken away; they are denied access to roads and often their living space, the Cheri on the outer fringes of the village, is encroached upon by the 'caste Hindus'; their access to clean drinking water is virtually non-existent and their wells are often poisoned during anti-Dalit riots; the majority of Dalits are agricultural labourers with low wages and long stretches of unemployment — the list appears to be unending. He also provides a long list of deprivation, (Nagaraj, K., Dalit situation in Tamil Nadu, K. Nagaraj, *The Hindu*, Book Review, August 23, 2005).

Classification of crimes

The NCRB broadly classifies crimes against persons belonging to Scheduled Castes into two major heads:

(1) Under the Indian Penal Code (IPC):

- (i) Murder
- (ii) Hurt
- (iii) Rape
- (iv) Kidnapping and abduction
- (v) Dacoity
- (vi) Robbery
- (vii) Arson
- (viii) Others (other classified IPC crimes).

(2) Under Special Laws (SLs)

- (i) The Protection of Civil Rights Acts, 1955
- (ii) The Scheduled Castes and the Scheduled Tribes (Prevention of Atrocities) Act, 1989.

Incidence Of Crimes

Data on various types of atrocities perpetrated on Scheduled Castes have been collected from National Crime Record Bureau for 13 years from 2000 to 2012 for this study. The rate of incidence of crimes committed against Scheduled Castes in Tamil Nadu and All India has fluctuated during the period of 13 years from 2000 to 2012. The year 2011 has witnessed a highest number of incidences of crime committed against persons belonging to the Scheduled Castes (Table 8.1).

Table 8.1: Incidence of crimes committed against Scheduled Castes during 2000-2012

Year	*Tamil Nadu*	*All India*
	Incidence	*Incidence*
2012	1647	33655
2011	4016	33719
2010	1631	32712
2009	1312	33594
2008	1618	33615
2007	1743	30031
2006	991	27070
2005	1206	26127
2004	1156	26887
2003	1495	26252
2002	2097	33507
2001	2336	33501
2000	1296	25455

Source: Crime in India, National Crime Record Bureau, Ministry of Home Affairs, Government of India (Various years).

Types of Crimes

Types of crimes committed viz. murder, rape, kidnapping and abduction, dacoity, robbery, arson, hurt, etc against the Scheduled Castes during 2000-2012 in Tamil Nadu is given in Table 8.2.

Murder

A total of 37 cases of murder of persons belonging to Scheduled Castes were reported in the year 2012 as compared to 12 cases in the year 2000, showing an increase of 208 per cent. The highest number of cases was reported in 2001 with 39 cases followed by 38 cases in 2001 in Tamil Nadu.

Rape

A total of 34 cases were reported in the year 2012 as compared to 17 cases in the year 2000, thus showing an increase of 100 per cent. The highest number of cases was reported in 2012 followed by 33 cases in 2002 in Tamil Nadu.

Kidnapping and Abduction

The incidences of kidnapping and abduction have increased by 400 per cent in the year 2012 over the year 2000 (from one case in 2000 to four cases in 2012). The highest number of cases was reported in 2001 with 16 cases followed by 10 cases in 2002.

Dacoity

Incidences of cases registered under dacoity was only one year that is five cases in 2001 and no such cases was reported in other years.

Robbery

A total of two cases were reported during the year 2012 as compared to one case in the year 2000, indicating an increase of 100 per cent in 2012 over 2000. The highest number of cases was reported in 2011 with four cases followed by three cases in 2010.

Arson

A total of five cases were reported in the year 2012 as compared to 18 cases in the year 2001 showing a decline of

Table 8.2: Types of crimes committed against Scheduled Castes during 2000-2012 in Tamil Nadu

Year	*Murder (Section 302 IPC)*	*Rape (Section 376 IPC)*	*Kidnapping and abduction (Section 363-369, 371-373 IPC)*	*Dacoity (Section 395-398 IPC)*	*Robbery (Section 392-394, 397, 398 IPC)*	*Orson (Section 435, 436, 438 IPC)*	*Hurt (Section 323-333, 335-338 IPC)*	*Protection of civil rights Act, 1955*	*SC/ST (Prevention of Atrocities) Act, 1989*	*Other offences*	*Total*
2012	37	34	4	0	2	5	191	9	1143	222	1647
2011	29	11	7	0	4	4	206	12	1011	107	1391
2010	20	11	0	0	3	4	149	3	1225	186	1631
2009	27	11	8	0	1	4	105	2	1047	107	1312
2008	31	17	2	0	1	8	147	3	1194	215	1618
2007	39	27	3	0	0	15	198	6	1064	391	1743
2006	26	21	3	0	0	7	136	84	468	246	991
2005	30	19	2	0	0	11	142	12	829	161	1206
2004	25	23	2	0	0	3	159	70	691	183	1156
2003	16	25	5	0	1	0	163	198	776	311	1495
2002	34	33	10	0	2	10	251	79	685	993	2097
2001	38	27	16	5	1	18	422	22	682	1105	2336
2000	12	17	1	0	1	0	654	-	-	-	-

Source: Crime in India 2012 Statistics, National Crime Record Bureau, Ministry of Home Affairs, Government of India.

278 per cent. The highest number of cases was reported in 2012 followed by 15 cases in 2007.

Hurt

A total of 191 cases were reported during the year 2012 as compared to 654 cases in the year 2000, thus showing a decline of 29.2 per cent. The highest number of crimes was reported in 2000 with 654 cases followed by 422 cases in 2001.

Protection of Civil Rights Act

A total of nine cases were reported during the year 2012 as compared to 22 cases in the year 2001, thus showing a steep decline in incidents of such cases in 2012 over 2001. The highest number of cases was reported in 2003 with 198 cases followed by 84 cases in 2006.

SC/ST (Prevention of Atrocities) Act

A total of 1,143 cases were reported during the year 2012 as compared to 682 cases in the year 2001, thus showing an increase of 167.6 per cent. The highest number of cases was reported in 2010 with 1225 cases followed by 1194 cases in 2008.

Disposal of Cases for Crimes By Police/Courts

The general trend of disposal of IPC and SLs (special laws) crimes by police and courts is shown in Tables 8.3 and 8.4. The average charge-sheeting rate for the crimes against Scheduled Castes stood at over 90 per cent crimes.

Disposal of cases by police as given in Table 8.3 shows that the pendency (percentage) rate has gone up from 10 per cent in 2001 to 33.6 per cent in 2012 for crimes against Scheduled Castes. On the contrary, the percentage of charge sheeting rate has gone down from 95.5 per cent in 2001 to

Table 8.3: Disposal of cases by police for crimes committed against Scheduled Castes during 2001-2012: Tamil Nadu

Year	Total number of cases for investigation including pending cases from previous year	Cases withdrawn by government	Investigation refused	Number of cases in which				Number of cases pending investigation at the end of the year	Pendancy (percentage)	Charge sheeting rate
				Investigation completed						
				Charge found false/mistake of fact or law etc.	Final report true submitted	Charge sheets submitted	Total			
2012	2416	0	0	313	112	1179	1604	812	33.6	91.3
2011	2048	1	0	318	75	885	1278	769	37.5	92.2
2010	2092	0	0	299	116	1020	1435	657	31.4	89.8
2009	1837	1	0	476	83	816	1375	461	25.1	90.8
2008	2079	0	5	516	65	968	1549	525	25.3	93.7
2007	1959	3	30	435	85	945	1465	461	23.5	91.7
2006	1227	0	4	184	46	777	1007	216	17.6	94.4
2005	1393	0	4	307	39	812	1158	236	16.9	95.4
2004	1727	4	18	281	429	803	1513	192	11.1	65.2
2003	2080	0	9	293	67	1140	1500	571	27.5	94.4
2002	2394	3	16	532	57	1470	2059	316	13.2	96.3
2001	2950	6	45	596	91	1925	2612	297	10.0	95.5

Source: Crime in India 2012 Statistics, National Crime Record Bureau, Ministry of Home Affairs, Government of India.

91.3 per cent in 2012. The average charge sheeting and the percentage of pendency vary over the years. The charge sheets found false/mistake of facts has come down but remains nearly one-fourth of the total number of cases.

As regards the disposal of cases by courts for crimes committed against Scheduled Castes clearly indicates that the rate of pendency (percentage) has gone up from 68.7 per cent in 2001 to 83.3 per cent in 2012 for crimes against Scheduled Castes. On the contrary, the percentage of conviction rate has gone down from 38.9 per cent in 2001 to 17.7 per cent in 2012. Data given in Tables 8.3 and 8.4 abundantly make it clear that the performance in disposal of cases for crimes against the SCs was not satisfactory.

Disposal of Persons Arrested by Police and Court

Disposal of persons arrested for committing crime against Scheduled Castes by police and court as given in Tables 8.5 and 8.6 shows that there was a poor performance in discharging cases, as the rate of pendency has gone up during 2000-2012.

Atrocities by Districts

The incidence and rate of crimes committed against SCs as given in Table 8.7 shows that there was a fluctuation in the incidence of crimes by districts. The incidence of cases reported was high in Madurai and Tirunelveli districts. The data further show that the rate cognisable crime was very low in all districts in Tamil Nadu. The incidence of total crimes to cognizable clearly indicates that the rate of cognizable crime was low in The Nilgiris, Tiruvallur, Kanchipuram and Chennai districts. There appears to no relation between percentage of population and the rate of cognisable crimes in Tamil Nadu.

Table 8.4: Disposal of cases by courts for crimes committed against Scheduled Castes during 2001-2012: Tamil Nadu

Year	*Total number of cases for trial including pending cases from previous year*	*Cases withdrawn by government*	*Compounded or withdrawn*	*Number of cases in which trial completed*			*Pending trial at the end of the year*	*Pendency (percentage)*	*Conviction rate*
				Convicted	*Acquitted or discharged*	*Total*			
2012	4039	0	0	119	555	674	3365	83.3	17.7
2011	3659	0	0	293	506	799	2860	78.2	36.7
2010	3568	0	30	187	577	764	2774	77.7	24.5
2009	3366	0	1	102	715	817	2548	75.7	12.5
2008	3394	0	14	140	690	830	2550	75.1	16.9
2007	3298	0	0	140	732	872	2426	73.6	16.1
2006	3081	0	0	176	552	728	2353	76.4	24.2
2005	3633	0	12	332	985	1317	2304	63.4	25.2
2004	4707	0	340	539	1007	1546	2821	59.9	34.9
2003	5335	1	7	403	1021	1424	3904	73.2	28.3
2002	5682	3	26	671	1334	2005	3651	64.3	33.5
2001	6136	14	50	727	1144	1871	4215	68.7	38.9

Source: Crime in India 2012 Statistics, National Crime Record Bureau, Ministry of Home Affairs, Government of India.

Table 8.5: Disposal by police, of persons arrested for committing crime against Scheduled Castes during 2000-2012: Tamil Nadu

Year	*Total number of persons under arrest including those from previous year*	*Number of*			*Pendency (percentage)*
		Persons released before trial	*Persons charge sheeted*	*Persons under investigation at the end of the year*	
2012	4717	690	2706	1321	28.0
2011	4447	202	2455	1790	40.3
2010	3750	102	2630	1018	27.1
2009	3168	182	2219	767	24.2
2008	2947	94	2031	822	27.9
2007	3017	88	2108	821	27.2
2006	2385	161	1795	429	18.0
2005	2569	134	2076	359	14.0
2004	2487	87	2026	374	15.0
2003	3277	90	2869	318	9.7
2002	4191	598	3012	581	13.9
2001	5556	704	4120	732	13.2

Source: Crime in India 2012 Statistics, National Crime Record Bureau, Ministry of Home Affairs, Government of India.

Table 8.6: Disposal by court, of persons arrested for committing crime against Scheduled Castes during 2000-2012: Tamil Nadu

Year	*Total number of persons under trial including those from previous year*	*Total number of persons whose*			*Number of persons convicted*	*Pendency (percentage)*
		Cases compounded or withdrawn	*Trial completed*	*Trial remained pending at the end of the year*		
2012	9025	0	1497	7528	275	83.4
2011	8193	0	1874	6319	419	77.1
2010	7831	30	2063	5738	364	73.3
2009	7247	0	2046	5201	310	71.8
2008	7252	28	2196	5028	311	69.3
2007	7448	0	2227	5221	327	70.1
2006	7304	0	1964	5340	358	73.1
2005	8050	30	2509	5511	474	68.5
2004	9518	67	3485	5966	1112	62.7
2003	10532	18	3022	7492	560	71.1
2002	11324	41	3378	7905	1084	69.8
2001	11386	194	2880	8312	891	73.0

Source: Crime in India 2012 Statistics, National Crime Record Bureau, Ministry of Home Affairs, Government of India.

Table 8.7: Incidence and Rate of Crimes Committed against Scheduled Castes during 2014

S.No	*District/City*	*Incidence*	*Percentage Contribution to State Total*	*Population of SCs (in Lakhs)*	*Rate of Total Cognizable Crimes*	*Rank as Per Rate of Total Cognizable Crimes*	*Rank as Percentage Share*
1	Ariyalur	13	0.8	1.71	7.6	24	30
2	Chennai	16	1.0	6.74	2.4	35	28
3	Coimbatore	36	2.3	3.32	10.8	16	19
4	Coimbatore City	9	0.6	2.17	4.1	33	34
5	Cuddalore	53	3.4	7.55	7.0	26	7
6	Dharmapuri	24	1.6	2.29	10.5	17	25
7	Dindigul	45	2.9	4.42	10.2	18	14
8	Erode	49	3.2	3.72	13.2	12	12
9	Kanchipuram	25	1.6	10.47	2.4	34	23
10	Kanyakumari	11	0.7	0.79	14.0	11	33
11	Karur	30	1.9	2.29	13.1	13	22
12	Krishnagiri	13	0.8	2.87	4.5	31	30
13	Madurai	195	12.6	2.07	94.3	1	1
14	Madurai City	13	0.8	1.92	6.8	27	30
15	Nagapattinam	22	1.4	5.00	4.4	32	26
16	Namakkal	33	2.1	3.38	9.8	20	20
17	Nilgiris	4	0.3	2.40	1.7	38	37

contd...

S.No	District/City	Incidence	Percentage Contribution to State Total	Population of SCs (in Lakhs)	Rate of Total Cognizable Crimes	Rank as Per Rate of Total Cognizable Crimes	Rank as Percentage Share
18	Perambalur	18	1.2	1.78	10.1	19	27
19	Pudukkotai	52	3.4	2.89	18.0	7	9
20	Ramanathapuram	44	2.8	2.55	17.3	8	15
21	Railway Chennai	0	0.0	0.00	0.0	39	39
22	Railway Trichy	0	0.0	0.00	0.0	39	39
23	Salem	25	1.6	4.22	5.9	29	23
24	Salem City	7	0.5	1.52	4.6	30	35
25	Sivagangai	72	4.7	2.29	31.4	4	4
26	Thanjavur	58	3.8	4.53	12.8	14	5
27	Theni	50	3.2	2.52	19.9	6	11
28	Thirunelveli	173	11.2	4.75	36.4	2	2
29	Thirunelveli City	31	2.0	0.92	33.7	3	21
30	Thiruvallur	16	1.0	8.49	1.9	37	28
31	Thiruvannamalai	52	3.4	5.52	9.4	22	9
32	Thiruvarur	39	2.5	4.29	9.1	23	17
33	Thoothukudi	53	3.4	3.34	15.9	9	7
34	Tiruppur	37	2.4	3.83	9.7	21	18

contd...

S.No	District/City	Incidence	Percentage Contribution to State Total	Population of SCs (in Lakhs)	Rate of Total Cognizable Crimes	Rank as Per Rate of Total Cognizable Crimes	Rank as Percentage Share
35	Tiruppur City	5	0.3	0.24	20.8	5	36
36	Trichy	42	2.7	2.92	14.4	10	16
37	Trichy City	4	0.3	1.76	2.3	36	37
38	Vellore	56	3.6	8.43	6.6	28	6
39	Villupuram	75	4.9	9.92	7.6	25	3
40	Virudhunagar	46	3.0	3.85	11.9	15	13
Total		**1546**	**100**	**143.67**	**10.8**		

Source: Crime Review –Tamil Nadu 2014, State Crime Record Bureau, Tamil Nadu.

Incidence, Rate and Percentage Contribution to State Total Crimes

The incidence, rate and percentage contribution to total state crimes as given in Table 8.8 clearly indicate that the percentage contribution to total crimes was high in Madurai and Tirunelveli districts in Tamil Nadu. Cases under protection of Civil Rights Act were reported only in Dharmapuri district. While the cases registered under the SC/ST Prevention of Atrocities Act were reported in all districts except in Ramanathapuram and Villupuram district in Tamil Nadu. It is to be noted that the highest percentage of atrocities cases were reported in Tirunelveli district. As regards the other offences, Madurai district tops the list with 35 per cent in Tamil Nadu.

Disposal of Cases by Police for Crimes

Disposal of cases by police for crimes committed against the SCs as given in Tables 8.9 and 8.9A clearly indicate that out of 2430 total number of cases for investigation including pending cases a little over 62 per cent (1509 cases) were under the category of SC/ST Prevention of Atrocities Act, 1989. The data further show that charge sheet found false, final report true submitted, cases pending investigation were high in Madurai and Tirunelveli districts. It is to be noted that the cases of atrocities reported was high in both the Madurai and Tirunelveli districts.

The data presented in Table 8.9B clearly indicate that charge sheeting by police was 100 per cent in crimes, such as, rape, kidnapping and abduction, robbery, arson, hurt and PCR Act. The charge sheeting rate was only 92 per cent in crimes relating to SC/ST Prevention of Atrocities Act, 1989. This indicates the unwillingness on the part of the police or problems associated with this SC/ST Act.

Disposal of Cases by Courts For Crimes

Disposal of cases by courts for crimes committed against SCs during 2014 is given in Tables 8.10, 8.10A and 8.10B. Out of 5089 cases of trial cases, (1041) 20.5 per cent of the cases ended in acquittal and only (89) 1.7 per cent of the cases ended in convicted. Of the total 89 cases of convicted, a little over 48 per cent of the cases were from the SC/ST Prevention of Atrocities Act, 1989. It is to be noted that nearly 78 per cent (3957 cases) were pending for trial at the end of the year (Tables 8.10 and 8.10B).

An analysis of the data by districts clearly indicates that total number of cases including pending cases from previous year was high in Madurai, Tirunelveli and Sivaganga districts. Out of 89 cases ended in conviction, Kanchipuram district tops the list with 23 cases followed by Theni district with 17 cases (Table 8.10A).

Disposal of Persons Arrested by Police

Disposal of persons arrested by police for committing crimes against SCs as given in Table 8.11 clearly show that out of 5392 persons under arrest including those from previous year, 33 per cent (2874 cases) from the SC/ST Prevention of Atrocities Act, 1989. Out of 2874 cases, 64.5 per cent of the persons charge sheeted and 34.6 per cent of the persons were under investigation at the end of the year.

Analysis of data on disposal by police on persons arrested by districts (Table 8.11A) clearly show that number of persons arrested by police was high in Cuddalore, Madurai and Tirunelveli districts and the number of persons charge sheeted were also high in these three districts. These three districts are known for caste sensitive districts in Tamil Nadu.

DISPOSAL OF PERSONS ARRESTED BY COURTS

Disposal of persons arrested by courts for committing crimes against SCs as given in Table 8.12 clearly indicate

Table 8.8: Incidence (i), rate I and percentage contribution to state total of crimes (p) committed against Scheduled Castes during 2014

S.No	Districts/city	Murder			Rape			Kidnapping & abduction			Dacoity		
		I	R	P	I	R	P	I	R	P	I	R	P
1	Ariyalur	0	0.00	0.00	0	0.00	0.00	0	0.00	0.00	0	0.00	--
2	Chennai	0	0.00	0.00	0	0.00	0.00	0	0.00	0.00	0	0.00	--
3	Coimbatore	0	0.00	0.00	0	0.00	0.00	0	0.00	0.00	0	0.00	--
4	Coimbatore City	0	0.00	0.00	0	0.00	0.00	0	0.00	0.00	0	0.00	--
5	Cuddalore	4	0.53	8.51	1	0.13	2.86	0	0.00	0.00	0	0.00	--
6	Dharmapuri	0	0.00	0.00	0	0.00	0.00	0	0.00	0.00	0	0.00	--
7	Dindigul	2	0.45	4.26	6	1.36	17.14	0	0.00	0.00	0	0.00	--
8	Erode	0	0.00	0.00	0	0.00	0.00	0	0.00	0.00	0	0.00	--
9	Kanchipuram	0	0.00	0.00	0	0.00	0.00	0	0.00	0.00	0	0.00	--
10	Kanyakumari	2	2.54	4.26	0	0.00	0.00	0	0.00	0.00	0	0.00	--
11	Karur	1	0.44	2.13	1	0.44	2.86	0	0.00	0.00	0	0.00	--
12	Krishnagiri	0	0.00	0.00	0	0.00	0.00	0	0.00	0.00	0	0.00	--
13	Madurai	3	1.45	6.38	4	1.93	11.43	4	1.93	57.14	0	0.00	--
14	Madurai City	1	0.52	2.13	0	0.00	0.00	0	0.00	0.00	0	0.00	--
15	Nagapattinam	0	0.00	0.00	0	0.00	0.00	0	0.00	0.00	0	0.00	--
16	Namakkal	1	0.30	2.13	0	0.00	0.00	0	0.00	0.00	0	0.00	--

contd...

S.No	Districts/city	Murder			Rape			Kidnapping & abduction			Dacoity		
		I	R	P	I	R	P	I	R	P	I	R	P
17	Nilgiris	0	0.00	0.00	0	0.00	0.00	0	0.00	0.00	0	0.00	--
18	Perambalur	1	0.56	2.13	0	0.00	0.00	0	0.00	0.00	0	0.00	--
19	Pudukkotai	0	0.00	0.00	1	0.35	2.86	0	0.00	0.00	0	0.00	--
20	Ramanathapuram	2	0.79	4.26	1	0.39	2.86	0	0.00	0.00	0	0.00	--
21	Railway Chennai	0	--	0.00	0	--	0.00	0	--	--	0	--	--
22	Railway Trichy	0	--	0.00	0	--	0.00	0	--	--	0	--	--
23	Salem	2	0.47	4.26	2	0.47	5.71	1	0.24	14.29	0	0.00	--
24	Salem City	1	0.66	2.13	1	0.66	2.86	0	0.00	0.00	0	0.00	--
25	Sivagangai	0	0.00	0.00	0	0.00	0.00	0	0.00	0.00	0	0.00	--
26	Thanjavur	0	0.00	0.00	1	0.22	2.86	0	0.00	0.00	0	0.00	--
27	Theni	0	0.00	0.00	0	0.00	0.00	0	0.00	0.00	0	0.00	--
28	Thirunelveli	11	2.32	23.40	4	0.84	11.43	1	0.21	14.29	0	0.00	--
29	Thirunelveli City	2	2.17	4.26	0	0.00	0.00	0	0.00	0.00	0	0.00	--
30	Thiruvallur	0	0.00	0.00	0	0.00	0.00	0	0.00	0.00	0	0.00	--
31	Thiruvannamalai	0	0.00	0.00	0	0.00	0.00	0	0.00	0.00	0	0.00	--
32	Thiruvarur	2	0.47	4.26	0	0.00	0.00	0	0.00	0.00	0	0.00	--

contd...

S.No	Districts/city	Murder			Rape			Kidnapping & abduction			Dacoity		
		I	*R*	*P*	*I*	*R*	*P*	*I*	*R*	*P*	*I*	*R*	*P*
33	Thoothukudi	7	2.10	14.89	3	0.90	8.57	0	0.00	0.00	0	0.00	--
34	Tiruppur	0	0.00	0.00	0	0.00	0.00	0	0.00	0.00	0	0.00	--
35	Tiruppur City	0	0.00	0.00	0	0.00	0.00	0	0.00	0.00	0	0.00	--
36	Trichy	1	0.34	2.13	0	0.00	0.00	0	0.00	0.00	0	0.00	--
37	Trichy City	0	0.00	0.00	0	0.00	0.00	0	0.00	0.00	0	0.00	--
38	Vellore	2	0.24	4.26	3	0.36	8.57	0	0.00	0.00	0	0.00	--
39	Villupuram	1	0.10	2.13	5	0.50	14.29	1	0.10	14.29	0	0.00	--
40	Virudhunagar	1	0.26	2.13	2	0.52	5.71	0	0.00	0.00	0	0.00	--
	Total	**47**	**0.33**	**100**	**35**	**0.24**	**100**	**7**	**0.05**	**100**	**0**	**0.00**	**--**

Source: Crime Review –Tamil Nadu 2014, State Crime Record Bureau, Tamil Nadu.

Table 8.8: (Continued)

S.No	Districts/city	Robbery			Arson			Hurt			Prot. of civil rights Act			SC/ST prev. of atrocities Act			Other offences			Total		
		I	R	P	I	R	P	I	R	P	I	R	P	I	R	P	I	R	P	I	R	P
1	Ariyalur	0	0.00	0.00	0	0.00	0.00	0	0.00	0.00	0	0.00	0.00	13	7.60	1.43	0	0.00	0.00	13	7.60	0.84
2	Chennai	0	0.00	0.00	0	0.00	0.00	0	0.00	0.00	0	0.00	0.00	16	2.37	1.77	0	0.00	0.00	16	2.37	1.03
3	Coimbatore	0	0.00	0.00	0	0.00	0.00	0	0.00	0.00	0	0.00	0.00	29	8.73	3.20	7	2.11	1.36	36	10.84	2.33
4	Coimbatore City	0	0.00	0.00	0	0.00	0.00	0	0.00	0.00	0	0.00	0.00	9	4.14	0.99	0	0.00	0.00	9	4.14	0.58
5	Cuddalore	0	0.00	0.00	2	0.26	13.33	0	0.00	0.00	0	0.00	0.00	0	0.00	0.00	46	6.09	8.93	53	7.02	3.43
6	Dharmapuri	0	0.00	0.00	0	0.00	0.00	0	0.00	0.00	8	3.49	100.00	16	6.98	1.77	0	0.00	0.00	24	10.47	1.55
7	Dindigul	0	0.00	0.00	0	0.00	0.00	0	0.00	0.00	0	0.00	0.00	37	8.37	4.08	0	0.00	0.00	45	10.18	2.91
8	Erode	0	0.00	0.00	0	0.00	0.00	0	0.00	0.00	0	0.00	0.00	25	6.72	2.76	24	6.45	4.66	49	13.17	3.17
9	Kanchipuram	0	0.00	0.00	0	0.00	0.00	0	0.00	0.00	0	0.00	0.00	25	2.39	2.76	0	0.00	0.00	25	2.39	1.62
10	Kanyakumari	0	0.00	0.00	0	0.00	0.00	0	0.00	0.00	0	0.00	0.00	9	11.44	0.99	0	0.00	0.00	11	13.98	0.71
11	Karur	0	0.00	0.00	0	0.00	0.00	0	0.00	0.00	0	0.00	0.00	25	10.93	2.76	3	1.31	0.58	30	13.11	1.94
12	Krishnagiri	0	0.00	0.00	0	0.00	0.00	0	0.00	0.00	0	0.00	0.00	13	4.52	1.43	0	0.00	0.00	13	4.52	0.84
13	Madurai	3	1.45	42.86	1	0.48	6.67	0	0.00	0.00	0	0.00	0.00	2	0.97	0.22	178	86.04	34.56	195	94.25	12.61
14	Madurai City	0	0.00	0.00	0	0.00	0.00	0	0.00	0.00	0	0.00	0.00	0	0.00	0.00	12	6.26	2.33	13	6.78	0.84
15	Nagapattinam	0	0.00	0.00	0	0.00	0.00	0	0.00	0.00	0	0.00	0.00	22	4.40	2.43	0	0.00	0.00	22	4.40	1.42

contd...

S.No	Districts/city	Robbery			Arson			Hurt			Prot. of civil rights Act			SC/ST prev. of atrocities Act			Other offences			Total		
		I	R	P	I	R	P	I	R	P	I	R	P	I	R	P	I	R	P	I	R	P
16	Namakkal	0	0.00	0.00	0	0.00	0.00	0	0.00	0.00	0	0.00	0.00	31	9.17	3.42	1	0.30	0.19	33	9.76	2.13
17	Nilgiris	0	0.00	0.00	0	0.00	0.00	0	0.00	0.00	0	0.00	0.00	4	1.67	0.44	0	0.00	0.00	4	1.67	0.26
18	Perambalur	0	0.00	0.00	0	0.00	0.00	0	0.00	0.00	0	0.00	0.00	17	9.54	1.88	0	0.00	0.00	18	10.10	1.16
19	Pudukkotai	0	0.00	0.00	0	0.00	0.00	0	0.00	0.00	0	0.00	0.00	51	17.63	5.63	0	0.00	0.00	52	17.98	3.36
20	Ramanathapuram	1	0.39	14.29	1	0.39	6.67	0	0.00	0.00	0	0.00	0.00	0	0	0.00	39	15.31	7.57	44	17.28	2.85
21	Railway Chennai	0	–	0.00	0	–	0.00	0	–	0.00	0	–	0.00	0	–	0.00	0	–	0.00	0	–	0.00
22	Railway Trichy	0	–	0.00	0	–	0.00	0	–	0.00	0	–	0.00	0	–	0.00	0	–	0.00	0	–	0.00
23	Salem	0	0.00	0.00	0	0.00	0.00	2	1.32	33.33	0	0.00	0.00	0	0.00	0.00	20	4.74	3.88	25	5.92	1.62
24	Salem City	0	0.00	0.00	0	0.00	0.00	0	0.00	0.00	0	0.00	0.00	1	0.66	0.11	2	1.32	0.39	7	4.62	0.45
25	Sivagangai	3	1.31	42.86	1	0.44	6.67	0	0.00	0.00	0	0.00	0.00	48	20.94	5.30	20	8.73	3.88	72	31.42	4.66
26	Thanjavur	0	0.00	0.00	0	0.00	0.00	0	0.00	0.00	0	0.00	0.00	52	11.48	5.74	5	1.10	0.97	58	12.81	3.75
27	Theni	0	0.00	0.00	0	0.00	0.00	0	0.00	0.00	0	0.00	0.00	50	19.87	5.52	0	0.00	0.00	50	19.87	3.23
28	Thirunelveli	0	0.00	0.00	7	1.47	46.67	1	0.21	16.67	0	0.00	0.00	118	24.84	13.02	31	6.52	6.02	173	36.41	11.19
29	Thirunelveli City	0	0.00	0.00	0	0.00	0.00	0	0.00	0.00	0	0.00	0.00	17	18.46	1.88	12	13.03	2.33	31	33.66	2.01
30	Thiruvallur	0	0.00	0.00	0	0.00	0.00	0	0.00	0.00	0	0.00	0.00	16	1.88	1.77	0	0.00	0.00	16	1.88	1.03

contd...

S.No	Districts/city	Robbery			Arson			Hurt			Prot. of civil rights Act			SC/ST prev. of atrocities Act			Other offences			Total		
		I	R	P	I	R	P	I	R	P	I	R	P	I	R	P	I	R	P	I	R	P
31	Thiruvannamalai	0	0.00	0.00	0	0.00	0.00	0	0.00	0.00	0	0.00	0.00	52	9.42	5.74	0	0.00	0.00	52	9.42	3.36
32	Thiruvarur	0	0.00	0.00	0	0.00	0.00	0	0.00	0.00	0	0.00	0.00	37	8.63	4.08	0	0.00	0.00	39	9.10	2.52
33	Thoothukudi	0	0.00	0.00	0	0.00	0.00	0	0.00	0.00	0	0.00	0.00	35	10.48	3.86	8	2.40	1.55	53	15.87	3.43
34	Tiruppur	0	0.00	0.00	0	0.00	0.00	0	0.00	0.00	0	0.00	0.00	37	9.66	4.08	0	0.00	0.00	37	9.66	2.39
35	Tiruppur City	0	0.00	0.00	0	0.00	0.00	0	0.00	0.00	0	0.00	0.00	5	20.83	0.55	0	0.00	0.00	5	20.83	0.32
36	Trichy	0	0.00	0.00	0	0.00	0.00	0	0.00	0.00	0	0.00	0.00	8	2.74	0.88	33	11.29	6.41	42	14.37	2.72
37	Trichy City	0	0.00	0.00	0	0.00	0.00	0	0.00	0.00	0	0.00	0.00	0	0.00	0.00	4	2.27	0.78	4	2.27	0.26
38	Vellore	0	0.00	0.00	0	0.00	0.00	0	0.00	0.00	0	0.00	0.00	51	6.05	5.63	0	0.00	0.00	56	6.64	3.62
39	Villupuram	0	0.00	0.00	3	0.30	20.00	3	0.30	50.00	0	0.00	0.00	0	0.00	0.00	62	6.25	12.04	75	7.56	4.85
40	Virudhunagar	0	0.00	0.00	0	0.00	0.00	0	0.00	0.00	0	0.00	0.00	35	9.08	3.86	8	2.08	1.55	46	11.93	2.98
	Total	**7**	**0.05**	**100**	**15**	**0.10**	**100**	**6**	**0.04**	**100**	**8**	**0.06**	**100**	**906**	**6.31**	**100**	**515**	**3.58**	**100**	**1546**	**10.76**	**100**

Source: Crime Review –Tamil Nadu 2014, State Crime Record Bureau, Tamil Nadu.

Table 8.9: Disposal of cases by police for crimes committed against Scheduled Castes

	Crime head	Total no. of cases for investigation including pending cases from previous year	Cases with-drawn by govt.	Investigation refused	No. of cases in which investigation was completed				No. of cases pending investigation at the ending of the year
					Charge found false / mistake of fact or law etc.	Final report true submitted	Charge sheets submitted	Total	
1	Murder	63	0	0	0	1	43	44	19
2	Rape	61	0	0	0	0	45	45	16
3	Kidnapping and abduction	8	0	0	0	0	4	4	4
4	Dacoity	0	0	0	0	0	0	0	0
5	Robbery	1	0	0	0	0	1	1	0
6	Arson	19	0	0	2	0	13	15	4
7	Hurt	24	0	0	0	0	12	12	12
8	PCR Act	12	0	0	0	0	8	8	4
9	SC/ST prev. of atrocities Act	1509	0	0	207	66	759	1032	477
10	Other crime	733	0	0	90	44	422	556	177
	Total	**2430**	**0**	**0**	**299**	**111**	**1307**	**1717**	**713**

Source: Crime Review –Tamil Nadu 2014, State Crime Record Bureau, Tamil Nadu.

Table 8.9A: Disposal of cases by police for crimes committed against Scheduled Castes during 2014 (districts/city-wise)

	Districts/city	Total no. of cases for investigation including pending cases from previous year	Cases with-drawn by govt.	Investigation refused	No. of cases in which investigation was completed				No. of cases pending investigation at the ending of the year	Pendency percentage	Percentage of pendency to state total	Charge sheeting rate ((col.8)/(col7+8)x 100)
					Charge found false / mistake of fact or law etc.	Final report true submitted	Charge sheets submitted	Total				
1	Ariyalur	13	0	0	3	0	9	12	1	7.7	0.1	100.0
2	Chennai	42	0	0	0	4	9	13	29	69.0	4.1	69.2
3	Coimbatore	52	0	0	10	2	21	33	19	36.5	2.7	91.3
4	Coimbatore City	14	0	0	3	0	1	4	10	71.4	1.4	100.0
5	Cuddalore	65	0	0	0	5	46	51	14	21.5	2.0	90.0
6	Dharmapuri	65	0	0	24	0	23	47	18	27.7	2.5	100.0
7	Dindigul	71	0	0	15	0	48	63	8	11.3	1.1	100.0
8	Erode	62	0	0	7	4	37	48	14	22.6	2.0	90.0
9	Kanchipuram	40	0	0	0	0	25	25	15	37.5	2.1	100.0
10	Kanyakumari	12	0	0	4	0	3	7	5	41.7	0.7	100.0
11	Karur	44	0	0	0	8	10	18	26	59.1	3.6	55.6

	Districts/city	Total no. of cases for investigation including pending cases from previous year	Cases with-drawn by govt.	Investig-ation refused	No. of cases in which investigation was completed				No. of cases pending investi-gation at the ending of the year	Pende-ncy perce-ntage	Percen-tage of pend-ency to state total	Charge sheeting rate ((col.8)/(col7+8)x 100)
					Charge found false / mistake of fact or law etc.	Final report true subm-itted	Charge sheets subm-itted	Total				
12	Krishnagiri	15	0	0	3	0	11	14	1	6.7	0.1	100.0
13	Madurai	372	0	0	21	33	157	211	161	43.3	22.6	82.6
14	Madurai Ciry	27	0	0	4	0	14	18	9	33.3	1.3	100.0
15	Nagapattinam	31	0	0	0	0	26	26	5	16.1	0.7	100.0
16	Namakkal	49	0	0	14	0	29	43	6	12.2	0.8	100.0
17	Nilgiris	5	0	0	1	0	3	4	1	20.0	0.1	100.0
18	Perambalur	22	0	0	1	0	17	18	4	18.2	0.6	100.0
19	Pudukkotai	73	0	0	22	0	44	66	7	9.6	1.0	100.0
20	Ramanathapuram	71	0	0	9	5	41	55	16	22.5	2.2	89.1
21	Railway Chennai	0	0	0	0	0	0	0	0	--	0.0	--

contd...

	Districts/city	Total no. of cases for investigation including pending cases from previous year	Cases with-drawn by govt.	Investig-ation refused	No. of cases in which investigation was completed				No. of cases pending investi-gation at the ending of the year	Pende-ncy perce-ntage	Percen-tage of pend-ency to state total	Charge sheeting rate ((col.8)/(col7+8)x 100)
					Charge found false / mistake of fact or law etc.	Final report true subm-itted	Charge sheets subm-itted	Total				
22	Railway Trichy	0	0	0	0	0	0	0	0	--	0.0	--
23	Salem	27	0	0	0	0	22	22	5	18.5	0.7	100.0
24	Salem City	14	0	0	0	1	1	2	12	85.7	1.7	50.0
25	Sivagangai	84	0	0	11	0	54	65	19	22.6	2.7	100.0
26	Thanjavur	96	0	0	0	0	62	62	34	35.4	4.8	100.0
27	Theni	65	0	0	1	13	40	54	11	16.9	1.5	75.5
28	Thirunelveli	271	0	0	25	21	113	159	112	41.3	15.7	84.3
29	Thirunelveli City	47	0	0	6	0	35	41	6	12.8	0.8	100.0
30	Thiruvallur	24	0	0	1	2	11	14	10	41.7	1.4	84.6
31	Thiruvannamalai	64	0	0	20	1	31	52	12	18.8	1.7	96.9

contd...

	Districts/city	Total no. of cases for investigation including pending cases from previous year	Cases with-drawn by govt.	Investig-ation refused	No. of cases in which investigation was completed				No. of cases pending investi-gation at the ending of the year	Pende-ncy perce-ntage	Percen-tage of pend-ency to state total	Charge sheeting rate ((col.8)/ (col7+8)x 100)
					Charge found false / mistake of fact or law etc.	Final report true subm-itted	Charge sheets subm-itted	Total				
32	Thiruvarur	43	0	0	5	1	34		3			
33	Thoothukudi	62	0	0	11	0	41	52	10	16.1	1.4	100.0
34	Tiruppur	54	0	0	17	0	32	49	5	9.3	0.7	100.0
35	Tiruppur City	21	0	0	0	0	16	16	5	23.8	0.7	100.0
36	Trichy	55	0	0	0	10	29	39	16	29.1	2.2	74.4
37	Trichy City	10	0	0	1	1	1	3	7	70.0	1.0	50.0
38	Vellore	120	0	0	13	0	84	97	23	19.2	3.2	100.0
39	Villupuram	116	0	0	36	0	47	83	33	28.4	4.6	100.0
40	Virudhunagar	112	0	0	11	0	80	91	21	18.8	2.9	100.0
	Total	**2430**	**0**	**0**	**299**	**111**	**1307**	**1677**	**713**	**29.3416**	**100.0**	**92.2**

Source: Crime Review –Tamil Nadu 2014, State Crime Record Bureau, Tamil Nadu.

Table 8.9B: Percentage disposal of cases by police for crimes committed against Scheduled Castes during 2014

	Crime head	Cases withdrawn by govt.	Investigation refused	No. of cases in which investigation was completed				No. of cases pending investigation at the ending of the year	Charge sheeting rate ((col.8)/(col7+8)x100)
				Charge found false / mistake of fact or law etc.	Final report true submitted	Charge sheets submitted	Total		
1	MURDER	0.0	0.0	0.0	1.6	68.3	69.8	30.2	97.7
2	RAPE	0.0	0.0	0.0	0.0	73.8	73.8	26.2	100.0
3	KIDNAPPING & ABDUCTION	0.0	0.0	0.0	0.0	50.0	50.0	50.0	100.0
4	DACOITY	0.0	0.0	0.0	0.0	0.0	0.0	0.0	--
5	ROBBERY	0.0	0.0	0.0	0.0	5.3	5.3	0.0	100.0
6	ARSON	0.0	0.0	10.5	0.0	68.4	78.9	21.1	100.0
7	HURT	0.0	0.0	0.0	0.0	50.0	50.0	50.0	100.0
8	PCR ACT	0.0	0.0	0.0	0.0	66.7	66.7	33.3	100.0
9	SC/ST PREV. OF ATROCITIES ACT	0.0	0.0	13.7	4.4	50.3	68.4	31.6	92.0
10	OTHER CRIME	0.0	0.0	12.3	6.0	57.6	75.9	24.1	90.6
	TOTAL	**0.0**	**0.0**	**12.3**	**4.6**	**53.8**	**70.7**	**29.3**	**92.2**

Source: Crime Review –Tamil Nadu 2014, State Crime Record Bureau, Tamil Nadu.

Table 8.10: Disposal of cases by courts for crimes committed against Scheduled Castes during 2014

	Crime head	Total no. of cases for investigation including pending cases from previous year	Cases with-drawn by govt.	No. of cases in which investigation was completed				Pending trial
				Compounded or withdrawn	Trials completed			
					Convicted	Acquitted or discharged	Total	
1	MURDER	140	0	0	2	10	12	128
2	RAPE	125	0	0	5	14	19	106
3	KIDNAPPING & ABDUCTION	12	0	0	0	3	3	9
4	DACOITY	1	0	0	0	0	0	1
5	ROBBERY	17	0	0	0	3	3	14
6	ARSON	27	0	0	1	5	6	21
7	HURT	66	0	0	0	20	20	46
8	PCR ACT	9	0	0	3	0	3	6
9	SC/ST PREV. OF ATROCITIES ACT	3451	0	2	43	630	673	2776
10	OTHER CRIME	1241	0	0	35	356	391	850
	TOTAL	**5089**	**0**	**2**	**89**	**1041**	**1130**	**3957**

Source: Crime Review –Tamil Nadu 2014, State Crime Record Bureau, Tamil Nadu.

Table 8.10A: Disposal of cases by courts for crimes committed against Scheduled Castes during 2014 (district/city-wise)

	Districts/city	Total no. of cases for investigation including pending cases from previous year	Cases with-drawn by govt.	No. of cases in which investigation was completed				Pending trial at the end of the year	Pendency perce-ntage	Perce-ntage of pendency to state total	Conviction rate ((col.6) / (col 8)x100)
				Compounded or withdrawn	Trials completed						
					Convicted	Acquitted or discharged	Total				
1	Ariyalur	43	0	0	0	17	17	26	60.5	0.7	0.0
2	Chennai	23	0	0	0	4	4	19	82.6	0.5	0.0
3	Coimbatore	76	0	0	0	31	31	45	59.2	1.1	0.0
4	Coimbatore City	11	0	0	0	1	1	10	90.9	0.3	0.0
5	Cuddalore	180	0	0	0	131	131	49	27.2	1.2	0.0
6	Dharmapuri	98	0	0	5	16	21	77	78.6	1.9	23.8
7	Dindigul	139	0	0	0	16	20	119	85.6	3.0	0.0
8	Erode	64	0	0	2	20	12	52	81.3	1.3	16.7
9	Kanchipuram	83	0	0	23	10	23	60	72.3	1.5	100.0
10	Kanyakumari	23	0	0	0	0	4	19	82.6	0.5	0.0
11	Karur	21	0	0	2	4	4	17	81.0	0.4	50.0
12	Krishnagiri	70	0	0	1	2	13	57	81.4	1.4	7.7
13	Madurai	565	0	0	8	12	73	492	87.1	12.4	11.0
14	Madurai City	32	0	0	4	65	19	13	40.6	0.3	0.0

contd...

	Districts/city	Total no. of cases for investigation including pending cases from previous year	Cases with-drawn by govt.	No. of cases in which investigation was completed				Pending trial at the end of the year	Pendency perce-ntage	Perce-ntage of pende ncy to state total	Conviction rate ((col.6) / (col 8)x100)
				Compounded or withdrawn	Trials completed						
					Convicted	Acquitted or discharged	Total				
15	Nagapattinam	58	0	0	0	15	0	58	100.0	1.5	--
16	Namakkal	107	0	0	2	0	10	97	90.7	2.5	20.0
17	Nilgiris	8	0	0	0	8	0	8	100.0	0.2	--
18	Perambalur	53	0	0	0	0	9	44	83.0	1.1	0.0
19	Pudukkotai	196	0	0	0	9	27	169	86.2	4.3	0.0
20	Ramanathapuram	228	0	0	6	27	63	165	72.4	4.2	9.5
21	Railway Chennai	1	0	0	0	57	1	0	0.0	0.0	0.0
22	Railway Trichy	0	0	0	0	1	0	0	--	0.0	--
23	Salem	84	0	0	0	0	9	75	89.3	1.9	0.0
24	Salem City	14	0	0	0	9	0	14	100.0	0.4	--
25	Sivagangai	458	0	0	2	0	50	408	89.1	10.3	4.0
26	Thanjavur	217	0	0	2	48	67	150	69.1	3.8	3.0
27	Theni	183	0	0	17	65	78	105	57.4	2.7	21.8
28	Thirunelveli	499	0	0	0	61	199	300	60.1	7.6	0.0

contd...

	Districts/city	Total no. of cases for investigation including pending cases from previous year	Cases with drawn by govt.	No. of cases in which investigation was completed				Pending trial at the end of the year	Pend-ency perce-ntage	Perce-ntage of pen-dency to state total	Convi-ction rate ((col.6) / (col 8)x100)
				Compounded or withdrawn	Trials completed						
					Convicted	Acquitted or discharged	Total				
29	Thirunelveli City	86	0	0	2	199	15	71	82.6	1.8	13.3
30	Thiruvallur	54	0	0	0	13	3	51	94.4	1.3	0.0
31	Thiruvannamalai	179	0	2	0	3	13	164	91.6	4.1	0.0
32	Thiruvarur	119	0	0	3	20	23	96	80.7	2.4	13.0
33	Thoothukudi	180	0	0	0	49	49	131	72.8	3.3	0.0
34	Tiruppur	65	0	0	0	0	0	65	100.0	1.6	--
35	Tiruppur City	37	0	0	0	16	16	21	56.8	0.5	0.0
36	Trichy	66	0	0	5	16	21	45	68.2	1.1	23.8
37	Trichy City	6	0	0	0	4	4	2	33.3	0.1	0.0
38	Vellore	132	0	0	0	0	0	132	100.0	3.3	--
39	Villupuram	429	0	0	2	72	74	355	82.8	9.0	2.7
40	Virudhunagar	202	0	0	3	23	26	176	87.1	4.4	11.5
	Total	**5089**	**0**	**2**	**89**	**1041**	**1130**	**3957**	**77.8**	**100.0**	**7.9**

Source: Crime Review –Tamil Nadu 2014, State Crime Record Bureau, Tamil Nadu.

Table 8.10B: Percentage disposal of cases by courts for crimes committed against Scheduled Castes during 2014

S.No.	Crime head	Cases with-drawn by govt.	Number of cases				Pending trial at the end of the year	Conviction rate (5/7x100)
			Compounded or withdrawn	Convicted	Acquitted or discharged	Total		
1	Murder	0.0	0.0	1.4	7.1	8.6	91.4	16.7
2	Rape	0.0	0.0	4.0	11.2	15.2	84.8	26.3
3	Kidnapping and abduction	0.0	0.0	0.0	25.0	25.0	75.0	0.0
4	Dacoity	0.0	0.0	0.0	0.0	0.0	100.0	--
5	Robbery	0.0	0.0	0.0	17.6	17.6	82.4	0.0
6	Arson	0.0	0.0	3.7	18.5	22.2	77.8	16.7
7	Hurt	0.0	0.0	0.0	30.3	30.3	69.7	0.0
8	PCR Act	0.0	0.0	33.3	0.0	33.3	66.7	100.0
9	SC/ST prev. of atrocities Act	0.0	0.1	1.2	18.3	19.5	80.4	6.4
10	Other crimes	0.0	0.0	2.8	28.7	31.5	68.5	9.0
	Total	**0.0**	**0.0**	**1.7**	**20.5**	**22.2**	**77.8**	**7.9**

Source: Crime Review –Tamil Nadu 2014, State Crime Record Bureau, Tamil Nadu.

Table 8.11: Disposal of persons arrested by police for committing crimes against Scheduled Castes during 2014

	Crime head	*Total no. of cases for investigation including pending cases from previous year*	*Persons released before trial*		*Persons charge sheeted*		*Persons under investigation at the end of the year*	
			No.	*Percentage to total*	*No.*	*Percentage to total*	*No.*	*Percentage to total*
1	Murder	322	0	0.0	221	68.6	101	31.4
2	Rape	65	0	0.0	46	70.8	19	29.2
3	Kidnapping and abduction	17	0	0.0	4	23.5	13	76.5
4	Dacoity	1	0	0.0	1	100	0	0
5	Robbery	13	0	0.0	11	84.6	2	15.4
6	Arson	93	0	0.0	85	91.4	8	8.6
7	Hurt	47	0	0.0	26	55.3	21	44.7
8	PCR Act	12	0	0.0	11	91.7	1	8.3
9	SC/ST prev. of atrocities Act	2874	27	0.9	1854	64.5	993	34.6
10	Other crime	1948	25	1.3	1335	68.5	588	30.2
	Total	**5392**	**52**	**1.0**	**3594**	**66.7**	**1746**	**32.4**

Source: Crime Review –Tamil Nadu 2014, State Crime Record Bureau, Tamil Nadu.

Table 8.11A: Disposal by police of persons arrested by police for committing crimes against Scheduled Castes during 2014

S.No	*Districts/city*	*Total no. of cases for investigation including pending cases from previous year*	*Number of*			*Pendency percentage*	*Percentage pendency to state total*
			Persons released before trial	*Persons charge sheeted*	*Person under investigation at the end of the year*		
1	Ariyalur	25	4	18	3	12.0	0.2
2	Chennai	25	0	9	16	64.0	0.9
3	Coimbatore	59	0	22	37	62.7	2.1
4	Coimbatore City	4	0	1	3	75.0	0.2
5	Cuddalore	553	0	355	198	35.8	11.3
6	Dharmapuri	114	0	89	25	21.9	1.4
7	Dindigul	190	0	169	21	11.1	1.2
8	Erode	71	0	57	14	19.7	0.8
9	Kanchipuram	76	0	25	51	67.1	2.9
10	Kanyakumari	9	0	3	6	66.7	0.3
11	Karur	69	0	34	35	50.7	2.0

contd...

S.No	Districts/city	Total no. of cases for investigation including pending cases from previous year	Number of			Pendency percentage	Percentage pendency to state total
			Persons released before trial	Persons charge sheeted	Person under investigation at the end of the year		
12	Krishnagiri	32	0	11	21	65.6	1.2
13	Madurai	599	4	307	288	48.1	16.5
14	Madurai City	41	0	21	20	48.8	1.1
15	Nagapattinam	37	0	26	11	29.7	0.6
16	Namakkal	64	0	42	22	34.4	1.3
17	Nilgiris	5	0	3	2	40.0	0.1
18	Perambalur	56	3	37	16	28.6	0.9
19	Pudukkotai	218	0	194	24	11.0	1.4
20	Ramanathapuram	128	0	86	42	32.8	2.4
21	Railway Chennai	0	0	0	0	--	0.0
22	Railway Trichy	0	0	0	0	--	0.0

contd...

S.No	Districts/city	Total no. of cases for investigation including pending cases from previous year	Number of			Pendency percentage	Percentage pendency to state total
			Persons released before trial	Persons charge sheeted	Person under investigation at the end of the year		
23	Salem	147	0	127	20	13.6	1.1
24	Salem City	22	0	1	21	95.5	1.2
25	Sivagangai	122	0	75	47	38.5	2.7
26	Thanjavur	119	0	67	52	43.7	3.0
27	Theni	66	0	52	14	21.2	0.8
28	Thirunelveli	845	0	456	389	46.0	22.3
29	Thirunelveli City	131	0	103	28	21.4	1.6
30	Thiruvallur	127	0	85	42	33.1	2.4
31	Thiruvannamalai	99	0	83	16	16.2	0.9
32	Thiruvarur	84	6	49	29	34.5	1.7
33	Thoothukudi	137	0	127	10	7.3	0.6

contd...

S.No	Districts/city	Total no. of cases for investigation including pending cases from previous year	Number of			Pendency percentage	Percentage pendency to state total
			Persons released before trial	Persons charge sheeted	Person under investigation at the end of the year		
34	Tiruppur	54	17	32	5	9.3	0.3
35	Tiruppur City	21	0	16	5	23.8	0.3
36	Trichy	182	18	109	55	30.2	3.2
37	Trichy City	13	0	2	11	84.6	0.6
38	Vellore	249	0	213	36	14.5	2.1
39	Villupuram	354	0	301	53	15.0	3.0
40	Virudhunagar	245	0	187	58	23.7	3.3
	Total	**5392**	**52**	**3594**	**1746**	**32.4**	**100.0**

Source: Crime Review –Tamil Nadu 2014, State Crime Record Bureau, Tamil Nadu.

Table 8.12: Disposal by courts of persons arrested for committing crimes against Scheduled Castes during 2014

S.No	*Crime head*	*Total no. of cases for investigation including pending cases from previous year*	*No. of persons whose*			*No.of persons convicted*	*Percentage of persons*	
			Cases compounded or withdrawn	*Trial completed*	*Trial remained pending at the end of the year*		*Whose trials remained pending (col.6 x 100 / col.3)*	*Convicted to trials completed (col.7 x100/col.5)*
1	MURDER	1047	0	49	585	7	55.9	14.3
2	RAPE	240	0	21	122	4	50.8	19.0
3	KIDNAPPING & ABDUCTION	26	0	5	10	0	38.5	0.0
4	DACOITY	1	0	0	1	0	0.0	--
5	ROBBERY	31	0	3	18	0	58.1	0.0
6	ARSON	131	0	24	84	1	64.1	0.0
7	HURT	416	0	37	184	0	44.2	0.0
8	PCR ACT	23	0	6	11	6	47.8	100.0
9	SC/ST PREV. OF ATROCITIES ACT	12916	5	1211	6169	105	47.8	8.7
10	OTHER CRIME	5139	0	589	2648	58	51.5	9.8
	Total	**19970**	**5**	**1945**	**9832**	**181**	**49.2**	**9.3**

Source: Crime Review –Tamil Nadu 2014, State Crime Record Bureau, Tamil Nadu.

Table 8.12A: Disposal by courts of persons arrested for committing crimes against scheduled castes during 2014 (district / city)

S.No	*Districts/city*	*Total no.of persons under trial including those from previous year*	*Total no. of persons whose*			*No. of persons convicted*	*Pendency percentage*	*Percentage of pendency to state total*
			Cases compounded or withdrawn	*Trial completed*	*Trial remained pending at the end of the year*			
1	Ariyalur	184	0	26	75	0	40.8	0.8
2	Chennai	73	0	8	33	0	45.2	0.3
3	Coimbatore	200	0	31	80	0	40.0	0.8
4	Coimbatore City	33	0	1	16	0	48.5	0.2
5	Cuddalore	1633	0	28	966	0	59.2	9.8
6	Dharmapuri	395	0	96	146	13	37.0	1.5
7	Dindigul	1087	0	76	552	0	50.8	5.6
8	Erode	147	0	14	88	2	59.9	0.9
9	Kanchipuram	163	0	24	70	24	42.9	0.7
10	Kanyakumari	47	0	4	21	0	44.7	0.2
11	Karur	164	0	10	89	8	54.3	0.9
12	Krishnagiri	245	0	62	66	5	26.9	0.7
13	Madurai	1349	0	185	643	19	47.7	6.5
14	Madurai City	65	0	27	16	7	24.6	0.2
15	Nagapattinam	124	0	0	75	0	60.5	0.8

contd...

S.No	Districts/city	Total no.of persons under trial including those from previous year	Total no. of persons whose			No. of persons convicted	Pendency percentage	Percentage of pendency to state total
			Cases compounded or withdrawn	Trial completed	Trial remained pending at the end of the year			
16	Namakkal	454	0	11	237	3	52.2	2.4
17	Nilgiris	13	0	0	8	0	61.5	0.1
18	Perambalur	283	0	31	129	0	45.6	1.3
19	Pudukkotai	1310	0	119	633	0	48.3	6.4
20	Ramanathapuram	586	0	150	186	13	31.7	1.9
21	Railway Chennai	0	0	0	0	0	--	0.0
22	Railway Trichy	0	0	0	0	0	--	0.0
23	Salem	509	0	25	293	0	57.6	3.0
24	Salem City	91	0	0	46	0	50.5	0.5
25	Sivagangai	935	0	55	450	3	48.1	4.6
26	Thanjavur	423	0	72	173	2	40.9	1.8
27	Theni	500	0	87	189	20	37.8	1.9
28	Thirunelveli	1560	0	284	724	0	46.4	7.4
29	Thirunelveli City	435	0	53	216	8	49.7	2.2
30	Thiruvallur	331	0	20	188	0	56.8	1.9

contd...

S.No	Districts/city	Total no.of persons under trial including those from previous year	Total no. of persons whose			No. of persons convicted	Pendency percentage	Percentage of pendency to state total
			Cases compounded or withdrawn	Trial completed	Trial remained pending at the end of the year			
31	Thiruvannamalai	1371	5	56	666	0	48.6	6.8
32	Thiruvarur	311	0	32	148	3	47.6	1.5
33	Thoothukudi	401	0	49	215	0	53.6	2.2
34	Tiruppur	164	0	0	98	0	59.8	1.0
35	Tiruppur City	100	0	37	21	0	21.0	0.2
36	Trichy	329	0	119	100	46	30.4	1.0
37	Trichy City	26	0	10	4	0	15.4	0.0
38	Vellore	405	0	0	309	0	76.3	3.1
39	Villupuram	3041	0	101	1570	2	51.6	16.0
40	Virudhunagar	483	0	42	293	3	60.7	3.0
	Total	**19970**	**5**	**1945**	**9832**	**181**	**49.2**	**100.0**

Source: Crime Review –Tamil Nadu 2014, State Crime Record Bureau, Tamil Nadu.

that out of 19970 cases for investigation including pending cases from previous year, 12916 cases (64.7 per cent) were under the SC/ST Prevention of Atrocities Act, 1989. Out of 181 persons convicted, 105 persons (58 per cent) were from the SC/ST Prevention of Atrocities Act, 1989.

Analysis of data by districts (Table 8.12A) clearly show that out of 19970 cases for investigation including pending cases from previous year, Villupuram, Tirunelveli and Cuddalore districts together accounted for 31 per cent of the cases.

Conclusion

The rate of pendency in disposal of cases for crimes by both the police and courts has gone up. The percentage of charge sheeting has come down in disposal of cases for crimes by police. Charge sheeting by police was around 90 per cent. The percentage of conviction rate has come down in disposal of cases by courts. It is to be noted that the highest percentage of atrocities cases were reported in Tirunelveli and Madurai districts. The Scheduled Castes and Scheduled Tribes (Prevention of Atrocity) Act, 1989 is an important milestone for the SCs as it aims to prevent atrocities on the SCs and STs and to eradicate the untouchability, but this law has not been effectively implemented in Tamil Nadu.

References

1. 'Reconciliation between Dalits, caste Hindus at Kavanampatti', *The Hindu*, January 20, 2005.
2. 'Dalit student's wrist slit 'for wearing watch' in Madurai', *Financial Express*, September 05, 2014.
3. 'Dalit boy stabbed for talking non-dalit girl', *Times of India*, 24-08-2013.
4. Marx, A., 'Kalvikkoodangalil Theendamai', *Makkal Kalam*, July 2012, also in *The Hindu*, 12-06-2012.

5. 'TN school excludes dalit children', *Deccan Herald*, 31-08-2012.

6. *Communalism Combat*, July 2000 Dalit Drishti.

7. Sampath, Progress and Struggle, Experiences of Struggles Against untouchability in Tamil Nadu, Pragothi, 15-05-2010.

8. Untouchability Declassified, anti-caste, on caste, women's oppression, communalism, and class struggle in South Asia from a Marxist perspective, June 12, 2010.

9. Nagaraj, K., Dalit situation in Tamil Nadu, *The Hindu*, Book Review, August 23, 2005.

9

Summary and Conclusion

Introduction

The SCs, in the past, were socially ostracised, economically exploited. They are widely spread all over India. Majority of them are depending on agriculture as landless agricultural workers. They are also engaged in traditional occupations, such as, scavenging, leather work and other menial and other low paid/income occupations. They were treated as slaves. The colonial government and Christian Missionaries have taken up various steps to provide education and land to the Depressed Class People. After independence, various ameliorative measures have been initiated by the government for the upliftment of weaker sections of society viz. Scheduled Castes and Scheduled Tribes. Despite the fact that several welfare and economic development programmes implemented by the state and central governments, the SCs could not come out of poverty and unemployment and various forms of economic and social discrimination and deprivation are highly prevalent in India. Even now they are unable to get adequate employment opportunities, in spite of development effort made by the government both at the central and at the state levels.

Methodology

Data relating to land, caste and gender in by social groups in Tamil Nadu were collected from All India Report on Agricultural Census for two points of time viz. 2005-06 and 2010-11 and the information on population were collected from the Census of India, 2011. The study has used two sets of data sources for delineating the occupational pattern among social groups viz Population Census, 2001 and 2011 and National Sample Survey (NSS) data for periods 2004-05 and 2009-10. Data on 1. Entrepreneur Development Institutes in India and Tamil Nadu, 2. Entrepreneur development programmes and economic development programmes implemented by National Scheduled Castes Financial Development Corporation (NSFDC), New Delhi and the Tamil Nadu Adi-Dravidar Housing and Development Corporation (TAHDCO), and Dalit Indian Chamber of Commerce and Industry (DICCI), and 3. Entrepreneurship and Development programmes implemented by other state controlled agencies in Tamil Nadu were collected from their respective websites.

Data relating to educational status by social groups have been collected from Census of India 1991, 2001, 2011; data regarding the enrolment in primary and upper primary school education by social groups were collected from the District Information System for Education (DISE), Cohort Study and Elementary Education Register (EER), Government of Tamil Nadu for the year from 1990-91 to 2007-08. Data were also collected from Annual Reports of the Department of School Education and Literacy and Department of Higher Education, Ministry of Human Resource Development (MHRD), Government of India. Health and per capita consumer expenditure related data, such as, mortality and morbidity were collected from the report on National Health and Family Welfare (Tamil Nadu Reports) for two points of time viz. 1998-99 and 2005-06 and differences in level of per capita consumption expenditure among socio-economic groups from

NSS Reports for two points of time viz. 1993-94 and 2004-05.

Data relating to Scheduled Caste Sub-Plan were collected for various years from 1. Performance Budget, Adi-Dravidar and Tribal Welfare Department, Government of Tamil Nadu, 2. Special Component Plan for Scheduled Castes: 2000-2001, Tamil Nadu, Adi-Dravidar and Tribal Welfare, Chennai, and 3. Annual Plan: Plan Budget Link. Information relating to the types of atrocities, cases filed and disposed of by police and court at the state level were collected from National Crime Record Bureau (NCRB) and the same information at the district level were collected from the Crimes Review (2014), State Crime Record Office, Chennai.

Findings of the Study

Land reform legislations were enacted mainly to redistribute land to the landless and other poor, but these legislations could not alter the agrarian structure as land operated by the SCs continued to be low even after fifty five years of implementation of land reform legislations. Access to land operated by SCs was low (with access index 0.37) as compared to STs (with access index 1.2) and Others (with access index 1.13). The land operated by the SCs is in the nature of small holdings. The Hindu Succession Act could deliver justice to women in getting their ancestral land, as the land controlled by women continued to be abysmally low even after several years of the enactment of Hindu Succession Act in Tamil Nadu. The percentage of land owned by women is disproportionately small considering their crucial contribution to agriculture. The wells and tube wells controlled by the STs and SCs forms less that 10 per cent which is disproportionately low in Tamil Nadu. The proportion of well and tube wells fitted with electric pump sets was high among Others and low among SCs and STs in Tamil Nadu both in 2005-06 and 2010-11. Distribution of area irrigated by diverse sources of irrigation viz. wells and tube wells was very low among SCs and STs as compared to Others in Tamil Nadu. It is evident from the data that other uncultivated land excluding fallow land, fallow land other than current fallows, cultivable waste land, total uncultivated and land not available for cultivation was low among SCs as compared to Others in Tamil Nadu which indicate that the SCs were efficient in utilising land.

As per the notification of the government, 6000 SCs women would financed for purchase of land in 2003-04. Till 2011-12 i.e. eight years of the implementation of the scheme, only 7,173 beneficiaries purchased 10576.97 acres of land under this scheme. If this scheme is genuinely implemented by the government, 72,000 women would have benefited and more than 1,00,000 acres of land would have been bought under this scheme by the SCs women alone. Thus, the data presented in Table 2.7 clearly point out that the land purchase scheme in not implemented properly.

Although, the trend towards occupational diversification of rural workforce across all social groups observed during the study period, 71 per cent and 79 per cent of the SCs and STs rural workforce respectively continue to be employed in agricultural sector. The disparity index of SCs as compared to non-SCs/STs workers remained above 1 which indicates a higher percentage of SCs workforce as against non-SCs/STs workforce. A majority of the SC workers (60 per cent in 2009-10) in rural areas work as agricultural workers. In 2001, only 15 per cent of the SCs rural workers engaged in cultivation as against the corresponding figures of 47 per cent of STs and 35 per cent non-SCs/STs rural workers. By 2011, this proportion declined to 10 per cent of the SCs rural workers, 34 per cent of STs and 27 per cent and non-SCs/STs among rural workers. NSS household data also substantiates the inter-social group disparities in rural occupation pattern that is SCs workforce constitutes 52.6 per cent, OBCs workforce with 30.4 per cent as against 35.7 per cent among all agricultural worker households.

The proportion of workforce engaged in household industry has declined, while the proportion of 'other workers' has increased for all social groups in 2011. However, during the study period, the proportion 'other workers' has increased sharply among SCs and STs. Further, the labour force displaced from agricultural sector is not absorbed in rural household industry but are engaged in 'other workers' with limited access to capital.

The SCs in urban areas in Tamil Nadu also occupy relatively disadvantageous position as compared to OBCs, as the percentage of self-employed SCs workers is lower about 10 percentage point in 2009-2010. As regards the casual labourers is higher about 20 percentage point than the corresponding figures for OBCs. The inter-group variation in the percentage of regular wage earners/salaried is much lower among SCs, STs and OBCs which indicate the positive role of the reservation policy for the SCs, STs and OBCs in Tamil Nadu. However, the proportion of workforce engaged in regular wage/salaried has declined among SCs, STs and OBCs, but the decline in regular wage/salaried is higher among SCs. This indicates that the brunt of slackening public employment during the economic reform period has fallen more heavily on SCs.

Analysis of the literacy rates by social groups clearly reveals that the rate of literacy has gone up substantially for all social groups in 2011 as compared to 1991 in Tamil Nadu. The rate of literacy was high among the non-SC/ST as compared to SCs and STs in Tamil Nadu. The rate of enrolment has gone up in the recent past, but the proportion of enrolment is still low among the Scheduled Castes and Scheduled Tribes in Tamil Nadu. The rate of drop outs has come down for all population, Scheduled Castes and Scheduled Tribes in 2005 as compared to 2001. The schools run by the government have enrolled more students as compared to the schools under private management.

The result of the study clearly shows that attendance rate, completion rate and transition rate were low among the SC as compared to non-SC/ST. The data relating to repetition rate was high among the SCs as compared to non-SC/ST at the school levels. Analysis of data by gender shows that repetition rate was high among the boys, completion rate was high among the girls and the transition rate remains more or less the same for both the boys and girls.

Mortality rates among children belonging to all social groups have declined in Tamil Nadu. The children who received Vitamin A supplementation was low among SCs children. The percentage of women who have received antenatal care was low among SCs women. The delivery assisted by doctors was high among OBCs, as compared to the delivery assisted by doctors among SCs. The food consumption by women viz. milk/curd, green leafy vegetables and fruits was low among SCs as compared to OBCs and Others. Prevalence anemia is much higher among women and children belonging to SCs. The prevalence of acute respiratory infection (ARI) was slightly high among the children belonging to SCs as compared OBCs in Tamil Nadu. Percentage of children received vaccination was low among the SCs children in both 1998-99 and 2005-06 as compared to MBCs. The percentage of households at the lower levels of monthly per capita consumer expenditure (MPCE) was high among the SCs and STs, while the percentage of households at the higher levels of monthly per capita consumer expenditure was high among OBCs and Others both in rural and urban areas.

Analysis relating to Scheduled Caste Sub-Plan vividly brings out the fact that the SCSP has not been effectively implemented in Tamil Nadu. The funds allotted under the scheme have been inadequate and less than the required allocation of fund from the state plan viz. allocation of fund should be equal to the proportion of the Scheduled Caste population in the State. A suitable law may be enacted for effective implementation SCSP with adequate provision for protection of fund only meant for the Scheduled Castes and the funds provided under the SCSP should be made non-divertible and non-lapsable. The hope of the deprived section of the people with regard to the effective implementation of the SCSP still remains a distant dream, due to lack of political will on the part of administrative machinery.

The rate of pendency in disposal of cases for crimes by both the police and courts has gone up. The percentage of charge sheeting has come down in disposal of cases for crimes by police. Charge sheeting by police was around 90 per cent. The percentage of conviction rate has come down in disposal of cases by courts. It is to be noted that the highest percentage of atrocities cases were reported in Tirunelveli and Madurai districts. The Scheduled Castes and Scheduled Tribes (Prevention of Atrocity) Act, 1989 is an important milestone for the SCs as it aims to prevent atrocities on the SCs and STs and to eradicate the untouchability, but this law has not been effectively implemented in Tamil Nadu.

Suggestion for policy implication

1. The land operated by SCs was low when compared to their size of population. Suitable measures may be initiated to provide adequate quantity of land to the SCs.
2. There is a need for reframing the land reform policies so that widows and deserted women would be given preference from government while distributing land to the beneficiaries.
3. Suitable policy may be initiated to provide irrigation to the farmers belonging to SCs, as the irrigated land controlled by SCs is disproportionately low.
4. The rate of drop outs has come down for all population, but it remains high in the case of SCs as compared to

non-SCs. Suitable incentive programmes for continuing education, like scholarship, hostel and implementation of reservation policy at higher secondary schools.

5. Schools run by government are enrolling more students as compared to the schools under private management. Government may start more and more educational institutions with hostels in backward areas.

6. Attendance rate, completion rate and transition rate are low among the SC students as compared to non-SCs. These occur mostly in the case of girl students. Special programmes like vocational training along with mainstream education and development of soft skill for them may be initiated to arrest the tendencies enlisted above.

7. Repetition rate was high among the SCs as compared to non-SCs. Suitable policy measures viz. remedial coaching may be initiated to control the repetition rate. Repetition rate is very high in the case SC students because of lack of facilities in their homes. Government may build suitable study centres in villages where more than twenty SC students are studying.

8. The proportion of workforce engaged in regular wage/salaried has declined among SCs, STs and OBCs, but the decline in is higher among SCs. Adequate employment opportunities may be initiated in the private sector to compensate decline in the workforce in government and public sector undertakings.

9. Skill development programmes may be initiated with adequate financial support for semi and unskilled workers belonging to SCs to enable them to take up self-employment.

10. Educational institutions run by the government have enrolled more students as compared to the schools under private management. Suitable measures may be

initiated to increase the educational institutions under the government management.

11. Children who received Vitamin A supplementation and prevalence of anemia and ARI was low among SCs children. The percentage of women who have received antenatal care, delivery assistance by doctor and consumption of essential foods was low among SCs women. Prevalence of anemia is much higher among women and children belonging to SCs. Suitable measures may be initiated to address health problems of children and women belonging to Scheduled Castes.
12. SCSP has not been effectively implemented in Tamil Nadu. The hope of the deprived section of the people with regard to the effective implementation of the SCSP still remains a distant dream, due to lack of political will on the part of administrative machinery. A suitable law may be enacted for effective implementation SCSP with adequate provision for protection of fund only meant for the Scheduled Castes. The funds provided under the SCSP should be made non-divertible and non-lapsable.
13. The Scheduled Castes and Scheduled Tribes (Prevention of Atrocity) Act, 1989 is an important milestone for the SCs as it aims to prevent atrocities on the SCs and to eradicate the untouchability, but this law has not been effectively implemented in Tamil Nadu. This Act was amended in 2014 to make it more effective. This Act may be implemented both in letter and spirit.

Conclusion

Access to land operated by the SCs is low and whatever land they cultivate, they are in the nature of small holdings. However, the proportion of workforce engaged in regular wage/salaried has declined among SCs, STs and OBCs, but the decline in regular wage/salaried is higher among SCs.

This indicates that the brunt of slackening public employment during the economic reform period has fallen more heavily on SCs. The result of the study clearly shows that attendance rate, completion rate and transition rate were low among the SC as compared to non-SC/ST. The data relating to repetition rate was high among the SCs as compared to non-SC/ST at the school levels. Health related provisions by the government have not been fully and properly utilised by SC women and SC children. Scheduled Caste Sub-Plan (SCSP) and The Scheduled Castes Scheduled Tribes (Prevention of Atrocities) Act, 1989 have not been effectively implemented in Tamil Nadu.

It is also worth noting that the Scheduled Castes and Scheduled Tribes (Prevention of Atrocity) Act, 1989 is an important milestone for the SCs as it aims to prevent atrocities on the SCs and STs and eradicate the untouchability. The SCSP is another landmark provision for the SCs as it mainly deals with the eradication of poverty among the SCs. But the authorities due to vested interests do not genuinely implement these two important provisions. If these two provisions were put into practice genuinely, the socio-economic problems, such as, poverty, unemployment and untouchability would have been vanished long ago among Scheduled Castes.

Bibliography

Annual Report, Sarva Shiksha Abhiyan, Tamil Nadu, 2009-10.

Annual Report, *Selected Educational Statistics*, Ministry of Human Resource Development, 1990-91 to 2007-08.

Balaji Pandey, Educational Development among Scheduled Castes, *Social Scientist*, Vol. 14, No. 2/3 (Feb. - Mar. 1986). pp. 59-68.

Chalam, K.S, "Caste Reservations and Equality of Opportunity in Education" *Economic and Political Weekly*, Vol. 41.13, No. 25, October-1990, pp. 2333-39.

Centre for Women Studies, *Property rights of women in Tamil Nadu*, Justice Basheer Ahmed Sayeed College for women, Chennai.

Census of India: 1991, 2001 and 2011 *Primary Census Abstract*, Series 23, Tamil Nadu, Volume-I.

Dalit Drishti, *Communalism Combat*, July 2000.

Dalit women right to land: A Fight for Survival, Dignity and Equality, Action Aid, Bangalore, India, April 2013.

'Dalit student's wrist slit 'for wearing watch' in Madurai', *Financial Express*, September 05, 2014.

'Dalit boy stabbed for talking non-dalit girl', *Times of India*, 24-08-2013.

Draft National Land Reforms Policy (24th July, 2013), Department of Land Resources, Ministry of Rural Development Government of India.

Dholakia, R and Iyenkar, S, "Access of Poor Household to Primary Education in Rural India", *Journal of Educational Planning and Administration*, Vol. XXII, No. 3, July 2008, pp. 255-271.

Economic Survey, Government of India – 2013-14.

Employment and unemployment among social groups in India, 1999-2000, NSSO, 55th Round, Department of Statistics, Government of India, New Delhi, 2001.

Employment and unemployment among social groups in India, 2004-05, NSSO, 61st Round, Department of Statistics, Government of India, New Delhi, 2006.

Ghosh, A.K, "The Gender Gap in Literacy and Education among the Scheduled Tribes in Jharkhand and West Bengal, Sociological Bulletin Vol. 56(1) (Jan.- April 2007), pp. 109-125.

Jayapal, S., "Social Welfare Programmes of Scheduled Castes in Tamil Nadu", M.Phil. Dissertation, Department of Economics, University of Madras, 2012.

"Jharkhand and West Bengal" *Sociological Bulletin*, Vol.56 (1), Jan-Apr 2007, pp. 109-125.

Jariwal, C.M., Constitution and Education, *Encyclopedia of Indian Education*, Vol. I, pp. 355.

Kamble, N.D., *The Scheduled Castes*, Ashish Publishing House, New Delhi, 1982.

Krishnakumar K, Tamil Selvan P, "Role of Commercial Banks in Socio-Economic Development of SCs and STs (A Study with Special Reference to Tahdco Schemes in Tamil

Nadu)" *Indian Journal of Applied Research*, Volume 4, No. 3, March, 2014.

Marx, A., 'Kalvikkoodangalil Theendamai', *Makkal Kalam*, July 2012, also in *The Hindu*, 12-06-2012.

Nagaraj, K., Dalit Situation in Tamil Nadu, The Hindu, Book Review, August 23, 2005.

Nambissan, G, "Equity in Education? Schooling of Dalit Children in India", *Economic and Political Weekly*, Vol. XXXI, No.16 and 17, April 20-27, 1996, pp. 1011-1024.

Nambissan, G, "Exclusion, Inclusion and Education; Perspectives and Experiences of Dalit Children", National Conference on Social Exclusion and Inclusive Policies, organised by *Indian Institute of Dalit Studies*, on 26-27-Oct-2007, pp. 95-126.

Parvathamma, C. *Scheduled Castes and Tribes: A Socio Economic Survey*, Ashish Publishing House. New Delhi, 1984.

Ratna and Nageswara, "Primary Education: Progress and Constraints", *Economic and Political Weekly*, Vol. XXXVIII, No. 12 and 13, March 22-29, 2003, pp. 1242-1251.

'Reconciliation between Dalits, caste Hindus at Kavanampatti', *The Hindu*, January 20, 2005.

Report of the Commissioner for SCs and STs (Various years).

Rubina, K., "Regional Returns to Education, Child Labour and Schooling in India", *Journal of Development Studies*, Vol.44, No.2, February-2008, pp. 233-257.

Sampath, Progress and Struggle, Experiences of Struggles Against untouchability in Tamil Nadu, Pragothi, 15-05-2010).

Seventh Educational Survey 2002, NCERT, New Delhi.

"Social Development of Dalit and Tamil Nadu Government budget: A Critique", Tamil Nadu People's Forum for Social Development, Year of the publication is not available.

Special Component Plan for Scheduled Castes, 2000-2001 Tamil Nadu, Adi Dravidar and Tribal Welfare, Chennai, January 2001.

"Tamil Nadu Social Development Report 2000", Tamil Nadu People's Forum for Social Development, 2000.

Thangaraj, M. "Land and caste in Tamil Nadu", in *Land reforms in India-Tamil Nadu: An Unfinished Task,* (Ed.), M. Thangaraj, Sage publications, New Delhi, 2003.

Thangaraj, M. "Access to land by Scheduled Castes and Scheduled Tribes in India", in *Dalits and the State,* (Ed) Ghanshyam Shah, Concept Publishing Company, New Delhi, 2002.

Thangaraj, M. "State and NGO Interventions in the distribution of land to the poor: A study of Tamil Nadu" in *Agrarian Reforms, Land Markets and Rural Poor,* (Ed.) Narasimha Reddy, Concept Publishing Company, New Delhi, 2009.

Thangaraj, M. "Economic development of the Scheduled Castes and Scheduled Tribes: A study of Tamil Nadu" in *Perspectives on Economic Development and Social Change* (Ed.) Yagati China Roa, Rawat Publications, New Delhi, 2009.

Thangaraj, M. "In the Service of Landless", *The Hindu,* December 12, 1993.

Thangaraj, M. "Special component plan for the Scheduled Castes in Tamil Nadu", Social Action, Vol. 57, No. 1, January-March 2007.

Thangaraj, M. "Analysis of Literacy by Social Groups in India", Indian Journal of Adult Education, Vol. 56, No. 4, October-December, 1995.

Thangaraj, M. "Demographic and Occupational Characteristics of the Scheduled Castes and the Scheduled Tribes in India", *MIDS Working Paper,* No. 134, September 1995.

Thangaraj, M, "Land Use Pattern in Tamil Nadu", *MIDS Working Paper*, No. 107, June 1992.

Thangaraj, M., "Occupational Pattern", in Thorat Sukhadeo and Nidhi Sadana Sabharwal (Ed), *Bridging the Social Gap: Perspectives on Dalit Empowerment*, Sage Publications, New Delhi, 2014.

The Laws of Manu, Penguin Books, 1991

The Tamil Nadu land reforms (Fixation of Ceiling on Land) Act, 1961, Government of Tamil Nadu, 1980.

Thorat Sukhadeo, "Oppression and Dalit: Dalit Discrimination in the 1990s", *Economic and Political Weekly*, February 2002.

Times of India, Barely one in ten women own land, brothers most anti sisters inheriting land: Survey, March 4, 2014.

'TN school excludes dalit children', *Deccan Herald*, 31-08-2012.

Uma, S. Hiremath, *Asian Journal of Home Science*, Volume 8, No. 1, June 2013, pp. 20-23.

Untouchability Declassified, anti-caste, on caste, women's oppression, communalism, and class struggle in South Asia from a Marxist perspective, June 12, 2010).

Velaskar, P."Education, Caste, Gender: Dalit Girls' Access to Schooling in Maharashtra" *Journal of Educational Planning and Administration*, Vol.XIX, No.4, October 2005, pp. 459-482.

Venkatanarayana, "Child Schooling in Community in Transition: A Case of Scheduled Tribe Community in Andhra Pradesh", *Journal of Educational Planning and Administration*, Vol. XX, No. 1, January 2006, pp. 1-25.

Vijay Kumar Baraik and P.M. Kulkarni, Health Status and Access to Health Care Services – Disparities among Social Groups in India, *Indian Institute of Dalit Studies*, Working Paper Series, New Delhi, Vol. 1, No. 4, 2006.

Wankhede, G.G, "Educational Inequalities among Scheduled Castes in Maharashtra", *Economic and Political Weekly,* May 5th 2001, Vol. 36, No. 18, p. 1553

World Bank study/survey report, as quoted in *The Hindu,* 21st January 2015, (Chennai edition).

http://www.businessdictionary.com/definition/entrepreneur.html.

http://india.gov.in/sectors/education.sarva_shiksha.php

Index

D

E

T